LEFT TURN

◆

THE RADICAL IMAGINATION SERIES
Edited by Henry A. Giroux and Stanley Aronowitz

LEFT TURN
Forging a New Political Future

STANLEY ARONOWITZ

Paradigm Publishers
Boulder • London

Copyright © 2006 by Paradigm Publishers

Published in the United States by Paradigm Publishers, 3360 Mitchell Lane, Suite E, Boulder, Colorado 80301 USA.

Paradigm Publishers is the trade name of Birkenkamp & Company, LLC, Dean Birkenkamp, President and Publisher.

Library of Congress Cataloging-in-Publication Data

Aronowitz, Stanley.
　　Left Turn : forging a new political future / by Stanley Aronowitz.
　　　p. cm.
　　ISBN-13: 978-1-59451-310-7 (hc)
　　ISBN-10: 1-59451-310-4 (hc)
　　ISBN-13: 978-1-59451-311-4 (pb)
　　ISBN-10: 1-59451-311-2 (pb)
　　1. Liberalism—United States.　2. United States—Politics and government—2001　3. Political planning—United States.　4. United States—Social policy—1993–　5. Democracy—United States.　I. Title.
　　JC574.2.U6A76 2006
　　320.51'30973—dc22

　　　　　　　　　　　　　　　　　　　　　　　　　2006015116

Printed and bound in the United States of America on acid-free paper that meets the standards of the American National Standard for Permanence of Paper for Printed Library Materials.

Designed and Typeset in ITC Bookman Light by Straight Creek Bookmakers.

10　09　08　07　06　　1　2　3　4　5

For Michael Pelias

Contents

◇

Preface

I write at a moment of danger and bewilderment. The elusive and secretive U.S. vice president accidentally shoots a supporter, some say while under the influence. The incident occurs in February 2006 on a 50,000–acre Texas ranch that has been groomed for hunting and, as Bill Moyers laments, is just one instance of the wealthy's squandering of wildlife, amid other environmental disasters created by their efforts to preserve their playgrounds. Members of Congress from both sides of the aisle condemn President Bush for his unauthorized use of executive powers to spy on American citizens; but there seem to be no consequences for a president whose candidacy for impeachment is eminently plausible—except to members of his own party who value loyalty over principle, and to members of the other party who compulsively place the value of their political survival over that of the constitution. A year since the apocalyptic effects of Hurricanes Katrina and Rita, New Orleans remains bereft, with only 160,000 residents, mostly in the affluent French quarter; the rest of the population dwells uncomfortably in the diaspora, having been threatened by the Federal Emergency Management Agency (FEMA) with eviction from hotels and other temporary quarters. At the same time, almost unnoticed by the media, tens of thousands of people along the Gulf Coast have yet to recover from the effects of Hurricane Rita's assault on their homes and their lives. Meanwhile, Iraq teeters on the edge of civil war following the bombing of a sacred Shiite mosque, the publicized evidence of wholesale corruption by the newly elected government leaders, and the obdurate refusal of the Bush administration to set a timetable for the withdrawal of American troops. Even as once-resolute hawks urge the administration to get out as soon as possible, Bush confidently declares that he can see the light at the end of the tunnel after more than three disastrous years of US and British military occupation.

We are witnessing the palpable disintegration of our national government, which seems unable to accomplish anything other than forcing through Congress the selection of two ultra-right-wing Supreme Court justices and a succession of huge military-laden budgets that starve the remnants of programs for the aged and the poor in America. The administration has also managed to accumulate unprecedented deficits resulting largely from humongous military expenditures and tax gifts to the rich—gifts that have secured the silence of many at the commanding heights of the economy who would otherwise be screaming about deficits and the unwarranted costs of an unadvisable war. Make no mistake: Bush is no conservative when it comes to federal intervention. His spending proposals would make any Democratic president since Roosevelt appear conservative by comparison. And with his record of meddling into the private lives of American citizens, he is the most authoritarian president since John Adams. In characteristic fashion the administration has misspent funds on disaster relief that seems to benefit only the White House's corporate friends and the politically connected such as Mississippi governor and former Republican national committee chair Haley Barbour. All this at a time when the putative opposition, the Democratic Party (DP), remains deeply ambivalent about the provision of social welfare, divided on the need to end the war in Iraq, and in conflict about whether to offer more than a token of resistance to a runaway executive's flagrant trampling of our civil liberties. For example, Senator Russell Feingold, long-time opponent of the Patriot Act, was able to round up only nine other votes against its reauthorization. For the remainder of the thirty-five Democrats in the Senate, digression was the better part of valor.

Of course the Democrats benefit from the widespread perception that, however callow their approaches to foreign policy and to domestic social and economic issues, their record and perspectives on race and religion are discernibly different from the GOP, which now seems joined at the hip with religious fundamentalism and has rigorously pursued racist policies.

In addition, the administration has successfully sought draconian cuts in social programs that heavily benefit blacks and Latinos, and has adopted an education policy that, despite its announced intention to equalize opportunity, has widened the gap between rich and poor.

The Democrats were far less flagrant in their contempt for immigrants and America's racial and ethnic minorities than the Republicans for whom racism is red meat. It is true that, in the wake of the mass black freedom movement's confrontations, Lyndon Johnson signed the Voting and Civil Rights acts, a gesture that signed away his party's national future for forty years. Thereafter, only a cautious and conservative candidate from the South was able to win a national election. Jimmy Carter, the first Democrat to occupy the White House after Johnson's departure, was a former Georgia governor. While his post-presidential role in world politics has often been exemplary, he was arguably the first neoliberal president, and his domestic agenda may have been partially responsible for the current plight of millions of Americans who have experienced plunging living standards and economic insecurity. Bill Clinton, in turn, cultivated a warm relationship with the black church and the civil rights establishment; he regularly accepted invitations to speak at black institutions and "felt the pain" of the assembled, while adhering to a neoliberal agenda of cuts in social spending and a foreign policy that, in many ways, foreshadowed that of the Bush administration. To the extent that symbolic politics is important, Clinton had an almost flawless talent for the genre. Yet, remember that it was Bill Clinton who signed the 1996 Welfare Reform Act, which restricted income support and forced millions to accept dead-end, below-poverty-level jobs in order to maintain their benefits—an outcome onerous to its white, black, and Latino victims. The Democrats do not enjoy the confidence of the fundamentalist Christian organizations because they are shamefacedly pro-abortion and, for the most part, do not oppose gay rights. But lest we forget, no Democratic president since Jimmy Carter has failed to proclaim that he is "born again," to attend church regularly, and to agree that religion is the bedrock of American values.

By now we should be accustomed to liberal centrism. After all, American liberalism has always been uncomfortable in opposition to established authority and habitually seeks to compromise with it; though a sometimes dissenting part of the establishment, it nonetheless shares the latter's nationalistic and many of its conservative values such as the idea that work, however degraded and poorly paid, is a religious principle. But the absence of a left in the public discussion and debate is troubling and potentially dangerous, especially at a time when the Bush administration has declared war on dissent and the left is beginning to resume its historic role in American politics as a favorite scapegoat, a target of right-wing ideological and legal abuse. Reeling from its many failures, the administration—especially elements of its right-wing base—does not hesitate to pursue arbitrary anti-radicalism. We can see evidence of this in the multiple assaults on academic freedom. Witness the nefarious work of former radical David Horowitz who recently published a scurrilous rant against the 101 Most Dangerous Professors, among whom I occupy a proud, if possibly undeserved, niche. A Brooklyn College sociologist resigned from his department chair amid loud protests against a statement on his website belittling those who held religious beliefs. A Middle Eastern professor in South Florida was dismissed because the government harbored unproven suspicion that he cavorted with terrorists. Other Arab-American and Arab professors have been harassed. And a prominent left-wing New York attorney faces years in prison after being convicted of giving aid to terrorist suspects by transmitting information from Guantanamo to the outside. Needless to say, not one prominent centrist politician has raised her or his voice against these flagrant assaults.

In 1986 I wrote a cover article for *The Progressive* titled "The Party's Over." There I argued that hope for the revitalization of the Democratic Party as a genuine tribune of popular interests was misdirected. The article appeared at a time when the Democrats had sustained a humiliating defeat in the recent presidential election, largely because its candidate failed to challenge the Reagan administration's relentless attacks against the historic achievements of the labor movement and the second New Deal. But Walter Mondale's weak campaign was only a symptom of the larger malady: Since Carter, the Democrats had all but shed their liberal veneer and openly proclaimed themselves as a party loyal to the largest corporations and to the political directorate. This evaluation, unfortunately, was vindicated by the rise of the Democratic Leadership Council (DLC) under the leadership of then–Arkansas Governor Bill Clinton and then–Tennessee Senator Al Gore, who insisted that the legacy of social programs and regulation—in their terms, "big government"—had all but ruined the party's chances of electoral success. The DLC urged the Democratic Party to adopt a strategy of moderation, meaning compromise with the conservative tenets of the traditional Republican Party: fiscal restraint, limited privatization, small government, and a politics that favored economic growth at the expense of regulation.

This strategy has been doggedly followed by the Democratic Party and has just as doggedly failed to improve its electoral position since the defeat of its first protagonist, Jimmy Carter. Its latest wrinkle is the new rage in left and liberal circles, Thomas Frank's *What's the Matter with Kansas?* There the villain is no longer Big Government or progressive economic programs. Rather, we are told, the Democrats now lose in the American heartland because they pander too much to constituents on both coasts who care about social and cultural issues; if they could divert their eyes from issues such as abortion and gay marriage and instead train their sights on working-class economic concerns such as the living wage, they could ride to victory. But Frank neglects to mention that the unions have been following such a course since the 1970s, when their top leadership refused to address abortion rights and other social issues. Since then, Organized Labor has experienced a free fall, having lost two-thirds of its strength. That the Democrats earned their reputation as a party of working people during the campaigns of William Jennings Bryan at the turn of the twentieth century (especially in the New Deal years of the 1930s), and yet have steadily retreated from that position for the last half-century, shows that myths outlive the real conditions that produced them. The left, broadly conceived, is stuck in its own political fantasies, while the conservatives within the party know exactly what they are doing: dangling the past before our eyes but acting as if the ideas that animated the DP's thirty-five years of dominance, 1933–1968, no longer retain their validity.

Twenty years ago the idea of a new radical party was regarded as plausible by only a handful of the familiar left organizations, a few labor activists, and a faction of the ecology movement. As it became clear in the 1990s that the Clinton Democrats had abandoned both the working class and the environment, two parties were formed to propose a political opposition and alternative: the Labor Party, which prematurely followed Frank's advice but soon fell into factionalism and was constrained by the affiliation of a half-dozen unions still committed to the DP; and the Green Party, which experienced a wave of initial success, especially in the 2000 election, but experienced multiple fissures after falling victim to the charge, endlessly repeated by the liberal opinion journals, that it was "splitting" the progressive forces. As I will discuss further in this book, the majority of the active left and liberal forces have either remained committed to the Democratic Party or, especially since the mid-1990s, renounced electoral politics and even the idea of fighting for power and, instead, dedicated themselves to protest and resistance. Meanwhile, the ideological and political right seems to be shrugging off its many scandals and remains assured that the cautious and increasingly conservative Democrats will barely lay a glove on them, as it dominates the political scene.

But maneuvers at the top do not tell the main story, which is that the Wealth Gap is now the biggest in American history, the power of working people has not been weaker since the late 1920s, and the social gains made by women and blacks in the 1960s and 1970s have been steadily pushed back. Frank argues that the conservative attack on abortion is a smokescreen for the right's economic insurgency, but in fact *Roe v Wade* is teetering on the edge of repeal. Even if the Supreme Court majority deems *Roe*'s complete abolition to be politically unfeasible, the invocation of states' rights is likely to make Kansas and twenty other states bastions of official, religiously based repression of sexual freedom. At the same time, even as liberals such as Michael Kazin, Jim Hightower, and Frank call for the return of Bryan-like populism within the Democratic Party (notwithstanding Bryan's blatant racism, of course), the Democratic congressional leadership is busy discouraging former representative and NAACP official Kwesi Mifune from seeking a Maryland Senate seat because he is simply too militant and "can't win" because of his "extreme" views. And, led by the senatorial campaign committee chair, New York's powerful Charles Schumer intervened to pressure an Iraq war veteran, Paul Hackett, to step down from his announced intention to enter the Democratic senatorial primary in Ohio, because his views on Iraq contradict the party's cautious support of the continuation of American military occupation—even though there is mounting evidence that it has contributed to prospects for a civil war in that beleaguered country.

My overall aim in this book is to argue that the left, which has been in thrall of the Democratic Party for seventy years, needs to organize itself as an independent radical political formation based on the country's social movements, the dissident wing of the labor movement, and radical intellectuals. Specifically, the party's immediate task is to form a genuine political opposition to the main drift, which is moving in an accelerated pace toward state authoritarianism. I also claim that it is time to develop and propose economic, social, and democratic political ideas different from those advocated by conventional liberalism and the traditional left. In this quest, a new political formation must invent new forms of discourse, of struggle, and of political and social theory.

For their comments and criticism on Chapters 1 and 2, I want to thank the following members of the *Situations* collective: Bill DiFazio, Julia Nevarez, Mark Zuss, Heather Guatney, Patrick Inglis, Ivan Zatz, and, especially, the co-managing editor of the journal, Michael Pelias, who read and criticized drafts of the entire manuscript and edited these first two chapters with discernment. As always, Ellen Willis has been my severest critic and an incredibly helpful editor. Rick Wolff commented on Chapter 2, and Robb Burlage organized a discussion among health advocates, based on their reading of the same chapter, from which I gained many useful insights. Thanks also go to Dean Birkenkamp, the publisher and editor-in chief of Paradigm, and my friend Henry Giroux, editor of the series in which this volume appears, for encouraging me to expand the first two chapters into a book.

◇

Introduction

Time for a New Radical Party?
American Politics on the Edge

There are few times in history when one can confidently declare that we stand at a dangerous crossroads. This is one of those times. We are in danger of abrogating many features of our imperfect liberal democracy and sinking into an authoritarianism, what George W. Bush terms "the unitary executive," that ignores Congress and the law in its quest for arbitrary power. The ancient left slogan composed by Rosa Luxemburg during World War I and reiterated by many in the era of fascist insurgency—that the fundamental choice confronting us is *socialism* or *barbarism*—has never been more pressing. George Bush's flagrantly unconstitutional, executive-driven practice of spying on American citizens without a warrant is countered by neither fear of impeachment nor censure by Congress. With the president's approbation, the US military maintains torture camps in Guantanamo, authoritarian Romania, Poland, and elsewhere; these are only the latest indications that we have entered a dangerous place in our political life. Moreover, the left and liberal organizations have been unable to thwart the Bush agenda to pack the Supreme Court and federal district courts with right-wing ideologues. Fatefully, the Democrats used their opposition to the nominations during the congressional hearings as a weapon in the midterm elections in 2006, depending on constituents' pressure on members of the Senate, along with a week of Senate hearings on each of Bush's two radical right nominees, to expose the ideological hue of John Roberts and Samuel Alito. These entreaties failed to prompt the Democrats

1

to filibuster the nominations. All but a handful of opponents, mostly professionals linked to the liberal establishment, remained otherwise demobilized as the public was reduced, by and large, to spectators to deliberations that were predesigned to approve the candidates. When on January 15, 2006, centrist Senators such as California's Diane Feinstein declared that a filibuster was an inappropriate way to derail Alito's nomination, it became clear that, whatever the inclination of the liberals (Feinstein finally reversed herself), they would not have the votes to defeat a cloture motion. The apparent explanation for the Democrats' callow refusal to invoke the filibuster was Tom Daschle's defeat in the 2004 senatorial race, a loss that was said to be attributable to his "obstructionist" tactics. What the Democratic establishment seems to have forgotten is that it is a minority and the putative opposition. And as such, if it does not use every measure at its command to stand up for principle, it may be convicted of complicity with the right's agenda.

We might also consider here Bush's brazen refusal to seriously address global warming. His decision not to sign the relatively mild Kyoto treaty because it might constitute a threat to economic growth is perhaps his most egregious threat to the survival of the planet's life forms. This posture has given new (and literal) meaning to the phrase "après nous la déluge" (after us the flood). The administration's openly anti-working- and middle-class fiscal and social policies constitute a direct assault on the poor—an expanding fraction of the US population—and on the once-stable sections of the working and professional managerial classes who daily can feel the ground shifting under their feet. The tepid response of Democrats, trade unions, feminists, and civil rights and environmental organizations—America's putative opposition class—only compounds the felonies. Although some opponents gathered around the ACLU during the reauthorization of the notorious Patriot Act in late 2005, and organizations like Move On sounded the alarm and temporarily thwarted the right, the level of fury and mobilization remains fairly weak. Most of the opposition seems to be waiting on Congress, the Democrats, or a fairy godmother to rectify the mounting accumulation of wrongs.

The left-liberals, no less than the moderates who control the Democratic Party, assume the lingering viability of the traditional strategy of putting pressure on the government and on representative institutions such as the legislatures to change social, foreign, and civil liberties policies. And during the 2004 presidential election they faithfully followed the idea-less Democrats on the road to almost certain defeat on the premise that its candidate, John Kerry, was not worse than Bush (in the ironic words of one commentator "not a lunatic").[1] They remained virtually silent as the Supreme Court awarded the 2000 election to George W. Bush by stopping the recount ordered by a lower court in Florida's heavily populated counties, even in the wake of overwhelming evidence that his minions had stolen the vote in Florida—the crucial state that, despite his loss of the popular vote, awarded Bush an Electoral College victory. In fact, Florida law disenfranchizes more than 800,000 otherwise eligible voters, most of them black. Against all evidence to the contrary, not the least of which has to do with the most ideologically loaded Congress and right-wing administration since Calvin Coolidge, the liberals have continued to place blind faith in the electoral process to reverse the current state of affairs. While some leaders of liberal and labor organizations are acutely aware of Democratic complicity, even collusion, in the pursuit of the Bush agenda (indeed, reports reveal that some congressional Democrats, including minority leader Nancy Pelosi, were informed by the Bush administration of its surveillance program but remained silent, perhaps because they were grateful to be "consulted"; others (associated with the DP's moderate and liberal wings) voted to authorize the administration's proposal to invade Iraq; and in 2001 all Senate Democrats save Russell Feingold of Wisconsin voted for the Patriot Act), they hold out hope that the Democrats will somehow see the light.

The liberals mobilize their constituents to write solemn letters to indifferent public officials, sign petitions, and even call their representatives, and these gestures pass for self-activity. Claiming the streets or organizing a genuine opposition political formation seems as far from their plans as going to Mars except, perhaps, when it comes to opposing the Iraq war. And even then, opposition has taken the form of a simple demand for withdrawal of US troops. The various wings of the anti-war movement have carefully avoided trying to offer an analysis for the intervention in the first place or to have taken the trouble to draw the consequences for Iraq of US withdrawal lest these split their ranks. War opponents have been willing to engage in mass demonstrations, but not in the complex work of providing to the public the tools of understanding. The anti-war forces do not believe in persuasion; otherwise, they would have emulated one of the most successful tactics of the anti–Vietnam war movement: teach-ins on college campuses, town meetings, studies, and white papers detailing the legal as well as political basis of the opposition.

And the left-liberal media, notably the magazines of opinion, staunchly refuse to examine the structure of the highest concentration of economic and political power in US history and the opposition's ideological integration, arguably the most important intellectual/political task of our own time. Specifically they have averted their eyes from the fact that elements of the top leadership of the Democratic Party are part of that concentrated power and have thwarted efforts to make the Democrats into an opposition party. Instead we are treated to a seemingly endless diet of Bush-bashing as if the Reagan revolution did not set the stage for both Democratic and Republican fiscal and social policies, and as if the bipartisan foreign policy forged in the aftermath of World War II does not still exist.

Nor are the left-liberal media willing to address in any serious way the bipartisan neoliberal consensus around trade, whose chief advocate was the Democratic president Bill Clinton. In this connection there is virtually no difference between the parties on the important question of supporting the activities of the World Bank, the International Monetary Fund, the World Trade Organization, and other agencies that are charged with managing the developing world in behalf of the neoliberal agenda of the leading powers. Nor is there a substantial debate in the legislative arena on whether capital should be able to move across borders at will. Capital's freedom to move anywhere it pleases has had dire consequences for US, European, and Latin American living standards. More than three decades of deindustrialization of the once-awesome US industrial machine followed Richard Nixon's abrogation of the Bretton Woods Agreement in the early 1970s, which had placed the dollar at the relatively stable center of world currencies—a fact that barely detains the liberals and has occupied the attention of only a small contingent of the labor left. This massive deindustrialization all but decimated the once-mighty industrial unions, reduced many of America's large and middle-sized cities to poverty, directly drove down living standards for millions of Americans who have been forced to seek employment in a retail sector that typically pays wages below the poverty line, and placed the economies of the more developed Latin American countries in jeopardy. For example, what are we to make of the discrepancy between the much-heralded low unemployment rate of under 5 percent in early 2006 and the fact that when Wal-Mart announced the opening of a South Chicago complex in January of the same year, and sought 365 employees, it received more than 24,000 applications. Yet apart from a few veteran labor advocates such as Michigan Congress member John Conyers, there is no congressional voice to address this question.

Until December 1999, when thousands converged on a Seattle meeting of the World Trade Organization, there was little protest in the streets as a significant portion of America's industrial base was being dismantled. But the United Steelworkers, the West Coast International Longshore and Warehouse union, feminists, anti-sweatshop activists, and a fairly large contingent of young "anarchists" (of which more in Chapter 5) came together in a disjointed, uneasy coalition. A portion of the protesters engaged in direct action and succeeded in shutting down the city for a few days; but, more dramatically, they called attention to the systematic anti-labor and anti–developing world actions of transnational capitalism and the US state. Until September 11, 2001, Seattle was the inspiration for a half-dozen major demonstrations in Europe and the Americas and for the organization of the World Social Forum, which remains to this day a gathering for the world's anti-globalization and global justice activists and intellectuals. As I argue in this book, there is a significant difference between the anti-globalization movement and those who seek global justice. The former unconditionally oppose the free flow of capital and the subordination of the developing world to its imperatives. "Global justice," like the issue of human rights, signifies an effort to improve the terms and conditions of subordination.

There is no doubt that the attack on New York's World Trade Center put a damper on direct action; in the fervor of patriotism and national unity that followed the disaster, many thought it unadvisable to protest in the streets of a wounded country.

Political reticence reigned on the broad left until February 2003, when, in an uncharacteristic burst of defiance, millions took to the streets in large and small cities to oppose the Bush administration's plan to invade Iraq. But after the invasion protest ebbed, opposition again took such traditional forms as letter writing and visits to Congress members.

After the swift removal of the Baathists and Saddam Hussein from power, Bush, donned in a combat jacket, confidently announced the end of the "military phase" of the war from the deck of an aircraft carrier. If the administration actually believed its own rhetoric, it was soon to be deeply disappointed. Having demobilized the Iraqi army, the US military neglected to disarm its more than 100,000 soldiers. Many of these former soldiers used their weapons against the conquerors and their Iraqi collaborators. By the summer of 2003 the military found itself fighting a guerilla war against a substantial fraction of the Iraqi population. As US and Iraqi casualties mounted, and the work of infrastructural reconstruction faltered, the Vietnam syndrome—earlier proclaimed dead and buried after September 2001—descended on the Bush administration: Recruitment to the voluntary military services declined, popular sentiment began to move away from support for Bush, and only the milquetoast Democrats stood in the way of his almost certain electoral defeat in the 2004 presidential election.

By the end of 2005 polls showed that a majority of Americans disapproved of the war, and despite Bush's narrow 2004 victory against an unimaginative Democratic opponent, his approval ratings had dropped from more than 75 percent following September 11 to about 43 percent. But while polls may be a rough measure of how a largely demobilized public responds to events and to the current political environment, it would be a serious mistake to rely on them as predictors of election outcomes, policy imperatives, or a reversal of fortune for the political party in power. Yet such reliance is exactly what has warmed the hearts of the opposition, such as it is. In the main, it seems to have forgotten the lessons of the past and present: The political system is rigged, its leading actors lack the elementary requirements of political independence from big money, and the Democratic Party is part of the problem, even if not at the cutting edge of perfidy.

Compromising Its Way to Oblivion

That the Democratic Party had largely abandoned its own New Deal legacy even before the so-called Reagan revolution remains a little-known fact to this day. It was Jimmy Carter, along with Ted Kennedy (arguably the leading liberal in the Senate), who introduced deregulation of banks and trucking in the late 1970s. These measures resulted in huge consumer interest rates and eventually compromised one of the sterling achievements of the Teamsters union long-distance hauling agreements: to take labor out of competition with itself on a national scale. And this was the period that witnessed the rise of global agencies such as the US-supported World Bank and International Monetary Fund, which increasingly took key responsibility for devising new forms of subordination of developing countries; chief among these was the award of billions in loans to the states of Africa, Latin America, and, as the Soviet economy slowly sank into stagnation and crisis, Eastern Europe. In return, these states agreed to temper redistributive programs such as social welfare, to pay back their loans at world interest rates, and to strengthen the hand of central governments to suppress land reform, workers' insurgencies, and other forms of popular protest. During the Carter years, a Democratic Congress and Democratic administration failed to enact a publicly financed national program, to end the thirty-year reign of the anti-labor Taft-Hartley amendments, and to restrain deregulated interest rates, which by the late 1970s had reached 15 percent or more. The left and the liberals were so enamored by Carter's foreign policy initiatives, especially his effort to bring Israel and Egypt together to make peace in the Middle East, that, except for a few unions that mounted something of a campaign against deregulation, they remained silent.

The last hurrah for the liberal wing of the Democratic Party was Ted Kennedy's unsuccessful primary fight in 1980 against the incumbent, Jimmy Carter. It proved to be an uphill battle owing to Chappaquiddick, but also because many of his erstwhile supporters were more loyal to the party than to liberalism. Hobbled by the seemingly endless Iran hostage crisis and the short-lived ideological split in his party, Carter's defeat in 1980 signaled a new wave of reaction. While the Reagan administration failed to privatize Social Security, this was perhaps the only significant setback of his administration's eight-year reign. But more crucial than legislative battles, the Reagan era marks the decisive shift in American politics of which we are still captive. Although Reagan was once viewed even by his Republican opponents (e.g., George H.W. Bush) as a right-wing lunatic, his political strategy has proven to be a blueprint for the right and has succeeded in driving the political debate. Reagan emerged largely unscathed from circumstances ranging from the arms buildup, ostensibly undertaken to bankrupt and ultimately overturn the Soviet Union—a program that provided the right with one of its sustaining myths that it was he who brought about the collapse in 1991—to the Iran/Contra affair, despite the Democrats' best but inadequate efforts to pin Reagan with the labels of corruption and violation of legality, and Reagan's own program of "starving the beast" of social programs, even as many of his associates were forced to resign in the wake of scandals. Dubbed the "teflon president," Reagan was able to survive mainly because of the Democrats' fear of impeaching him for blatant violations of the law. To this day, the prevailing national policy remains military keynesianism amid incessant efforts to reduce social spending, privatization of almost every major federal function, and an aggressive interventionist foreign policy designed to overthrow or undermine socially progressive or anti-American authoritarian regimes. When, in the wake of Bill and Hillary Clinton's woefully ill-conceived and failed efforts to provide universal national health care through the private insurance companies, and other fumbled policies, the Republicans won both houses of Congress in 1994 for the first time since 1946, any chance for a new beginning in providing public goods was indefinitely postponed.

The Democratic leadership has drawn lessons from the Reagan era: The old policies of imposing a progressive tax system on the wealthy, and the potential resort to deficit spending to provide jobs and income for the long-term unemployed, public housing, and a genuine national health program based on the principle of public financing, are forever deep-sixed. Instead, the party's platform is to maintain and to defend what social movements won from the 1930s through the 1960s—the shards of the New Deal, especially Social Security and higher minimum wages—but also, wherever possible, to accommodate to the right's foreign and domestic agenda without offending its base of Organized Labor, blacks, Latinos, environmental organizations, and women. This delicate balance is abetted by the subordination of Organized Labor and the old social movements to the national party, right or wrong. Since Clinton, the Democratic Party has stood for free trade, favored moderate nominees for the Supreme Court and district courts, justified its support of deregulation, and renounced Big Government by making a balanced budget its fiscal signature. In short, the party is deeply committed to the center-right. In the 1990s the liberals fretted and fussed and wrung their hands but were reticent in the face of Clinton's rightward swings because he seemed to be able to frustrate the most atrocious policies of the ultra-right. During this period the liberals disappeared as an independent force.

The basic question is, Why do liberals and a considerable fraction of the left cling to the Democrats? The superficial justification is that in a winner-take-all system of electoral politics, third-party progressive or radical electoralism is widely perceived as "throwing away my vote." Consequently, strategies range from building citizen pressure on key issues to keep a recalcitrant Congress in line to constructing a "party within the party" that, in its most articulate expression, would one day dominate the Democrats' program. Such was the implicit aim of Howard Dean's dramatic rise during the 2004 presidential primaries, which, beyond the candidate's own moderate domestic program, managed to scare the party's establishment. Remember, after sustaining a string of defeats at the upstarts' hands, a coalition of the various elements of the establishment—the Clintons and their wide network as well as the main line of the AFL-CIO and the media—waged a witheringly frontal attack on Dean, which catapulted the Senate back-bencher but independently rich and decorated Vietnam veteran John Kerry to the nomination. The party's left swiftly shifted its loyalty, money, and energy to Kerry, who proceeded to run a typical Democratic snooze-mongering race.

But a deeper analysis is needed to understand why the strategy of "a party within the party" is improbable and, from a practical perspective, nearly impossible. After all, it may be argued, didn't the right take over a moderate to conservative Republican Party by the early 1990s? And didn't the left liberals nominate George McGovern to the Democratic presidential candidacy in 1972? These appear to be parallel cases of successful insurgencies. But a closer look at the two cases reveals an underlying difference. The right-wing campaign to take over the Republican Party was a well-planned thirty-year effort marked by a level of ideological radicalism unknown in recent American history, at least within the major parties. McGovern captured the nomination because he opposed the Vietnam war, even as most of the party heavyweights stood by Nixon, or at least refused to take a flat-out stand of opposition. He was, in effect, a single-issue insurgent. In contrast, the right presented a full-blown vision for America that embraced almost every major political issue. Despite the fact that McGovern was a good liberal on domestic issues, he probably could not have been nominated without the support of the grassroots anti-war movement and the pro- versus anti-war splits within the Democratic Party and the corporate establishment.

McGovern's defeat led to a major shakeup within the party. The peace forces were routed from their newly won party offices by a centrist coalition of leaders of the congressional party, major funders (most of whom were corporate types and rich individuals), and the all-important leaders of the AFL-CIO who, with a few exceptions, notably the United Auto Workers and the public employees unions (but not the Cold War–led Teachers Union), sat out the election campaign after their candidate was defeated at the convention, thereby ensuring McGovern's rout. By 1974 the center-right had reclaimed the national party and the interlopers had been cleaned out of most state and local Democratic committees. Heartened by Richard Nixon's troubles, the centrist Democratic leadership, in alliance with an important coterie of members of the Eastern financial establishment, which had organized as the "Bi-Lateral Commission," prepared to regain the presidency after eight years in the cold. The corporate types were determined to restore the legitimacy of the capitalist state and clearly asserted that only a squeaky-clean Democratic centrist who was free of the taint of beltway politics could win. They looked at the demographics of the country, which had already indicated a decisive population shift toward the South and Southwest, and nominated a moderate former Georgia governor, Jimmy Carter.

After waging a ferocious battle within the party for power between 1967 and 1972, what did the liberals do? Discouraged by their defeat and, without the war to propel their dissent, they returned to the fold and supported Carter, despite his social conservatism—a capitulation that revealed the essential opportunism of their support for women's rights and for sexual freedom. Some were awarded portfolios within the Carter administration, but none achieved cabinet status, except perhaps the secretary of Health and Human Services, Joseph Califano, whose liberal credentials were somewhat suspect. As is the wont of liberals, they compromised their principles and gave up their fight for power within the party. But the now victorious centrists, sobered by their earlier intraparty loss, vowed never to be caught napping again. In 1984, after fielding one more liberal who, nevertheless, tempered his New Deal past and presented himself in the Carter mold, former Vice President Walter Mondale of Minnesota was humbled by a seemingly invulnerable Ronald Reagan. Four years later, in 1988, with the Republican presidential candidate, incumbent Vice President George H.W. Bush, reeling from the perception that he had completely yielded to the right in his party, and with a White House scandal under way, the Democrats nominated the governor of Massachusetts, Michael Dukakis, who ran an issueless campaign that revealed the party's new centrist orientation. Dukakis trumpeted his administrative and technical abilities, an approach that foreshadowed Al Gore's technocratic claims twelve years later. Unfortunately, however, Dukakis lacked the elementary rhetorical skill required of a national candidate and, like every Democrat since Harry Truman, pandered to the right on national security—and when he failed to address the crime issue in an appropriate way when the Republicans mounted the "Willie Horton affair," he went down in flames. Trying, somewhat absurdly, to portray himself as a strong proponent of national defense, he appeared in a photo atop a tank, dressed up in a military uniform. But acknowledging the need for a strong military establishment—as well as the existence of a skewed tax system that favors the wealthy, and, consequently, a relatively weak social welfare state—is a formula for permanent political marginality, a condition that even the charming, but deeply conservative, Bill Clinton was unable to remedy. Recall that Clinton won the presidency because of the split in the Republican Party, which culminated in the third-party candidacy of billionaire businessman Ross Perot.

Victorious and with a solid Democratic Congress, Clinton presided over nearly a decade of political stalemate, White House scandals, and the erosion of an already weakened welfare state. Despite his badly mismanaged health care proposal, Clinton made history. Fearing that he was losing support because he had been tagged by the right with the "L word" and weakened by a resolute Republican Congress, he signed away income guarantees for the poor in the 1996 Welfare Reform Act, as only a Democrat could do.

Modern liberalism is, by definition, a movement of compromise because it is deeply committed to the capitalist status quo and attempts only to make it somewhat more humane by providing some relief for those without resources and securing a limited menu of rights for labor, racial minorities, women, and the disabled. It is essentially, as was its predecessor, progressivism, a movement from the top; its primary constituency is the disaffected middle class, but its key agents are a fraction of the political directorate and the corporate bourgeoisie who, a century ago, recognized that untrammeled capitalism might rouse a genuine opposition and ultimately lead to dire consequences for the system. That it was brilliantly successful for sixty years had much to do with a roused working class that carried the burden of the 1930s economic crisis on its own shoulders and demanded more radical measures than even the New Deal had initially been prepared to institute, the complaints of farmers, and the new middle class of professionals who were similarly encumbered with foreclosures, high unemployment rates, and class degradation. For the past forty years liberalism has been at bay and, since the Reagan era, has been rendered illegitimate by an unyielding and incessant rightist campaign of vilification that has transformed the term "liberal" into an epithet to which the liberal response has been to say "Who me, liberal?" and accuse its adversaries of waging ideological combat.

Precisely. The right has been victorious because, unlike the liberals and their leftist supplicants, it offers a coherent account of the economic, political, and social situation based on fear, nationalism, religious moralism, and militarism—an ideology that it wears proudly. The right is by no means encumbered by electoral maneuvers. It has waged political, cultural, and ideological warfare on a broad front. Over a forty-year period it has maintained an uncompromising legislative program intended to strengthen the coercive powers of the state, to reduce social spending to its absolute minimum, and to assert US imperial interests on a world scale to the point of engaging in military action, when necessary. Its institutions have trained two generations of intellectuals to write, speak, and perfect its ideas; cultivated a corps of candidates and other public officials to carry its ideas into the electoral arena and to the institutions of private and public education, social and national security, and health policy; and acted like a movement dedicated to cleaving society around its claims.

And the right has been able to accept loss in order to assert its principles, as it did during Barry Goldwater's 1964 presidential catastrophe. After 1964 it conducted a thirty-year effort to conquer the state. Well financed by money from foundations such as Olin, and from leading figures in oil, arms, and food corporations, among others, it established a phalanx of think tanks including the Heritage Foundation, the American Enterprise Institute, the Manhattan Institute, and a host of others; it bankrolled magazines and newspapers such as the *Weekly Standard*, which is edited by William Kristol (the son of Irving Kristol, the Godfather of neoconservatism); and formed or supported public relations firms that fed the media with right-wing propaganda masquerading as news. In this regard Fox News Channel, a Murdoch-owned television station, is an entirely reliable voice of the right. It did not hesitate to intervene in intellectual as well as political life, supporting the organization of the National Association of Scholars and the Center for Popular Culture, whose main mission is to wage a red-baiting campaign on the academic left, even as liberal publications such as *Commentary* became, under the about-face of editors such as Norman Podhoretz, conservative to right-wing sheets or, like Martin Peretz's *New Republic* (a magazine that seems to have adopted the global playbook of neoconservatism, but remains moderate to liberal on domestic matters), economically relatively progressive, politically centrist, and socially liberal to conservative.

The right is radical and has ideas about how to comprehensively organize society to benefit its base, which consists of large corporations, fundamentalist religious institutions, small-town merchants and other business interests, and a considerable fraction of the professional-managerial class. The liberals are neither radical nor committed to the interests of their base. They stubbornly cling to a piecemeal approach toward societal problems and disdain coherence because it might get them labeled as ideological. But they have a seemingly infinite capacity for compromise. In fact, especially on trade, military spending, social issues, and civil liberties, they have been willing to sacrifice the interests of their base in order to prove their mainstream credentials. The right targeted the Republican Party because, except for its ability to win presidential elections, and until the advent of its most effective political intervention, Reaganism, the party wandered in the wilderness in most Democratically controlled state houses, cities, and, of course, Congress. The reinvigorated right drove out congressional caretakers such as Robert Michel, the perennial minority leader, and replaced them with bona fide Southern ideologues such as Trent Lott, Bill Frist, Newt Gingrich, and Tom Delay, who vowed to take no prisoners in their march to power. During these thirty years it operated as an independent force and refused to be subordinated to the compromises that Republican legislative leaders felt obliged to make with the liberals and moderates. Assisted by the politically astute Reagan administration, during which the liberals found themselves outmaneuvered and outthought—but also by the center-right Clinton White House, which, in its first two years, was effectively stymied by its own confused identity and conservatism—the right, in the 1994 midterm congressional and state elections, was ready to make its move with Newt Gingrich's "Contract with America," the manifesto of a New Right that outlived Gingrich's rule over the House of Representatives. His demise illustrates another key feature of our times: the delusional liberal faith that corruption scandals involving leading right-wing politicians are enough to guarantee their victory. The right can bear these setbacks because it has a party line that outweighs individuals. It can always bring up new cadres to replace the deposed. From scandals involving Oliver North to Gingrich to Louis Libby, it barely felt the heat. In contrast, the liberals have only the memory of their heroic past, a host of personalities without substance, and the will to accommodate a restive and suspicious electorate. But Hollywood stars and glamorous young politicos do not a party make. By the time Gingrich went down in 1998, the liberals and the left had compromised themselves to the point of helplessness.

The New New Social Movements

The abject failure of liberals to hold the line—let alone make significant gains, even in the direction of piecemeal reform—and the firm hand of the Republican right over repressive state apparatuses such as the police, the vast prison system, the courts, and the military have prompted many to form strong anti-electoral, almost anti-political grassroots movements and advocacy organizations that have no organic ties to the older civil rights, feminist, and environmental groups. Since the mid-1990s a new generation of activists has occupied the space of opposition. It is uncompromising and often anti-capitalist. Its forms are mainly: anti-globalization protests; union organization by graduate assistants at prestigious private as well as public universities; undergraduate campaigns against sweatshops and, more recently, against the Coca Cola company's anti-labor policies in Latin and Central America (with the result that this soft drink has been driven from a host of campuses); resistance against gentrification and organized movements that occasionally elect radical local officials; the World Social Forum and several regional social forums (outgrowths of the anti-globalization movement that support efforts to reconstitute a new civil society); and a variety of "social justice" initiatives on the labor, anti-hunger, and human rights fronts that have posed new challenges to the flagging older feminist and civil rights movements. To which we might add the Green Party and the Labor Party, which, albeit in different modalities, share many of the anti-establishment values of the newer movements. There has emerged a "generational divide" because the older organizations have, at least in the eyes of their younger beholders, lapsed into a lethargy born of both bureaucratic rot and co-optation by the Democratic Party establishment.

These movements and organizations operate quite autonomously and independently from each other. As we shall see in the next chapter, they share, often unwittingly, what I call a postmodern approach to politics. That is, conditioned by the failure of the Old Left, the left Democrats, and the "new" communist parties to offer significant oppositional politics, they tacitly and explicitly avoid forming an alliance that might offer a systemic alternative to the prevailing transnational capitalism. Instead, they have advanced the slogan and the practices of "protest and resistance" and, in the main, have settled for a politics that, I contend, behind their backs ends up as a radical version of pluralism, the leading political ideology of American liberalism.

This book is an argument for the formation of a new radical party of the left. I try to integrate the perspectives of the new grassroots radicalism with a new concept of the "party." While I am critical of the anarchist wing of the anti-globalization movement, I appreciate its creativity, energy, and anti-authoritarian impulses. Although I believe that Marx and the democratic radical tendencies in marxism can offer much to this project, I do not intend to reproduce the serious distortions of the past: undemocratic centralism, dogmatism, third worldism and the egregious tendency of many to justify or apologize for the authoritarian practices of "socialist" countries, whether the former Soviet Union, Mao's China, Vietnam, or Cuba. Altogether I am convinced that without a new political formation that can combine the characteristics of an electoral vehicle with those of the extra-electoral—cultural activity, education, the strengthening and building of grassroots movements, and the creation of new communities—the dire predictions of Luxemburg and of the anti-fascists of the 1930s and 1940s will likely be realized. The greatest danger is that we will remain burdened by the past. Under these circumstances the left will find itself caught in the tangled web of fragmentation and, for this reason, will sink even further into marginality and oblivion.

Note

1. Ellen Willis, "Symposium on 2004 Election," *First of the Month* (Fall, 2004).

1

The Retreat to Postmodern Politics

What Is Postmodern Politics?

"Postmodernism" is a term of multiple definitions and meanings. Following Jean-Francois Lyotard's declaration that postmodernism is, essentially, not so much an attitude as a "condition" from which its philosophical and intellectual forms derive, the condition of which Lyotard speaks signifies a kind of social being in which the precepts of modernity are overturned, or at least severely tested.[1] Fredric Jameson has argued that postmodernism is the cultural logic of late capitalism; as opposed to modernism—which, even as it depicts estrangement of the subject from itself, retains the dream of the whole person—its forms of artistic representation may be understood in the modes of pastiche and parody.[2] Postmodern art surrenders to the fractured self and the fragmented social world. Art and politics follow no set rules, but they do obey a few of the imperatives that the Enlightenment dictates: deep respect for scientific thought as much as the results of science; a profound quest for rationality, if by that term we mean the search for explanatory propositions about the natural and social worlds; strict obedience to the rules of evidence upon which to base judgments; and, above all, a renunciation of myth and religious symbols as guides to conduct. While Freud tries to understand the unconscious in order to control it for rational ends, postmodern philosophy acknowledges the reign of the

This chapter initially appeared in *Situations* 1, no.1 (spring 2005). Reprinted by permission of the author Stanley Aronowitz.

irrational and, implicitly, argues that any effort to conquer it or, indeed, to understand the unconscious with the use of rational categories and scientific methods—even of symptomatic reading—is an exercise in futility.

As a social and political philosophy, postmodernism often connotes the renunciation of "grand narratives"—that is, the point of view of the totality. In its social scientific expression it may be identified with "social construction," a conception of social things that is radically anti-foundational: Since, according to its precepts, social phenomena are constructed by actors and their sediments, one does not need a theoretical framework consisting of concepts and algorithms in order to engage in social investigation or commentary. In fact, Erving Goffman's *Frame Analysis* may be read as self-critique since Goffman was among the most persuasive writers in the social construction-ist canon. But postmodernism also leads to suspicion of social and political theory itself since the concept of "theory" implies a web of relations that are interconnected. Theory wants to "make sense" of the world by creating concepts of understanding that link otherwise disparate phenomena to each other in schemas that make individual events and phenomena intelligible. In other words, frames. Postmodern thought presumably revels in grasping the essential incoherence of social and cultural things and, in effect, constructs understanding by patchwork and montage.

A second and no less powerful application of some of these predispositions may be found in politics. Postmodern politics may share the marxist critique of contemporary society—that it is increasingly dominated by capital, for example—but has refused to propose a systemic alternative such as socialism or communism—of the social-democratic no less than the leninist or anarchist varieties—on the grounds that these are closed systems that inhibit creative thought and action. This break with both the liberal and marxist pasts of Hobbes, Locke, Hegel, and Marx has come to signify a certain celebration of the fragmentation of the social world because, among other virtues, it can protect the autonomy of individual expression and group identity against concepts such as class or other types of social interest linked to a collectivity that it perceives as oppressive. The reply to the centralization of power by capital is to undermine it from below, to avoid making sweeping, generalized indictments of the system, but instead to resist its power on a piecemeal basis. In this sense postmodern politics has an elective affinity with pragmatism, perhaps the earliest and the most compelling of postmodern political philosophies. Since there are no underlying ideological criteria from which to evaluate the system taken as a totality, pragmatist political theory proposes a piecemeal approach that "tinkers' with the system.

Beyond theoretical objections to the standpoint of the totality stands the historical failure of the social-democratic and Communist projects to fulfill the dream of human emancipation. In fact, some the most terrible violations of individual and collective freedom have been perpetrated by "really existing" socialist societies such as China and the Soviet bloc, ostensibly in the interest of "emancipation." And social democracy has become, in its European varieties like modern liberalism in the United States, no better than a version of welfare state liberalism: Politics is now a contest over which political force can best manage the capitalist state in a manner that protects human rights and provides for the welfare of the poor, but there is no challenge to the concept and the rule of capitalism itself and whether it can meet popular needs, especially in the era of post-fordism (when the tie between production and consumption within a national economy is broken). Precisely because late capitalism has become the unchallenged presupposition of social democracy no less than liberalism, the best they can offer is a largely exhausted doctrine of political pluralism. As I argue throughout this book, postmodern politics adds one new dimension: the hope that social movements, particularly those of feminism, black freedom, and ecology and, in a different register, a kind of radical urbanism can, in some way, supplement—or replace—the labor movement and its political parties—Labor, Socialist, Communist, Democratic—as the linchpin of social transformation. But since this hope is rooted in their rejection of marxist orthodoxy according to which the working class alone, or in leadership of a class-based coalition, stands in a privileged position to change the social world, in the main they have been unable, even in the few instances when they were willing, to provide a political vision of transformation. Rather, they offer the program of "resistance" to prevailing state or transnational capital's policies. To the old vision that the object of the radical project is to create the "whole person" from the thrall of alienation and fragmentation, while acknowledging the accuracy of Marx's analysis, postmodernism refuses his implied prescription of a new society, especially because the political parties that have invoked his name, and purport to follow his prognostications, have so distorted the emancipatory project that it is no longer worth preserving, at least in its extant form.

At the same time, the notion of "vision" itself is criticized on two principal grounds: To propose a totalizing future is to give an example of "bad" utopia. It becomes a "line of march" from which there can be no deviation without dire consequences for the dissenters. From this perspective the vision constitutes a kind of determinism, against which the creativity of practice is measured, usually to the detriment of the latter. So, in the interest of combating dogmatism, postmodern politics tends to lapse into a kind of realism that, in its own way, becomes the mirror image of party marxism. Since utopian thought is strictly precluded, the conversation revolves around the possible. Needless to say, the predilection of postmodern politics is to refuse and denounce the party formations, past, present, and future. In effect, if not in intention, it tends to merge with liberal pluralism: even when—as in Germany and France, the ecologists, for example, formed their own parties that are postmodern in character because they refused to counterpose their vision of a new society to the prevailing versions—the new social movements have gradually taken on the role of pressure groups within a Democratic or Social-Democratic coalition. That they have influenced the parties to become somewhat "greener" there can be no doubt. But they have been unable to counter the hegemonic neoliberal framework of contemporary political parties, right and center. And they have stubbornly clung to a failed coalition politics that generally leaves them ultimately in the cold.

Perhaps the most characteristic aspect of postmodern politics is the degree to which it has accepted the idea that marxism—indeed, all prescriptive and utopian political thought—is identical with its stalinist version. That there are significant trends in contemporary marxism and anarchist social thought that reject the notion that society can be constituted as a consensual identity seems to have escaped their notice. Here I want to carefully distinguish Theodor Adorno's concept of the "nonidentical" and Jacques Derrida's nonmarxist idea of "differance" (the play of the distinction between "defer" and "differ") from the idea that the totality itself is authoritarian. The concept of the nonidentical connotes the fallacy of the reconciliation of opposites into a new state of identity that preserves as it transforms. Derrida insists on difference but does not posit a permanent gulf between knowledge and its object, nor between the categories of understanding and those of existence or being. He merely wants to defer the notion of identity or the unified self as long as such ideas avoid deconstructing the myths of the Enlightenment.[3]

I want to argue that the "totality" need not be conceived as the point of arrival in a new identity shared by all of humankind. For example, capitalism as the name for the economic, political, and social totality of our time is constituted by its contradictions, and by the opposing actors who embody them. It is not only a question of the nonidentity of the subject and object within the alienated totality of capitalist social relations. It is as well the statement, most forcefully enunciated by Louis Althusser, that communism would not abolish contradictions nor the conflicts among participants.[4] That is, the new society will not result in the end of politics because neither "interests" nor problems of recognition of, among others, individuals, social formations such as women and their relation to men, and racial formations can be abolished without generations of struggle. Moreover, a new society would inevitably generate unforeseen new contradictions that would surely be different from those that prevail in capitalist social relations.

The period of the long transition to even rough equality in work relations, those in neighborhoods and other forms of association, will undoubtedly be protracted. While we should engage in the effort to overcome these rifts—indeed, politics will consist largely in the conflicts arising from these efforts—we should not expect them to be healed in short order, nor should healing imply the end of social conflict as such. In this respect, utopian hope is a radical futurity, the enunciation of the not-yet, but a full recognition that, in the slogan of the anti-globalization movement, another world is "possible" even when it appears as a vanishing horizon. That postmodern politics cannot accept the not-yet as a legitimate goal for a radical movement reveals its failure of radical imagination.[5]

Needless to say, not all postmodern political thought shares the same perspectives on all questions. In some of its forms, postmodern politics converges with liberal conceptions of a radical democracy (one that, in effect, leaves the workplace to capital because it cannot envision a different workers' movement save one that remains ensconced in the struggle for bread and butter), but tries to fix the disabled system of representation; in another register, it correctly insists on the importance of the new social movements, although what some writers mean by the "new" refers largely to those that sprung into being in the 1950s and 1960s, partially in protest against the tyranny of the left political parties and organizations that acted like proto-parties. And still another tendency, most often identified with contemporary anarchism, refuses to engage the state in a positive struggle for hegemony. Instead, this tendency wants to concentrate on the restoration of the autonomy of civil society against state interventions. In the words of anthropologist Pierre Clastres and philosopher Michel Foucault, it wants to defend "society against the state."[6] We shall have occasion to return to these themes in Chapters 3 and 4.

In what follows I want to examine the work of Sheldon Wolin, one of the major political theorists of our time. Wolin exemplifies a pastiche of radical analysis that borrows, among other sources, from historical materialism, while refusing to depart from the conclusion that postmodernism provides the best chance for a radical politics.

Postmodern Political Theory

Since the appearance of his landmark work of political philosophy, *Politics and Vision,* in 1960, Sheldon Wolin has been a major influence in turning the study of politics from its abstract ethical orientation toward social theory. The main presupposition of social theory is that the possibility for what Wolin terms "participatory democracy" is immanent in the totality of economic, political, and social relations. Inspired largely by his example, but also appalled by the slow erosion of democratic institutions in the United States and around the world, a considerable fraction of succeeding generations within political theory has adopted the stance of social theory rather than remaining within the orbit of conventional political philosophy concerned with the old questions: What are the first principles of politics? How can politics be autonomous from economic and social influences? How do political philosophers free themselves from the pernicious influences of Machiavelli and Rousseau, let alone Hegel and Marx, all of whom insisted that politics was integral to class power?

The turn that began with *Politics and Vision* signifies that for a left-liberal American political theory class, inequality, power, and the role and obligations of the capitalist state have been thrust from the shadows to center stage. So it was with anticipation that the expanded edition of his classic text appeared in 2004,[7] especially given that, in the more than forty years since the first edition, Wolin has arguably become the leading left-liberal political philosopher in the United States. While he has lost none of his capacity for brilliant, often scorching commentary on the tepid liberalism that dominates today's intellectual landscape, Wolin's conclusion confirms not only the end of the liberal phase of political philosophy but the crisis in social theory that seems unable to rise above the despair that marked most of the history of the Frankfurt School—which, in the aftermath of the fascist era and the apparent betrayals of workers' power by the states of the Soviet orbit, concluded that the rule of law within a liberal democratic regime was the best we could expect. Indeed, in this new edition, it is glaringly apparent that Critical Theory has influenced Wolin, including the resignation to the prevailing setup that marked its late development.

Like Benjamin Barber, Robert Weibe, Robert Dahl (whose migration from the pluralist ideology was a stunning aspect of his later writings), Amy Guttmann, Mark Warren, and many others, Wolin's project is to determine the prospects for, and conditions of, democratic renewal in the wake of what he perceives as a near-complete corporate capitalist takeover of the modern state. In the light of this project I will try to assess what he has and has not achieved and what remains to be theorized in order to realize the project. My chief conclusion is that, despite a sincere and often trenchant analysis of the current state of affairs, Wolin's retreat to a modest, episodic (he calls it "fugitive") democracy is a symptom of the isolation of many left-liberal intellectuals from actual oppositional movements, and of their refusal to take seriously a sophisticated marxist analysis; his misreading of Marx and contemporary marxism prevents Wolin from taking the point of view of the totality and produces only a fragmented vision, which he calls postmodern. In Chapter 6, I outline a different direction for social and political theory to take if the project of radical democracy is to be realized.

The Decline of Liberal Democracy

Ours is a time when a relatively honest election almost anywhere in the world is greeted by many as a triumph because wide participation in the act of voting has become the virtual definition of citizenship and of democracy. A citizen confers consent on the prevailing system of political rule, choosing among contenders for power who, nevertheless, are pledged to manage and reproduce the liberal state. To be sure, this is a definition as old as the origins of liberal democratic governance in seventeenth-century England. One may question whether representative democracy is real democracy because elections are rigged by, among other means, legislative decisions about districts, exclusion of some voters from entering the process, and the huge funds needed to run a credible campaign. But in this reactionary era we are admonished to accept the idea that the farthest horizon of democracy consists in legal protections for individual and collective political expression, short of insurrection; a justice system that guarantees individual civil and criminal rights before the law; and representative government in which citizens confer consent on the prevailing system of political and economic power through the transparent exercise of the franchise and are free to choose among competing parties that offer platforms that promise to rule in a lawful way corresponding to accepted practice. This view is hegemonic in all liberal democracies, whether ruled by conservatives, the authoritarian right, or labor and socialist parties. In the American system, private property shields its owner(s) from being required to share decision-making with workers or nongovernmental citizens, and only collective bargaining agreements ensure a degree of worker voice in decisions affecting a limited range of enterprise activities; many aspects of economic life are not democratic but, indeed, correspond to the most authoritarian practices of anti-democracy. Recall Andre Gorz's characterization of the industrial workplace as a "prison factory."[8]

In the sphere of state functions, Wolin's pithy comment says it all: "The citizen is shrunk to the voter: periodically courted, warned and confused but otherwise kept at a distance from actual decision-making and allowed to emerge only ephemerally in a cameo appearance according to a script composed by the opinion-takers/makers."[9] Wolin attributes this reconstitution of the "civic culture" to the emergence of capitalist subsumption of all aspects of society, including its political institutions, under a fundamentally anti-democratic regime of domination. Echoing Critical Theory's concept of the "totally administered society"—uniformly derided by pluralists and much of the left—in this new form of repressive totalization, Wolin notes: "The unity of theory and practice is ironically realized in the optical illusion of all utopias: in uncollapsed and totalizing capitalism no one seems able to see 'beyond.' Consequently the notion of alternative appears irrational."[10]

Certainly, even from the perspective of representative process, some countries are more democratic than others. Israel and Germany have systems that permit the smaller parties' representation in parliament if they meet a threshold of votes. And France, where representatives are elected by district, ensures that the winner has received a majority of the votes by mandating, in cases of pluralities, a runoff of the top two candidates a week after the general election. Contrary to the popular myth that the United States is marked by political pluralism, its "winner take all" system and the absence of a runoff provision in federal and state electoral processes in most instances effectively thwarts the emergence of third parties, but also signifies that, in a sharply divided electorate, and one in which half the voting population does not cast ballots, a large majority may be disenfranchised. Thus, in the recent past, victorious president candidates were elected by about 30 percent of eligible voters.

An electoral majority or plurality itself, no matter how narrow the margin, and no matter what proportion of the electorate has chosen or has been coerced not to participate, is taken as a mandate for the implementation of a series of policies that may or may not be popular. Witness the 2000 and 2004 Bush victories. All the dominant party needs is a sliver of legislative members of the putative "opposition" party to go along in order to implement its program. For example, although polling data showed that a majority of voters opposed or were skeptical of the justice of the Bush administration's huge permanent tax cuts for the rich, and had serious reservations about privatizing Social Security, it behaved as though it had a mandate to move forward on these and other proposals to implement reverse redistributive justice.

In the alternative view, democracy has been defined as the participation of the "people" in decision-making. In the context of the nation-state, the citizenry intervenes on a continuous basis in the decisions affecting their everyday lives as well as the life of the community, whether the national or a local jurisdiction. This concept, often termed "radical" democracy, has been variously identified with the "cooperative commonwealth" (the old Anglo-Saxon term for "socialism")—a self-managed society of producers of social as well as economic goods, in which the "state" either disappears or is relegated to administrative (i.e., coordinating) functions but, in any case, does not impose its will from above. This bottom-up regime does not necessarily mark the "end" of politics, but it sharply restricts the sovereignty of bureaucratic, centralized institutions. Representatives are chosen by popular assemblies of workers, members of the armed forces, and neighborhood residents and merchants. These assemblies may elect delegates to make decisions subject to the popular will. Radical democracy confirms the right to recall representatives at any time. In Wolin's conception, the state, but perhaps only the local state, becomes a site for popular decision-making, and politics consists in genuine debate and discussion about what constitutes the community interest. Sadly, in the wake of the collapse of the "official" institutions of popular sovereignty—the workers' councils—these conversations have all but vanished in contemporary political discourse, largely due to the virtual disappearance of radical and revolutionary movements, let alone "socialist" societies where the abridgement of these principles often spurred oppositional movements from the left. Of course, where popular decision-making is on the political agenda, even if not essentially operative—in Brazil and Argentina, for instance—the public conversation revolves precisely around these questions. More of this later in the present chapter and in Chapters 4 and 5.

Despite the sound and fury surrounding the 2000 and 2004 US national and state elections, the differences among contestants, in the United States, and in many countries of Europe, have narrowed so much that some observers argue that national electoral politics is little more than the granting of collective consent to the prevailing neoliberal consensus. And in the United States we have been in a state of near-total military mobilization for sixty years of putative peace, a policy that crosses partisan political lines. Neither major political party stands for isolationism. Certainly not even the Democrats challenge the main drift of foreign policy. Election opponents differ only on matters of strategy and tactics of how to secure global US economic and political hegemony, no longer on principle. And it is not exclusively a question of whether the major parties agree that the prevailing system of capitalist power is off the political table. In the United States, the bipartisanship that has dominated executive and legislative decision since the Spanish American War has withstood the rancor of sporadic partisan debate generated by the emergence of anti-war movements that reflect the views of a substantial portion of the population. In one of the rare instances of public airing of the question of whether to go to war—the congressional debate over the 1991 Gulf war—many in the opposition argued that the decision was hasty and should be delayed or should be referred to UN jurisdiction, not that the war itself was unjustified. In the American discourse about war, liberals and moderates sometimes differ from the war party over tactics. But the Bush administration's 2003 rush to the Iraq war saw the Democrats divided, with its eventual presidential candidate, John Kerry, voting for the war resolution. And during the presidential campaign Kerry was consistent in his refusal to oppose the war, even when it became clear that, as with Vietnam, there was little to no chance of a clear-cut military victory, let alone winning the peace.

During the 2004 presidential election, at least at the level of political programs the two parties were not far apart. Kerry accused the Bush administration of bungling the Iraq war and promised to pursue its resolution more intelligently and with increased military force. Despite his often blistering criticisms of his opponent on particulars such as sending too few

soldiers to protect a swift military victory over the Iraqi government forces, Kerry never once questioned the war itself. The
Democrat took the stance of the bipartisan post–World War II
US foreign policy, which was committed to multilateralism, in
which the Western alliance, through either the United Nations
or NATO, was designated as the proper vehicle for conducting
wars against rogue regimes and other threats to international
stability. Only in areas where the Great Powers maintained their
sphere of influence, as determined by the Big Three at Potsdam
and Yalta and in previous agreements, were they permitted to
take unilateral military action. Indeed, Harry S. Truman received UN sanction for intervening in the Korean conflict, but
Dwight Eisenhower sent troops into Central America without a
multilateral cover since, before the Cuban Revolution, he knew
that neither the Soviet Union nor Western European powers
would actively contest the right of the United States to promote
its interests in the region. Similarly, when the Soviet military
crushed the Hungarian Revolution in 1956 and sent tanks
into Prague in the spring of 1968 to suppress reform, neither
Eisenhower's nor Johnson's administration lodged more than
formal protests.

Since the end of World War II there has also been bipartisan
agreement that the state of permanent war requires sacrifices
of public goods. Moreover, since the 1970s the Democrats
have acknowledged that the privatization of public goods may,
under some conditions, be desirable, although they have been
hesitant to support plans to privatize the national pension
program, Social Security, largely because a substantial fraction
of its constituency directly benefits from the program. Thus,
consistent with the failed plan advanced by the Clinton administration to provide universal health care through the private
sector, Democratic presidential candidate John Kerry agreed
with the Republican, George W. Bush, that a government-fi-
nanced and administered universal health care system was out
of the question. The challenger offered instead a complex and
largely undecipherable scheme that left the system, including
its most costly feature, prescription drugs, in the hands of
private corporations and suggested government subsidies as a
way to bring the uninsured into the privatized system. Similarly,
on the question of trade policy—which, since the passage of
NAFTA in 1993, has elicited considerable opposition from the

unions, among other sources—Kerry stood firmly for free trade, a cardinal plank of neoliberalism, and promised only to revisit the issue after the election, but only for minor tinkering.

These experiences remind us that even in a liberal democracy, at the commanding heights of political power no less than at the local level, the parties in power steal votes, "persuade" members of the state and federal courts to thwart legitimate procedural challenges to elections, and, through a network of local officials committed to victory at any price (broken machines, intimidation, bogus challenges, and planned understaffing of voting sites), rob opposition constituencies (largely black and working-class voters) of their ballots. For example, there is reason to believe that the Bush reelection victory—which, because of the arcane Electoral College system, depended crucially on the Ohio results—was purchased by the widespread use of these tactics by county Republican election officials and sanctioned by the Republican election commissioner, who was George Bush's campaign chairman for the state.

For more than three decades the public has been treated to a veritable avalanche of scandals involving high elected officials who have taken bribes and used their offices to benefit cronies, campaign funders, and lovers; a president's administration that used drug money to finance illegal counterinsurgency activities in Nicaragua, though it would surprise few if other presidents were involved in similar shenanigans; and, thanks to an outrageous Supreme Court decision granting candidates the right to ignore campaign finance regulations, in 2004 both candidates were able to circumvent these badly crafted campaign finance restrictions, exempting them from public accountability. At the federal level, regulatory agencies such as the Securities and Exchange, Environmental Protection, Food and Drug, and Federal Communications commissions have been so compromised by congressional underfunding (which, in the administrations of both parties, corresponds to the administration's complicity with major corporation lobbies who often write the regulatory codes, that the laws they are constituted to enforce are often inoperative—a sign of both parties' complicity with lobbies representing major corporations and the agencies' indifference to corporate flaunting of these regulations. Bipartisanship was illustrated by the Clinton administration's "voluntary" program of corporate regulation and the use of a market exchange to allow companies to avoid compliance with environmental rules. Moreover, Clinton's budget chronically underfunded inspection and other regulatory personnel. While the US example is perhaps most flagrant, these practices are widespread in Eastern Europe and Latin America and some nations of Western Europe. That the opposition Democrats in both presidential elections bowed to the will of the courts and to the realities of local political power indicates that democracy, even in its representative guise, is at best episodic in the current conjuncture or, as Sheldon Wolin has argued, "fugitive": "Above all, it should be recognized that in the contemporary world democracy is not hegemonic but beleaguered and permanently in opposition to structures it cannot command. Majority rule, democracy's power principle, is fictitious. Majorities are artifacts manufactured by money, organization, and the media."[11] For these reasons he concludes that

> small scale is the only scale commensurate with the kind and amount of power that democracy is capable of mobilizing, given the political limitations imposed by prevailing modes of economic organization. The power of a democratic politics lies in the multiplicity of modest sites dispersed among local governments and institutions under local control (schools, community health services, police and fire protection, recreation ...). Multiplicity is an anti-totality politics.[12]

So ends the expanded edition of Wolin's much-praised magnum opus *Politics and Vision,* first published in 1960 and reissued with five new chapters in 2004.

In the original chapters, which remain unaltered in the new edition, Wolin treats his readers to a breathtaking survey and commentary on the history of political theory that revolves around a dominant theme: Is it possible to realize the hope of political philosophy since Plato to create an autonomous politics? Machiavelli, who broke from medieval political philosophies, which were based on ecclesiastical dogma, was the first modern political thinker insofar as he helped establish politics as "an independent area" of inquiry and rigorously excluded religion and other nonpragmatic issues while focusing almost exclusively on the problems of power. According to Wolin, he "offered a new science of statecraft" based on the then revolutionary idea that the prince's sovereignty depended, crucially, on the consent of the "people" and could no longer rely on heredity or the absolute sovereignty of the medieval prince to exercise rule.

Leading philosophers of the prerevolutionary period in France (such as Montesquieu and Rousseau), but also political economists (notably the Scottish Adam Smith and the English Thomas Malthus), argued that the economy and, by extension, nature as the ground of production and reproduction of physical life, occupied pride of place in society. As Wolin showed in his earlier writing, even seventeenth-century proponents of natural right, such as Locke, and of the priority of the political order as the genuine site of the general interest (as opposed to the particular interests of economically dominated civil society) were fatally drawn to the idea that the self—the basis of political life—is fundamentally conditioned by its social surroundings in which private property plays a pivotal role, and by the natural conditions that form the basis of productive activity. In turn, informed by private property the social was infused with private interests that complicated the task of constituting a unified, sovereign state, and forming a polity that could reach consensus concerning their common problems, was fated to be frustrated.

The concept of the autonomy of politics from social and economic relations was severely challenged in the eighteenth century, even as the bourgeoisie, to facilitate its dominance in the production sphere and civil society (which had been reduced to market relations), demanded control over the state form as a necessary complement to its economic and social hegemony. Wolin terms the rise of economic and social thought "anti-political" in the sense that statecraft, as much as popular participation in state decision-making, was theoretically as well as descriptively undervalued. Needless to say, the anti-political tendencies within liberalism itself prepared the ground for what became known as the "managerial revolution" associated with the twentieth century, and forcefully argued, in different ways, by Thorstein Veblen, A. A Berle, and, most popularly, the erstwhile American marxist James Burnham, whose book *The Managerial Revolution* became a best seller in the immediate years before World War II.

Written at the end of the 1950s during the Cold War and amid confident declarations of unparalleled prosperity, even as theorists of the American celebration such as Robert Dahl (who later changed his mind) proclaimed the pluralism of US power, and the increasing concentration of corporate wealth dominated the media and other sources of public information, *Politics and Vision*'s explication of an "Age of Organization" thesis strongly resembles Daniel Bell's contemporaneous contention that we had arrived, at least in the West, at the "end of ideology." Bell tends to approve, if not entirely celebrate, this development. In contrast, Wolin insists that, by its focus on class and other sectoral interests and categorizations, social science had neglected the "general" dimension of society, the need for integration of disparate groups, which remains the function of politics and cannot be replaced by administration. Wolin deplores the elevation of the large corporation to the level of a quasi-state and the consequent elevation of the business executive to the status of "statesman." In sum, in 1960 Wolin retained his critical ethical stance against the anti-politics of bureaucratic and corporate domination of society, but offered neither prescription nor theoretical discourse that pointed to new agents capable of restoring to the polity its central place in decision-making. In the absence of any but ethical alternatives, the earlier essay trails off.

The essential contention of the long concluding chapter of the earlier edition was that politics had been eclipsed by the "Age of Organization." In concert with Max Weber's theory of rationalization, Wolin argues that modern societies were dominated by technical rationality. Decision-making had conclusively passed from political elites and property owners—and certainly from the demos—to managers and experts who exercised bureaucratic control of the functions of the economy as well as government, whether in "American capitalism, British Socialism or Soviet Communism."[13] Thus, the emancipatory doctrines of liberalism and marxism had been fatefully displaced by the requirements of large-scale organizations for efficient and "neutral" management. For example, conditioned by the balance of nuclear terror between the world's two superpowers, wars were all but excluded that were not officially sanctioned by them as "local." This is surely a judgment that could not withstand the Cuban Revolution and the subsequent Cuban missile crisis of 1961, in which the Soviet Union apparently attempted to establish a military and economic beachhead in the Western hemisphere—a perception fueled by the spread of insurgencies throughout Latin America that were inspired by the survival of the revolution; the global implications of the Vietnam war, and the concomitant spread of communism in Southeast Asia; and the intensification of turmoil in the Middle East.

Nor, one might add, were Wolin and his colleague John Schaar—then professors at the University of California—unaffected by the 1964 student Free Speech Movement at Berkeley, which challenged the corporate university with democratic demands, especially the right of students to engage in national politics on campus. In fact, Wolin collaborated with Seymour Martin Lipset on an edited collection of commentary on the movement and its demands and, with Schaar, wrote a fairly sympathetic assessment of the movement that contrasted with Lipset's and other professors' generally hostile comments.[14] After Wolin moved to Princeton in the early 1970s, his political ideas became much more radical. At the end of the decade he founded and edited a short-lived journal, *Democracy,* that was, de facto, a dialogue between marxists and radical democrats. Wolin's seminar at Princeton mirrored his belief that Western marxism, associated chiefly with the Frankfurt School, might offer some clues to the resolution of the crises of liberalism and orthodox marxism, of which he was acutely aware.

In the new chapters added for the 2004 edition of *Politics and Vision,* Wolin frontally addresses some theorists and philosophers who have captured the attention of considerable fractions of the intelligentsia during the past forty-five years: Marx, Nietzsche, "rationalists" such as John Dewey and Karl Popper, and the leading liberal philosopher, John Rawls. Wolin argues effectively that the "new" Nietzsche, celebrated by a legion of philosophers and literary critics beginning with Bataille in the 1930s and concluding—if not irrevocably—with Derrida and Deleuze, is misdirected because it ignores Nietzsche's elitist, anti-popular, anti-political "and therefore anti-democratic" and authoritarian side. In fact, notwithstanding outbursts of right-wing populism that are deployed opportunistically in electoral campaigns, Wolin seems to argue that we are living in a Nietzschean World.

Of course, this aspect would not give Martin Heidegger pause. His celebration of Nietzsche's anti-democratic railings was fully consistent with his own denigration of the everyday and of the concerns of ordinary people, especially their penchant for solidarity with friends and family, but also on the basis of their common interests in society. Wolin argues that it is this side of Nietzsche, rather than his often trenchant arguments against "laws" of history, and other scientistic dogmas, that is characteristic of his writings. Against those twentieth-century French philosophers who attempt to rescue Nietzsche from the charge of being pre-fascist and anti-semitic, Wolin aggressively demonstrates, with a kind of overkill of quotations from a broad range of his writings, that the traditional characterization is right, if incomplete, because it ignores Nietzsche's importance as a political thinker.

Nietzsche's main concern, as with other political philosophers, is with power. As with all of the critiques, Wolin proceeds from the question of how is democracy possible and finds Nietzsche an impediment rather than an ally of this project. His argument suggests that the protagonists of the Nietzsche revival are either naïve or complacent regarding the fate of the Enlightenment in the twentieth century. Wasn't the twentieth century a time when the Enlightenment project was brutally deformed, not only by the rise of fascism and the degeneration of communism, into a bureaucratic nightmare? As Horkheimer and Adorno argued, it was challenged from within its own precepts, raising the question of whether it is possible that society could be organized rationally and particularly according to scientific precepts.[15]

The will to scientificity—which Nietzsche identified with the will to power—has given rise, at all levels of social organization, to the rule of managers and other experts with its concomitant usurpation and denigration of the sovereignty of the ordinary citizen. Indeed, Wolin critically invokes Karl Popper's identification of the "open society" with the rationality of science.[16] Recall that in view of the impossibility of devising a method to affirm the truth of any scientific proposition, Popper sought to evaluate the claims of science by the criteria of falsifiability. Any scientific proposition not subject to repeatable experiment would be adjudged poetry or worse.[17] But, as Wolin correctly notes, to organize society on these principles would require that only qualified experts be entitled to access to rule. Of course, the educational system would bear heavy responsibility for training such people but, parallel to Walter Lippmann's famous argument in *Public Opinion* (1921), the role of the polis in the management of society is reduced to the ritual of approving or disapproving the performance of professionals trained in rational methods of governance. Wolin justly derides this phantasm as impractical and, contrary to Popper's prattle about the "open" society, ultimately undemocratic. Despite this claim, Popper's discourse is a version of the rationality that informs the ideology of the modern capitalist state, no model of participatory democracy itself.

The second effort to bring rationality to political affairs while retaining a small-town version of participatory democracy finds Wolin far less critical. While remaining skeptical of John Dewey's attempt to offer a prescriptive participatory model based on face-to-face interaction among equals because it remains ensconced in conditions of rural and small-town life, whose time in industrialized urban society is all but past, Wolin's own views are closely parallel.[18] In view of his recognition that the conditions of contemporary economic, political, and social life have so reduced citizenship on the large scale, Wolin holds out hope that democracy has a chance to flourish at the grassroots level in such issues as education, health, and the environment. His own embrace, albeit somewhat despairing, of a postmodern democratic politics retains a strong affinity to the underlying assumptions that inform the social psychology of Dewey and his colleague George Herbert Mead. We know the world and ourselves in the process of face-to-face interaction with "significant others." The social process of abstraction signified by the dominance of the mass media and other large-scale state and economic institutions such as the corporation are, for Wolin, barriers to genuine communication and therefore undermine real democratic decision-making.

Wolin reserves his most biting criticism for John Rawls's doctrine of redistributive justice not only because Rawls was the most influential theorist of the post–World War II generation of political philosophers but also because his work remains almost identical to modern postutilitarian liberalism. Liberalism, in Wolin's lights, fails because it leaves the socioeconomic system intact and offers only palliatives to redress the blatant inequalities of capitalist economic relations. And, as Wolin points out, Rawls's *Theory of Justice* (1971) is careful to renounce any effort to address these relations. Insofar as Rawls stays within the confines of the current political and economic arrangements, his proposals for redistributive justice must ultimately fail because, by accepting the status quo institutions, they would reproduce the inequality (and other injustices) they intend to mend:

> Rawls' liberalism accepts democracy as a formal principle of "free and equal citizens." The revealing passage is where he explicitly condemns the "civil humanism"—a code word for expressing participatory democracy—and sides with the more elitist classical republicanism. Civic humanism/participatory democracy is denounced as a comprehensive doctrine that "man is a social, even a political animal, whose essential nature is most fully achieved in a democratic society in which there is widespread participation in political life." Participation, Rawls remarks disparagingly, is trumped not merely as a right but as a "privileged locus of the good life."[19]

Wolin has arrived at the position of radical democracy by means of a comprehensive critique of the limits of political philosophy—including its liberal variant, which retains a too narrow vision of society. This leaves him with two alternatives: a radical democratic marxism, whose critique of capitalism, he readily acknowledges, is unmatched by any other paradigm; and what Wolin terms "postmodern democracy," which incorporates large chunks of the contemporary neomarxist critique of late globalized capitalism but ultimately rejects both its designation of the proletariat as capitalism's gravedigger and Marx's conviction that it must be transformed root and branch.

That Wolin addresses Marx in a fairly wide compass indicates his political and theoretical evolution since the early 1960s. It is a courageous intellectual act, considering that even the most liberal and social democratic of his peers carefully avoid taking this step. Wolin combs the *Economic and Philosophical Manuscripts, Capital,* and the historical and political writings to discover whether, despite the general discredit to which Marx and marxism have been subjected, especially since the collapse of the Soviet Union, there is anything left to salvage. Wolin's reading of Marx is filtered through the lens of political philosophy, especially the problem of power. In this project he traces Marx's early and later perspectives on the prospects for democracy and for revolutionary transformation of society.

While accurately showing that, in general, Marx favored proletarian engagement in the institutions of liberal democracy (indeed, Marx argued that the struggle for suffrage was the "last" great working-class struggle under capitalism), Wolin argued that in a system of class exploitation, these institutions were unable to secure social freedom, let alone justice for its subjects. Contrary to the liberal expectation that elections are the proper forum for settling major political issues or the more sophisticated contention that civil society is the space for the resolution of social differences and conflict through debate and dialogue—Habermas's public sphere—Habermas himself argued in his great early work *The Structural Transformation of the Public Sphere* (1962) that the institutions of "civil society" generated by the bourgeois revolutions of the eighteenth and nineteenth centuries are reduced to the marketplace, thereby inhibiting the emergence of a public sphere in which rational discourse might clarify and solve social issues. As Hegel showed, commodities and commodity-exchange become the substance of civil society where buyers and sellers are perennially antagonistic to each other.[20]

In the cauldron of the capitalist market the proletariat, whose only saleable commodity is its labor power, is the class in "radical chains ... in but not of society." Marx argued that the proletariat was a revolutionary class out of necessity, not moral suasion. Uniquely situated as the fundamental source of capital accumulation, the labor process, but under conditions of ruthless exploitation, the proletariat is "designated" by Marx as the agent of historical change that, through its struggle over basic needs that capital in its relentless pursuit of profit cannot permanently satisfy, develops a vision of the new society. Under these circumstances, in and through revolutionary action, which always evolves from unmet demands for elementary needs, the working class may realize the potential for human freedom inherent in, but betrayed by, capital's relentless pursuit of its own interests after it calls society as a whole to defend freedom.[21]

At the same time, capital's great achievement was to abolish the institutions of past feudal societies that fettered the forward march of history, particularly a system of land tenure that, relatively speaking, protected, intergenerationally, the peasants' right to remain on the land. The betrayal, manifested infamously in the enclosures of the commons, consisted chiefly in capital's refusal to make good on its declaration of universal human freedom. While it often was obliged to concede political liberty and the right of the people to confer formal consent on the political forms of its rule, it was unable and unwilling to extend democracy to the sphere of social production, nor did it concede voting rights for the propertyless, and for women, without a fierce and prolonged struggle. The divine right of property is the absolute limit of capital's commitment to democracy.

Wolin detects a contradiction in Marx's naming of the proletariat as the historical agent capable of liberating humanity from the thrall of capitalist social relations. On the one hand, Marx shows that capital reduces the worker spiritually and physically to a cog in the machine of commodity production. One of the crucial features of the past that capital all but destroys is the power of the craftsperson over the labor process. As we know, by the turn of the twentieth century the last vestiges of workers' control, rooted in the skills inherited from a much earlier time, were co-opted and appropriated by systems of rationalized production such as taylorism and fordism. Even the ostensible legatees of the artisanal mode of production, such as toolmakers, carpenters, and tailors, are no longer the masters of production.

All but a few skilled workers repair or maintain the machinery or the commodity and become subject themselves to the capitalist division of labor. Equally significant, as Marx shows in the last chapter of *The Grundrisse*, is that with the application of science to the labor process, the machine and other technologies have become largely "self-activating"—a concept whose prescience was richly verified in the mid-twentieth century when automation and computerization gradually dominated the processes of industrial production. Now the worker had definitively become the object rather than the subject of the production process. At the turn of the twenty-first century, nearly all sectors of industrial production, distribution, communications, and state and corporate administration have become subject to the vicissitudes of cybernetic technologies in which the entire labor force follows the rules intrinsic to the digitalization of nearly all economic activity; the computer—the characteristic machine of late capitalist production and reproduction—invades, with force, our social and psychic lives as well. Production occurs without the direct intervention of the worker who, as Marx remarks, has been relegated to a "bystander," pushing buttons, watching and reporting on gauges, and reporting breakdowns or irregularities to mechanics and managers.

Capital is a "social relation," meaning that its hidden character is that it owes its existence to the appropriation of the labor time of both intellectual and manual labor. A condition of its expansion is the subsumption of labor under its rule. Yet, on the other hand, despite computerization—numerical controls atop lathes and other standard machines, automatic feedback mechanisms, and robots—living labor, in its various forms, remains crucial to the production process insofar as, despite the relative marginalization of its direct role in production by technology, it retains its regulative function. The motive power of the machine is supplied by labor; machines only partly produce other machines; the intellectual and manual labor of design, tool-making, and mold-making are the absolute condition of mass production. Almost universally ignored by political philosophers who have detected the end of the working-class intellectual, the labor involved in operating automated equipment, transporting commodities from the shop to the truck or train, and bringing the product to warehouses or markets remains vital to realizing and transforming capital from its material form to its money-form.

In Volume 3 of *Capital,* Marx argues that the relentless reduction of the part played by direct labor in the production of the commodity in the intensive regime constitutes a crisis since labor time remains the basis of value. The value of the commodity is constantly cheapened by incredible labor productivity, the so-called multiple powers of labor. This puts enormous pressure on profits, which, after all, are derived from surplus labor. But if surplus labor for each unit of production is reduced to nearly the vanishing point in industries such as chemicals and oil refining, monopoly and oligopoly can mitigate the crisis through price-inflation in certain products and, most important, by further intensifying the technological fix, but only for a time. Under conditions of competition between highly centralized capital (examples in the computer industry include Hewlett Packard, Compaq, IBM, and other PC makers), after the initial stage of expansion based on high prices—which partially cover the costs of research and development—prices tend to fall precipitously, and mergers and acquisitions ensue because the smaller and weaker corporations—even many technical pioneers—cannot withstand the price wars and can no longer raise capital. At the end of the process, only a few firms are left standing, but capital still scrambles to get rid of inventory. After all, no matter how relentless the cost-cutting practices of technological innovation, in the end the product must be exchanged for money. Hence, for example, the realization crisis that afflicted computer makers from 1998 to 2004.

After suffering what its apologists termed a crisis of productivity during the 1960s—a symptom of the vigor of workers' resistance to the logic of capital—the last three decades of the twentieth century were marked by a systematic and largely successful effort, promulgated by new global institutions such as the World Bank and International Monetary Fund, and national states under the hegemony of Western capital, to drive the working classes of the advanced capitalist societies into submission. This class war is still under way; but it must be admitted that, through globalization and decentralization of production, reductions of the social wage and, above all, the weakening of workers' movements, capital achieved most of its objectives. The strike wave that ignited during the last two years of the 1960s may have subsided in the West, but, in the face of brutal suppression both by client governments of the United States and by former Communist regimes, it has been taken up by the newly industrialized workers in the developing world.

Since Wolin is, in the main, unconcerned with exploring the question of capitalism as a system of social relations or the real processes by which capital is produced, its fundamental unit being the commodity and the inherent relations that are reified in its material forms, his focus on politics and power leads to a bleak conclusion about the uses to which Marx's analysis of capitalist social relations might provide for democratic social transformation. The new social forces that arise as a consequence of the complex changes in the modes of material and ideological production largely elude his analysis. So, apart from the influence of Critical Theory's powerful analysis of the cultural and political contradictions of late capitalism—which are exemplified by Marcuse's *One Dimensional Man* and Horkheimer and Adorno's *Dialectic of the Enlightenment*—Wolin remains impressed chiefly by the failures of what may be termed the "real socialism" of the Eastern bloc and China. That is, if it can be shown that, overcome by the powers of technology and capitalist organization, the working class is no longer capable of confronting a much stronger adversary, global capitalism, the whole project of a self-managed socialism and its "midwife," the social revolution, is rendered obsolete.

Against his own intentions, Wolin arrives at the postmodern turn. While rhetorically endorsing the dialectical concept of the totality, Wolin concedes that fundamental social transformation is now off the table because socialism—which promised to transform the social world root and branch—has failed. Concomitantly he is pessimistic about the chances of achieving democracy beyond the local level. Democratic struggle must, he admits, confine itself to reinforcing "fugitive" democracy, which is necessarily episodic and limited in scope. However accurate is this evaluation of the current state of affairs, its consequences are dire for the fate of theory and practice. The piercing metaphor of "fugitive democracy" suggests that it has become outlaw, but also marginal in advanced capitalist societies. While immanent in the concept of fugitive democracy is a piercing critique of the claims of liberal and authoritarian states alike to have achieved some kind of "end" of history, this concept is not only bereft of hope but never rises to the concrete because it fails to identify countervailing tendencies, especially outside the United States, which, after all, is not the center of the world.

Wolin is not alone in his stripped-down version of democracy and social justice. Others—such as Benjamin Barber, Michael Walzer, and, indeed, a veritable legion of former marxist intellectuals including Chantal Mouffe, Ernesto Laclau, and, although retaining his radical edge, Sigmund Bauman—have taken the postmodern turn: They have abjured "grand narratives" (anti-totality) and utopian visions, and have abandoned the search for a new or significantly altered paradigm of social transformation. Although most call themselves "radical" democrats, they advocate the "realistic" politics of what Cornel West and Roberto Unger have settled for: pragmatic tinkering with the institutions of liberal democracy. In this sense Habermas is right to argue that modernity remains an unfinished project if, in most cases, it has led left intellectuals back to liberalism—albeit not without critique.

The Decline of the Public Sphere

In concert with traditional political philosophy some liberals, as well as an important strain of modern philosophers whose farthest horizon has been the possibility of an autonomous political sphere, are experiencing tremendous anxiety in the wake of overwhelming evidence that the economic, social, and cultural spheres are, both theoretically and practically, structures of dominance in the configuration of political life. More precisely, the autonomy of the nation-state—especially its coordinating role of the economy, and its ability to unify and mobilize the underlying population around its program—has been called into question by (a) the argument recently advanced by Benedict Anderson that the nation is a fiction, an "imagined community" rather than a social "fact," and by (b) the reemergence of large corporations, especially those that are transnational, as key political actors after their relative recession in the era of state regulation, which abruptly came to a close in the 1970s. Capital's concomitant abrogation of the informal social contract between capital and labor in the most advanced industrial societies—which, to a large degree, was facilitated by the postwar agreements designating the dollar as the stable international currency—has produced a slow but steady slide in real wages. Wage stagnation is mitigated only by the proliferation of part-time, contingent, and temporary employment of women and youth, the combination of which has precariously maintained the household wage, even as social wages—popularly designated as the "welfare state"—have plummetted.[22]

With the decline of the European and US labor movements and the consequent deterioration of the remnants of civil society and the public sphere, the capitalist state is undergoing a fairly prolonged period of transition. Contrary to some recent arguments, the national state has not disappeared; instead, its core functions have shifted from the legitimating institutions such as those of social welfare to, on the one hand, providing the monetary and fiscal conditions for the internal but spurious expansion of (fictitious) capital, among whose elements is a reverse redistributive program and, on the other, supplying a vastly expanded regime of coercion—that is, the growth of the police powers of government at home and abroad directed against the insurgencies that object to the growing phenomenon of an authoritarian form of democracy. In this form the procedural institutions of liberal, representative government are preserved, but, owing to vast centralization of capital and of economic and political power, the substance of participation is equivalent to conferring consent.

This shift does not mean that all aspects of the social wage are subject to repeal; but in the United States it does suggest the transfer of a considerable quantity of public goods to private hands. The law remains powerful, but now the taxing powers of government are a mechanism for the transfer of wealth from the working class to large corporations and wealthy individuals. Lacking a concerted counterattack by workers and other sections of the relatively powerless class, this reverse transfer payment inevitably will result in the decline—both absolutely and relatively—in the share of national budgets devoted to the social wage. If these trends have been displayed more haltingly in Europe, this is due not to some vague concept of "political culture" but, rather, to the specific resistance of the labor movement and its allies. For example, when the rightist governments of France and Italy proposed pension and health care reductions, sometimes in the form of reducing the number of employees in the public sector, they were met with labor-led mass demonstrations and strikes and were forced to scale back or withdraw their plans. However, recent proposals to reinstitute the forty-hour work week from the prevailing thirty-five hours in Germany and France have not provoked the same level of working-class opposition because many have been convinced that one can no longer decrease hours in a single country or a small group of European nations as long as the United States and the developing world, especially China, are still mired in overworking and underpaying the workers.

In the United States and most countries of Western Europe, democracy is reduced to a voting ritual in proportion to the decline of civil society and the public sphere. Habermas had already noted the decline of the "bourgeois" public sphere by the late eighteenth century. But with the advent of mass consumer society and its entailments, especially suburbanization and the relatively easy credit system, lacking the political and social will by workers' organizations and their parties, the development of what Negt and Kluge term the "proletarian" public sphere[23] was effectively thwarted.

In the United States during the first half of the twentieth century, the chief sites of the democratic sphere were the local unions of the insurgent industrial working class and the neighborhoods they inhabited. Even as the top layers of the labor movement became more centralized and bureaucratic in the 1940s and 1950s, and given that the largest multi-worksite local unions in the big cities were really "little" national unions in their practices and ideology, there were thousands of single worksite local unions whose democratic practices exhibited a high level of membership participation both on the shop floor—where wildcat strikes were not uncommon—and in the administration of union committees. And many other sites of working-class conviviality remained: the bar, social clubs closely linked to industrial labor, ethnic societies, and, yes, ladies' auxiliaries of local unions and nationality-based institutions such as the Polish National Home and Ukranian, Jewish, and Russian mutual aid societies. The rank and file tended to show up at membership meetings where, in many instances, they spoke without fear and intimidation. In the Auto, Steel, Electrical, and Rubber Workers unions, winning an election to the local union office was often a sign that the candidate had gained the confidence of the most militant and vocal section of the rank and file. And when their choices turned out to be corrupt or otherwise failed to serve members' needs and interests, the membership did not hesitate to throw the rascals out of office.

By the early 1950s a combination of laws and contract concessions had eroded the shop-floor militancy that protected and extended formal and informal worker-imposed restrictions on management's power to speed up the assembly-line and otherwise unilaterally set production standards, and limited the right of the unions to bargain over changes in the way the company does business. Unions began to sign long-term contracts that, among other shackles, restricted the use of the strike weapon to the expiration of the contract or, in the best scenarios, permitted strikes during the life of the contract only for a limited group of issues. Many unions watered down their rank-and-file steward systems by making stewards full time and enlarging their jurisdiction, which effectively reduced the number of activists and gave shop floor leaders a vested interest in holding union office (hardly anybody voluntarily returned from the full-time union office to the line). These changes provoked a rash of wildcat as well as official strikes in the last half of the 1950s and, in the current of opposition and insurgency of the1960s, led to the mass organization of public employees, to a veritable revolt among black auto and steel workers against racist union policies, to a brief rebellion among young workers and members of the armed forces in Vietnam and at home, and to the birth of a new feminist movement whose breadth has still to be adequately chronicled. But these insurgencies were short lived. Their agents either were drummed out of the shops, settled for less than they once were prepared to accept, or won union office only to find that the forces of conformity were stronger than those of innovation and dissent.

When the black freedom movement and locally based community organizations turned their attention in the 1960s to what they perceived to be vast corruption and discrimination in municipal services, they found no trade union allies except among a handful of long-time left unions such as the Longshore, Electrical, and some of the newly formed state and municipal unions that had large black, female, and Latino memberships. By this time, labor was already split on the Vietnam war, to a lesser extent on the Democratic Party, and on the so-called social issues raised by feminists, blacks, and gays. By the 1970s many production sector unions were fighting the specter of deindustrialization and, after Reagan's presidential victory, were caught in the vortex of contract concessions amid membership losses. In sum, in these environments labor fulfilled C. Wright Mills's judgment that unions had become a "dependent variable" in the political economy. In several fundamental respects, in the past quarter-century, except in national elections and some local contests, labor's voice has been muted as unions have withdrawn from civil society and especially the public sphere. In turn, labor's *cause*, which still faces a mountain of unfinished business, has lost considerable public support since the farm workers' organizing campaigns of the 1970s, the fights of low-waged hospital workers, and the battles for public employees' unionism that electrified the labor movement and middle classes.

The Revival of Natural Law?

Political philosophy is, with the exceptions noted above, a normative science. Since Plato, its prevailing project has been to ask whether the realities of politics and of the state—the Is—reach the standard of the Ought. The tradition of political philosophy arising from *The Republic* seeks a prescription that links the current state of affairs to the Good. The Good is the self-evident set of values derived from natural law or from *a priori* religious precepts. In either case the first principles of the political order are fixed, prior to any possible consensus arrived at by argument or by convention. The main questions for those who follow the precepts of natural law are what are the elements of the Good and how do we arrange our political relationships so as to correspond to virtue, which, in political philosophy, is often taken as a synonym for the Good.

Of course, modern political theorists—confronted with the growing distance between, on the one hand, the concentration and centralization of capital (oligarchic control over large sections of the global economy and the consequent disappearance of the era of the small- and medium-sized producers) and, on the other, a political system that is prone to take direction from these corporations—have lowered their expectations. At the same time, since there is no political theory of the global metastate(s), contemporary political philosophers cling to the nation-state as the only possible context for politics. Thus communitarians, no less than the liberals they criticize, write as if global capitalism and its discontents are part of a distant universe. Alisdair McIntyre (another erstwhile marxist of the hegelian variety), Charles Taylor, and Michael Sandel remain locked in arguments derived from Kant, the empiricists, and their latter-day accolytes: What is the moral life, and how can the self achieve it?[24] But even they, like Rawls—whose theory of redistributive justice Sandel has sharply criticized—are obliged to acknowledge the power of the question of justice, even economic justice, in the constitution of politics.

It may be argued that almost alone among twentieth-century political philosophers, Leo Strauss and his followers are the last before the last, among practitioners of the profession, to proclaim the Good and the search for its contents as the sole task of political philosophy. As I shall argue at the end of this chapter, the very last is the great marxist utopian Ernst Bloch, whose defense of natural law is perhaps the best argument for freedom in our time. Strauss and Bloch go back to the early Greeks but draw radically different conclusions. Bloch wants to show that the impulse to freedom is relatively autonomous from historical determinations. But Strauss seeks to reclaim the ancients for a very contemporary project of political reaction; his real object is to erase history except the history of ideas, especially those about morality. While acknowledging the social nature of humans, Strauss denies the historicity of ethics and politics; his definition of historicity is that everything, including philosophical concepts, inevitably passes away. Of course, he is confusing historicity with historicism; for Strauss, "historicity" preeminently stands for marxism. In a revealing passage Strauss imputes to marxism the view that a thinker's class origin determines or at least strongly influences her or his ideas:

> According to a view which today is rather common and may be described as marxist or crypto-marxist, the classics preferred the rule of the urban patriciate because they themselves belonged to the urban patriciate or were hangers-on of the urban patriciate. We need not take issue with the contention that, in studying political doctrine, we must consider the bias, and even the class bias of its originator. It suffices to demand that the class to which the thinker belongs be correctly identified. In the common view the fact is overlooked that there is a class interest of the philosophers qua philosophers, and this oversight is ultimately due to the denial of the possibility of philosophy.... [T]he selfish or class interest of the philosophers consists in being left alone, in being allowed to live the life of the blessed on earth by devoting themselves to the most important subjects.[25]

Presumably, by this little joke Strauss means to reveal marxism's vulgarity and the absurdity of any attempt to link class origins or class interest to philosophical ideas. Moreover, the "common people" had little sympathy for philosophy until the nineteenth century, "due to a complete change in the meaning of philosophy"—that is, when the concept of natural right was replaced by utilitarian, constitutional, and other deontologized conceptions of justice. Since, according to Strauss, all true philosophy concerns ontology, until Heidegger, ideas about nature as the ground of all aspects of human existence disappear. And it was Heidegger who went back to the Greeks to rediscover the "first principles."

Strauss claims that humans have lost or forgotten the true meaning of political philosophy: the quest for "first things," the principles or things that are "imperishable"—not subject to the vicissitudes of history. One must avoid seeking virtue in conventional meanings—that is, in conceptions that derive solely from "ancestral" authority or from divine revelation. For in these instances, political philosophy, which presupposes that we do not yet possess the knowledge of these principles, becomes unnecessary. Indeed, genuine political philosophy, as opposed to political theory and especially political science, seeks its object neither in convention nor in divine law but in "Nature," the term Strauss employs to designate the "eternal." But since Nature is hidden it must be discovered. The discovery does not nullify the ancestral or customary, but "uproots" it from its position of first principle. But "[b]y uprooting the authority of the ancestral philosophy recognizes that Nature is *the* authority."[26] In turn, this move nullifies the distinction between reason and authority. And this is the fundamental distinction between "classical" and "modern" natural right. Following Plato—the founder of classical political philosophy, for whom man was essentially a political and social animal—the straussian task is to discover the forms of the specifically political without regard to the sociohistorical conditions under which they exist. At the same time, in concert with only Rousseau among modern philosophers, Strauss locates the origin of virtue in the ancient Athenian and Roman cities.

Rousseau, whose famous proclamation of natural law in the first chapter of *The Social Contract,* "Man is born free," which implies a state of "nature" prior to "his" entrance into the social world where "everywhere he is in chains,"[27] advocated a return to "nature" while in civil society, invoking a kind of democracy that entails economic and social equality and "conscience"—derived from instinct and sentiment—as twin paths to freedom.[28]

Yet Rousseau was ambivalent about the Enlightenment, viewing science with considerable skepticism (see his *First Discourse on the Sciences and Arts*) and believing that civil society was, in the last instance, "closed and a site of inequality rather than providing a basis for its remedy." At the conclusion of the *Discourse on the Origin of Inequality*, Rousseau acknowledges the huge distance between the natural state of freedom and the social reality of inequality, whereby the stronger and more talented inevitably have more rights than others, and the distinctions between the leaders and the led in civil society lead to political despotism. Hence natural right, with its exhaltation of the state of nature and of the heavenly city as its social repository, becomes a utopian declaration of hope rather than a practical way to freedom.

If Rousseau may be claimed by social science as one of its modern founders, he was also the last of the great bourgeois political philosophers—last because, while he proclaims nature as the foundation for social critique, he no longer finds the origins of inequality in natural distinctions among people but, rather, attributes them to social arrangements. Under the influence of Rousseau and Hegel, the doctrines of natural right and natural law suffer partial eclipse in the nineteenth century, as ethics itself submits to the criterion of human ends as its basis and becomes deontologized. In this respect, historical materialism occupies a somewhat ambiguous place. Conditioned by the level of development of human knowledge of nature and embodied in science and technology, Marx notes that, alone among members of the animal world, humans create the object first in the imagination and then in its material form. Ends are conditioned by means but are in essence prior as well. It is important to assert that Marx was no social determinist: From the *German Ideology* to *Capital* he never tired of reminding us that the physical organization of man is the first premise of social production and therefore human history. Among the components of this physical organization is the brain, capable of imagining new objects and new relations before they can assume material form. In turn, this physical organization is conditioned by the natural environments into which communities are thrust. As Alfred Schmidt, Herbert Marcuse, James O'Connor, Joel Kovel, and John Bellamy Foster, among others, have pointed out, the dialectic of labor is, in the first instance, the relation between humans and "nature"—both that which is prior to their existence and the built environments inherited by succeeding generations. That balance with nature—its ecology—is vital for reproduction of the species these writers declare are already integrated by Marx into his critique of capitalist social relations. Marx's ecology consists precisely in his discovery that the imperative of labor, with its organic origins and consequences, is inherent in the fundamental proposition that humans are part of natural history.

In this regard Ernst Bloch's spectacular effort to restore the concept of natural law and natural right to marxism proceeds from the premise that human history is itself conditioned by human striving for freedom, an "ideal" (his term) that cannot be realized under all social conditions but which appears within every mode of production. Bloch's great insight is that there is a limit to historicity in the dialectic between the transhistorical and the historical. Bloch argues from philosophical evidence that, for example, Epicurus and the stoics already contain this striving in the Epicurean "law of pleasure" that stands outside of institutions of the status quo. "Of course," Bloch adds, "that the desires and life of the slaves could also be taken into consideration when securing such guarantees (against mutual injury and harm) is not even a possibility in a society of slave owners with its Epicurean garden for the elite. The Epicurean right to pleasure needed calloused hands to sustain it."[29] Thus Bloch retains the fundamental assertion of historical materialism of the primacy of the dialectic of labor: "[N]ature is the mother" of humans, but social relations configure these relations. In this discourse, history is the constraint to the natural law of the ineluctable striving by subordinate classes to human dignity, but not the determination of the law itself. The great Spartacus revolt in Ancient Rome, the eighteenth-century slave revolt in Haiti, and the early-nineteenth-century slave uprising in the American South may have been somewhat mythologized by historians and social theorists, but they are only a few of many "premature" challenges to the prevailing order by chattel slaves whose powerlessness was presupposed by masters and their acolytes. Similarly, the 1381 "Wat Tyler" peasant rebellion in England prefigured the uprisings of the English workers four centuries later—those of the luddites and the ranters—just as the appearance of the German and French working classes within the democratic revolutions led by the bourgeoisie in 1848 took place when capitalism had not yet reached its maturity in these countries. Unexpectedly, the signs of proletarian autonomy were not to be even partially realized for a quarter-century. Eric Hobsbawm and George Rudé have documented the activity of the "crowd" in the French Revolution, and in the Italian countryside. These so-called primitive rebels defied the expectations of their betters, and while rulers labeled them "dangerous criminals," according to Hobsbawm "bandits" were really agents of rebellion. And how do we account for the recent factory occupations in Argentina where, refusing to accept the decision of the employers to abandon the plants, workers have opened them and adopted a regime of self-managed cooperatives. Don't they know that the working class is only a potentiality, and no longer corresponds to the conditions of the globalized world?[30]

Wolin's trajectory tracks a path from the political morality characteristic of political philosophy before Rousseau to a recognition of the historicity of any possible ethical basis for politics. When the political philosopher discovers what Rousseau, Smith, Hegel, and Marx argue—that all modern (and postmodern) politics are class politics and are about power and hegemony, and that the state and its institutions are irrevocably linked to economic and social relations—the retreat to the postmodern constitutes, like all politics of despair, a profound, if unintentional, conservative ideological shift. This shift occurs because of the surrendering of a concrete vision of a new series of social arrangements and of political agents to address the transformations needed to realize them. Or, to be more exact, the postmodern political philosopher's vision of radical democracy remains hollow because it no longer provides a ground for hope, but merely restates a sophisticated version of pragmatic rationality. Needless to say, despite many "fugitive" actions by apparently defeated workers, there is much ground for pessimism, for precisely the reasons given in *Politics and Vision:* The traditional left opposition has been largely defeated, as have the "new" social movements, many of which have devolved into "nongovernmental organizations" (NGOs) and have become mouthpieces for liberal democratic regimes in the developing as well as the advanced capitalist worlds.

But the judgment that this is no time for world-historical theorizations or for a vigorous dialogue about alternatives to traditional formulae and expectations demonstrates the impoverishment of both analysis and an entailment of an anti-utopianism, which, in the last instance, is a de facto acknowledgment of the permanence of the current setup. Lacking not only a concrete conception of possible futures but also a sober assessment of incipient social forces, the political philosopher becomes overwhelmed by the forces of domination and can only urge us to be content to narrow our compass and our vision. Perhaps, as with Sartre and Marcuse, revival of the only chance of reversal of these ruminations will come when rebellion is reignited.

Taking the Next Step

I face a conundrum. On the one hand, I don't have the luxury of ending this chapter on a note of defeat since I have argued that the dialectics of defeat, enunciated with great eloquence by Critical Theory during and after World War II and repeated with numbing regularity by its legatees, no longer suffices, if it ever did. More to the point, this attitude reflects the growing isolation of intellectuals from movements of the global opposition. It may be argued that in the dim twilight of really existing socialism and the bankruptcy of the social democracies of Western Europe and their proto-equivalents in the North America, Critical Theory had nowhere else to turn. In the wake of the abandonment of the concrete utopia by the putative forces of opposition for most of the last half of the twentieth century, keeping alive critical analysis of the givens of the social world was—and remains—an important program. At the same time, I reject the cockeyed optimism of much of the left, which, on the whole, is bereft of even a fraction of the acuity of Wolin's analysis of the main features of advanced capitalism's betrayal of what, following the felicitous phrase enunciated first in the SDS's manifesto *The Port Huron Statement,* he calls "participatory democracy"—a concept that is still foreign to much of the left—and that certainly offers little more than the same formulae that failed in the past century. In this sense I follow Bloch in accepting the obligation of declaring and, even more, specifying reason for hope, without engaging in the phantasm of empty revolutionary rhetoric. The question is: Is the postmodern turn away from totality—the possibility of the emergence of a new subjectivity that can "grasp" the sprawling object and constitute itself as a new subject/object of freedom—as ineluctable as it is ubiquitous?

Introduced in "Note on the Dialectic," the new preface to *Reason and Revolution: Hegel and the Rise of Social Theory*, Herbert Marcuse's concept of the Great Refusal was an acknowledgment that the conditions of possibility for this eventuality resided only in the excluded masses: the working poor of the advanced industrial societies and of the colonial and postcolonial world. The preface was written in 1960, just after the victorious Cuban revolution against the ghastly Batista dictatorship; in it, Marcuse invokes the power of negativity as "hope against hope" against the increasingly narrow horizons wrought by the smooth repressive desublimation of technologically suffused late capitalism. Four years later, in *One Dimensional Man*, he declared that only from those entirely excluded from the blandishments of consumer society could critical theory derive solace. In any case, the possibility of agency within the scope of late capitalism itself was strictly proscribed by the universalization of technological rationality.

Published just a year before the most politically significant anti-war demonstration in two generations, Marcuse's monumental dialectic of defeat, *One Dimensional Man*, had a curious effect: It inspired precisely the proponents of participatory democracy, the young opposition that emerged out of the civil rights movement, out of the boredom of the smooth repression of suburban life, out of the profound discontent students experienced with the prospect that they could take their places as loyal supplicants of the bureaucracies of late capitalism and, especially, the war machine. And virtually obliterated from contemporary history were the movements of working-class struggles against the capitalist production machine—in France, Italy, and the United States. Marcuse's vivid description of their condition had the opposite effect intended by its author: Together with C. Wright Mills's powerful indictment of the ruling circles in *The Power Elite*, and with Paul Goodman's searing indictment of the educational system in *Growing Up Absurd*, *One Dimensional Man* was among the most influential political texts for the New Left.

Critical Theory failed to acknowledge the fundamental significance of feminism, ecology, and black freedom as expressions of opposition, even as a new class politics reflected both the isolation of left intellectuals from new social movements and the limits of the negative dialectic. Elsewhere I have argued that holding to the criterion that no social movement has world-historical significance unless it represents the "determinate negation" of the prevailing social order is too high a standard.[31] Moreover, in its enslavement to the past, it cannot grasp the new when it does not dismiss it entirely. What was new in the late 1960s influenced some elements of the camp of Critical Theory. But many remained true to the masters: For example, Paul Piccone, editor of the influential journal *Telos*, dubbed the New Left and the social movements of which it was a part as examples of "artificial negativity"; and Russell Jacoby wrote an interesting study of *The Last Intellectuals* that, while containing the grain of truth that academia had absorbed much of the revolt against late capitalism, nevertheless ignored the emergent intellectuals of the new social movements. But Andre Gorz, Tony Negri, and Mario Tronti insisted that intellectuals who would theorize world history keep their ears and noses to the ground. Toward the end of his life Marcuse came to recognize the irony of Critical Theory's failure to embrace feminism, black freedom, and the episodic but powerful workers' revolts on the shop floor. But Marcuse's shift away from the politics of despair had little influence on his "children," many of whom began to shift to the center in the 1980s.[32]

I would argue that these judgments were symptoms of the parochialism of late Critical Theory, which, although disdaining the postmodern retreat, failed to integrate a global perspective into its analysis. For the preponderance of Critical Theorists only Western Europe and North America were worthy of concern. And then only white males were capable of entering history. Although this attitude was somewhat engendered by a healthy rejection of the third worldism of much of the 1970s left, for which no displacement of subjectivity was too extreme to embrace, it also produced considerable intellectual blindness. What many could not see were the profound implications of the emerging global vision of the ecology, feminist, and labor movements for the creation of a new opposition to transnational capitalism. The Seattle demonstrations of December 1999, the subsequent mass demonstrations at Quebec, Genoa, and Madrid against the key institutions of global capital, and the development of the World Social Forum, whose location in Brazil's Porto Allegre was symbolic of a global shift, as both an attempt to create a new civil society and as a post-9/11 continuation of the protests, present new possibilities, the ignorance of which leave social and political theory stranded in the past.

Even as Europe drifts rightward and an entrenched far-right regime maintains its power in the United States, what are we to make of the dramatic shift in Latin America from the morass of military dictatorships that prevailed until the 1980s to today's center-left governments? Note well, most of these are by no means radical: Indeed, Chavez's Venezuela is far from a radical democratic regime. Yet the factory occupations in Argentina and the government's rejection of IMF and World Bank austerity plans, the Workers Party government in Brazil, and the electoral victories by anti-neoliberal parties, supported by social movements in Chile, Bolivia, Uruguay, Peru, and Ecuador, are signs of major change in the region. While it would be foolish to neglect the still-powerful influence of neoliberalism over these parties and governments, especially in Brazil—the largest and one of the most industrially advanced countries in Latin America—it would also be a mistake to dismiss the new context for social struggles. Already, forces to the left of these parties have sharply criticized them for their accommodation to global finance capital. While the electoral center-left promises more equality, its base insists on more democracy as well. Compare the world's response to the resurgence of US militarism to any similar development in the twentieth century. In the eyes of much of the world, including perhaps half the American people, the Bush administration stands condemned of gross violations of human rights, and its legitimacy has been widely questioned.

And despite the right-wing victory in the United States, under the radar screen is the largest burst of activism in thirty-five years. Anti-war and anti-sweatshop movements, fierce discussions in black circles about the future of a people whose gains are being wiped away in slow but steady measures, a new student activism, and even the outpouring of hundreds of thousands of anti-Bush liberals and leftists to aid John Kerry's failed 2004 presidential campaign despite his center-right platform indicate the existence of a popular opposition, however fragmented and visionless it might remain. The task of social and political theory is plain: to make sense of these developments, and to address those already in motion to propose an alternative. We might speculate that the disparity between activism and theory is a symptom of new circumstances, the dimensions of which we are only dimly aware because theory lags behind events.

What has become clear, however, is that the old forces of the opposition—the parties of the labor, communist, and social-democratic left—have exhausted their capacity for struggle, except for the occasional demonstration to stall the shredding of the welfare state. In some instances they are the embodiments of what Sartre termed the "practico-inert"—a play on Marx's famous remark in the *18th Brumaire* that "the traditions of all the dead generations weigh like a nightmare on the brains of the living." In consequence, despite the revolution of 1989, and the subsequent rapid collapse of really existing socialism, many still cling to the past but, more to the point, insist that it should rule the present and the future. Ensconced in tradition, the left seems unable to assume the position of the opposition. One explanation for its relatively tepid response to the anti–social right offensive is that the working-class composition of the parties is thinning as almost all of them become parties of government and, more to the point, as the traditional Western industrial working class retreats, however slowly, into history. Moreover, without a sharply altered conception of what it might be, socialism has become a statement of moral hope, mostly bereft of content and certainly not on anyone's political agenda.

What is emerging as an urgent, but also radical, departure from the old formulae is an ecological perspective rooted in the implausibility of continuation of the 300–year legacy of carboniferous capitalism, and of one of its primary presuppositions, economic growth on the basis of urban and suburban sprawl, dirty energy, and the consequent automobile culture. Radicals need to reject the penchant of social and political theory to leave questions of our ecological relations to the scientists and engineers or to the "Greens." They must become involved in the politics of land use, water, and energy if alternatives to the current setup are to be at all possible. Social theory must address questions of our relation to the ecological context, which conditions the character of social relations, and must be able to examine the effects of exploitative social relations on the environment and then to consider alternatives, many of which have been worked out but languish for lack of strategic theorizing. "Global warming"—or, to be more precise, structural climate instability and shift—may be the catalyst for the invention of new economic, social, and cultural arrangements or at least the development of a program of regional, democratic delinking of communities from the global system. This would entail programs of import substitution, new modes of cooperative ownership of enterprises, limits to the market as regulator of economic activity, and the forging of a new international labor movement, the seeds of which were born in Seattle in 1999. Note the contradictory character of these proposals: Delinking seems to contradict global solidarity. This may be true; but if current trends continue, the main strategy for maintaining historical living standards in the West will be to raise the wages and living conditions of workers in developing countries while, at the same time, conceiving new modes of life that reduce or otherwise undermine capitalist interdependence.

For instance, *The Take*—the film documentary depicting the attempts by a network of Argentine workers to reopen abandoned industrial plants on a cooperative basis—might be considered an exemplary instance of initiative from below and could have broad application in the so-called advanced capitalist societies, especially the United States where millions of relatively well-paid jobs were lost in the last thirty years without opposition or alternative initiatives taken by workers, their unions, and their communities. The Argentines did not emulate so-called worker-controlled industries, which preserved the top-down managerial style of the fordist system; rather, they tried to effect a broad democratic management in which workers participated and ownership did not revert to the former owners. Of course, within a market system, these efforts met with only mixed results; some attempts failed to get off the ground. The question for us is, How to comprehend such a development? And again, what to make of the landless movement in Brazil, which is driving the Lula government crazy as it demands agrarian reform? (Note that 2,500 troops were deployed in February 2005 to break up a peaceful demonstration for land redistribution. Eight hundred demonstrators were arrested, and several were killed.) Is democracy from below possible? And if so, under what circumstances? How can workers take the initiative to defend their own living standards without resorting to protectionism, concessionary bargaining, and other forms of collaboration with capital?

I invoke these examples to suggest that beyond hand-wringing and surrender to liberal institutions, beyond pure defense of the gains of the past, lies considerable uncharted territory. Our task is to draw the maps.

Notes

1. Jean-Francois Lyotard, *The Post Modern Condition* (Minneapolis: University of Minnesota Press, 1984).

2. Fredric Jameson, *Postmodernism: The Cultural Logic of Late Capitalism* (Durham: Duke University Press, 2001).

3. Theodor Adorno, *Negative Dialectics* (New York: Seabury Press, 1974); Jacques Derrida, "Differance," in *Speech and Phenomena* (Evanston, IL: Northwestern University Press, 1973).

4. Louis Althusser, "Marxism and Humanism," in *For Marx* (New York: Vintage Books, 1969).

5. For a discussion of the concept of the not-yet, see Ernst Bloch, "Non-Synchrony and Dialectic," in *Heritage of Our Times* (Cambridge, MA: MIT Press, 1988).

6. Pierre Clastres, *Society Against the State* (New York: Zone Books, 1989); Michel Foucault, *Society Must Be Defended* (New York: Picador, 2003).

7. Sheldon Wolin, *Politics and Vision,* expanded ed. (Princeton: Princeton University Press, 2004).

8. Andre Gorz, Strategy for Labor (Boston: Beacon Press, 1967).

9. Wolin, *Politics and Vision,* expanded ed., p. 565.

10. Ibid., p. 566.

11. Ibid., p. 601.

12. Ibid., p. 603.

13. Daniel Bell, *The End of Ideology* (Glencoe, IL: The Free Press, 1960).

14. Seymour Martin Lipset and Sheldon S. Wolin, *The Berkeley Student Revolt* (New York: Doubleday and Co. 1965).

15. Max Horkheimer and Theodor W. Adorno, *The Dialectic of the Enlightenment* (Stanford, CA: Stanford University Press, 2002).

16. Karl Popper, *The Open Society and Its Enemies,* 2 vols. (London: Routledge and Kegan Paul, 1945).

17. Karl Popper, *The Logic of Scientific Discovery* (1934).

18. John Dewey, *The Public and Its Problems* (New York: H. Holt and Co., 1927).

19. Wolin, *Politics and Vision,* expanded ed., p. 549.

20. G.W.F. Hegel, *The Philosophy of Right* (London: Oxford University Press, 1952).

21. Karl Marx, "On the Jewish Question," in *Early Writings* (London and New York: Penguin Books, 1975).

22. Stanley Aronowitz, *Just Around the Corner: The Paradox of the Jobless Recovery* (Philadelphia: Temple University Press, 2005).

23. Oskar Negt and Alexander Kluge, *The Public Sphere and Experience* (Minneapolis: University of Minnesota Press, 1992).

24. Michael Sandel, *Liberalism and Its Critics* (New York: New York University Press, 1984); Charles Taylor, *Sources of the Self* (Cambridge, MA: Harvard University Press, 1989).

25. Leo Strauss, *Natural Right and History* (Chicago: University of Chicago Press, 1953), p.143.

26. Ibid., p. 92.

27. Jean-Jacques Rousseau, "The Social Contract," in *Basic Political Writings*, edited by Donald A. Kress (Indianapolis/Cambridge: Hackett Publishing Co.), p. 141.

28. Jean-Jacques Rousseau, "Origins of Inequality," in *Basic Political Writings*, edited by Donald A. Kress (Indianapolis/Cambridge: Hackett Publishing Co.); Strauss, *Natural Right and History*, p. 256.

29. Ernst Bloch, *Natural Law and Human Dignity* (Cambridge MA: MIT Press, 1986).

30. Eric Hobsbawm and George Rudé, *Captain Swing* (Chicago: Phoenix Press, 2001).

31. Stanley Aronowitz, *How Class Works* (New Haven: Yale University Press, 2003), ch. 2.

32. Ibid.

◊

2

On Left Political Organization

From the New Deal to the New Left

The United States is the only nation in the "advanced" capitalist world without a significant left party. Although labor and
socialist/communist parties have long existed at the local
level—many cities had workingmen's parties, the Socialist
Party was a national organization that made important electoral inroads at the turn of the twentieth century, and the
Communists were key organizers of the mass industrial union
and other social and cultural movements in the 1930s and
1940s—in general Americans have been tied to the two-party
system. The question is whether the absence of a left political
formation of significant influence and constituency is a function of "American Exceptionalism"—as was first argued by the
German sociologist Werner Sombart, whose book *Why Is There
No Socialism in the United States?* first appeared in 1906, when
the Socialists were in a phase of rapid growth—or whether far
more concrete, "subjective" influences have prevented the sus-
tenance of a left party of national influence. Sombart's essential
argument is that in the absence of a feudal tradition in the
United States class consciousness was never formed; in other
words, historical materialism applies only to Europe. America's
artisan and yeoman past, which constituted a sustaining myth
of individualism; its surfeit of natural resources, which permit

This chapter was published initially as "Is It Time for a New Political Party?
A Meditation on Left Political Organizations," *Situations* 1, no. 2 (winter
2005–2006). Reprinted by permission of the author Stanley Aronowitz.

cheap energy and cheap food; its mobility opportunities, which parallel Frederick Jackson Turner's frontier thesis; its populist urban political machines, which absorbed class discontent; and its ethnically diverse working class all constituted unbreachable obstacles to class solidarity. With two major exceptions—Henry Wallace's Progressive Party presidential campaign of 1948, and the Green Party's 2000 campaign in behalf of Ralph Nader—by the end of World War II progressives and many radicals had been swept up in Franklin D. Roosevelt's New Deal Coalition or had conceded that radicalism was permanently incapable of attracting a popular constituency.

We saw the consequences of the absence of a coherent and forceful left in the 2004 presidential election, when most on the left and the center-left rallied behind a centrist Democratic candidate while the third-party forces were hopelessly divided. Leaving aside the historical left abdication of the space of the opposition to the Democrats, the fact is the Democrats do not occupy that space, except in electoral terms. Their campaign was bereft of sharply defined issues: They neither defended their social liberalism nor mounted an attack against the Bush administration's war and economic policies, which have been directed against the working class, and they barely mentioned the Bush betrayal of the environment or challenged his claim that the US economy was on the mend.

The left was led by the nose by the de facto American liberal party, which emerged as a serious political force during the primary season when former Vermont governor Howard Dean came out of nowhere to challenge the party establishment with his mild anti–Iraq war position and a grassroots fund-raising campaign that helped energize a citizens' movement at the local level. The demise of Dean's presidential candidacy was not nearly as important as his legacy: the creation of a new middle-class liberal movement that has taken the novel form of Internet communication both through a series of webzines (to add to the hard-copy journals of opinion such as *The Nation* and *The Progressive*) and through issues organizing by MoveOn.org, which has shown a phenomenal ability to assemble a mass online constituency that can be mobilized to write letters, visit legislators, and give money to promising electoral campaigns. But in the end, left-liberals supported the centrist John Kerry, whose major domestic plank was to offer tax breaks for employers who created jobs for the unemployed and who criticized Bush for not sending enough troops to get the job done in Iraq.

In order to explain this appalling state of affairs, we must briefly address the historical choices that led large sections of the left to abdicate the position of opposition. For the sad situations of the last two decades that produced liberal hegemony over what was once a promising radical movement were the outcome of a long process that can be traced to two signal events that shaped the American left: the admission by Nikita Khrushchev that the "crimes" of Stalin against the peasantry, a large cohort of old Bolsheviks, and countless others marked the twenty-five years of his undisputed rule; and the left's response to the rise of fascism during the 1930s and 1940s, when most of its organizations suspended the class struggle, chose to give qualified support to liberal capitalism, and consequently subordinated itself to the Democratic Party. Under these circumstances, it is no wonder that the question of political organization was relegated to the back burner.

Since the 1960s, the American left has, with few exceptions, accepted the view that the question of political organization was resolved by the collapse of communism, initiated quite unintentionally by Khrushchev's revelations at the 1956 Twentieth Soviet Party Congress of the repressive and sometimes terroristic character of Stalin's rule. Among its features was the moral and political corruption of the Bolshevik project, especially the vision of a society in which workers, peasants, and other exploited strata would, through popularly elected councils, manage all of the crucial economic and social functions. Particularly loathsome were the details surrounding the Moscow Trials of 1936–1937, during which the cream of the old Bolshevik revolutionaries were wiped out by a "legal" process that offered little room for defense, let alone dissent. Equally abhorrent was the knowledge of the formation of a new class of party apparatchiks and state bureaucrats who enjoyed a monopoly of power and material privilege. Far from a force for pointing the way to a more egalitarian future, the Communist Party (CP) became, itself, a new ruling class. After 1956, these revelations drove thousands of dedicated Communists from the American party, which, after a prolonged debate, remained staunchly apologetic for the Soviet oligarchy; more, the stain carried over to succeeding generations of young leftists for whom the concept of "party" was itself an epithet. Even as private property in the ownership of the means of material production was largely abolished, state "socialism" brought neither freedom nor prosperity to the mass of Soviet citizens. But the immense authority of the Soviet Union on the left—especially during the 1930s, when its economic achievements were heralded as proof of the superiority of socialism over capitalism, and during the 1940s, when the Red Army vanquished the mighty Nazi war machine at Stalingrad and arguably paved the way for the Allied victory—became a nightmare for millions of dedicated radicals and revolutionaries whose faith was shattered by the truths they had vehemently denied, or for which they had offered apologies for decades. The aftermath was not only mass resignations from many of the parties of the West, including the United States and the United Kingdom, but a slow but steady deterioration of the entire socialist project.

With the collapse of the Soviet Union, the end of "really existing" socialism triggered a tidal wave of criticism, confusion, and recriminations that resulted in the stunning decline of the once-powerful mass Communist parties of Italy and France. The crumbling Soviet Empire prompted the Italian party to change its name to the Democratic Party of the Left, which preserved some of its electoral appeal but signaled a radical loss of confidence in its own heritage and vision. Soon after the name change, two new formations arose, the Rifundazione group and the Italian Communists, which sought to retain the revolutionary aims of the historical Italian Communist Party. After 1991, the less flexible French party rapidly lost most of its electoral constituency and some of its trade union hegemony and, equally important, ceased to be a magnet for a considerable fraction of the intellectuals whose cultural and ideological role in French society remains to this day important. What saved these parties from virtual extinction was their long-held ironic attitude toward the Soviet Union and its supplicants.

This was not the case with the American party and its once-substantial periphery. Although it had sustained losses during the bleak first half of the 1950s, especially among its leading trade unionists (who were prohibited by law from holding union office if they were openly Communists), Khrushchev's speech proved utterly devastating to its member rolls and to the remnants of its influence. The key reason was that since the party's inception in 1919, the American Communists were true believers. Particularly damaging to its survival, even in a weakened state, was the slavish subordination of much of the leadership to the Soviet party—which itself can be explained by, on the one hand, the strong representation of fiercely pro-Soviet immigrant and first-generation Eastern Europeans within the party and, on the other, by the almost complete lack of cultural and political circumspection within its ranks. The latter feature was a symptom of the degree to which American communism was truly American: puritanical, humorless—for example, it lacked the capacity for self-mockery—and self-abnegating when it came to matters of religion and other forms of authority. For members of the party core, which was mostly bereft of theoretical and historical perspective, marxism and communism were the twin pillars of their religion. Their fervent profession of marxism scarcely hid the bald fact that few Communists enjoyed even a superficial mastery of Marx's critique of political economy, let alone the materialist conception of history. Instead, many party faithful were imbued with Stalinist dogmatism culled from a few texts. And Stalin himself was elevated by the official line to the status of a demi-god, which made it all the more difficult to change the party's course, especially when the authority of the Soviet party was being severely tested and its leading figures had no time for the troubled Americans. After several years of debate, two thirds of its membership left the party and its voice was reduced to a whisper.

Other parties of the left were similarly enfeebled. The two main Trotskyist formations—the Socialist Workers Party (SWP) and the Independent Socialist League (ISL)—had suffered government attacks but mainly lost ground for two distinct reasons: The CP, whose relative strength once gave them a reason for being and sustained their opposition, was in shambles; and, as with other socialists, many of its activists, especially of the ISL, became trade union and liberal functionaries, positions that drove them to silence or, worse, collaboration with the prevailing Cold War, liberal consensus. Others were pleased to find academic jobs, positions that had been denied them either by McCarthy-like university policies or by party discipline. Although the SWP experienced a brief revival during the anti–Vietnam war movement, managing to attract some young intellectuals and soldiers, it was unable to overcome the general decline of the left or its own lack of any but tactical imagination.

Questions of political organization typically occupy social movements and political formations during periods of popular upsurge. Members of the New Left, which, in 1960, arose in the ideological vacuum produced by its ancestors—many were "red diaper" babies imbued with their parents' will to change the world but not necessarily sympathetic to their political affiliations and methods—were, in the zenith of their influence, obsessed with the question of what to do in the wake of the spread of the movement beyond the universities, to professions such as medicine, social work, and teaching and even to the ranks of young workers and members of the armed forces. Their decision not to form a new "party" of the left, or even to build a national movement for a "democratic society" parallel to Students for a Democratic Society (SDS)—arguably the leading formation of the New Left—was fateful for the future development of American radicalism for this was the first time since the 1930s that the left had a popular base. As Wini Breines has demonstrated, the fact that attempts to build a permanent organization failed was the outcome not of a mood drift but of a quite deliberate decision.[1] The main voices of the New Left, including the leadership of the mass anti–Vietnam war movement, were convinced that party formations would inhibit the mass character of the movement and lead to bureaucratization and, worse, to the inevitable integration of the movement into the liberal mainstream. These views were not only fueled by the prevailing libertarian sentiment among many sections of the movement, which disdained ideas such as party discipline and centralization, but also were conditioned by the tawdry history of international communism. Since the Cold War was the ineluctable context for politics, the words of C. Wright Mills rang in the ears of many. In his influential *Letter to the New Left,* Mills left little room for doubt: Do not become entangled in the "Russian Question" but build a movement directed to American society and particularly its politics and culture.[2]

And these arguments were tinged by more than a small dose of participatory democratic concepts, according to which power must reside in the "people" rather than in tightly organized party elites composed chiefly of middle-class intellectuals. In

SDS, "participatory democracy" stood in not only for a healthy affirmation of a politics that required the direct participation of the people "in the decisions that affect[ed] their lives" but also for a populist, even anarchist, suspicion of a political center that might have influence over the movement.[3] These ideas were mixed in with the heavy dose of anti-intellectualism that permeated the later SDS.[4]

Of course, not every fraction of the left was imbued with antipathy toward the concept of a revolutionary or radical party. For a brief moment the organizational question dominated conversations in the New Left and its leading organization, SDS. The debate was fomented by one of the sects, Progressive Labor (PL), a self-proclaimed Maoist organization founded in 1960 by a small group that had split from the Communist Party, accusing it of "revisionism"—a term that connoted deviation from revolutionary politics. In its search for a wider political base, PL had made SDS a special concentration since 1966. While most SDS leaders rejected PL itself as an organizational alternative to the relatively loose SDS structure, many were attracted to its argument that without a party to lead and unify the opposition to capitalism and imperialism, the movement would inevitably ebb and perhaps disappear.

How was PL able to refocus the organization's attention away from its preoccupation with the Vietnam war toward a season of introspection? One factor was the enormous prestige of North Vietnam and the National Liberation Front, its South Vietnam affiliate. Several leading New Left figures, including SDS founder Tom Hayden and Staughton Lynd, had visited Vietnam and returned with glowing reports about the anti-imperialist resistance and favorable impressions of its Communist leadership. The main debate within SDS in 1968 and 1969 was whether the organization should transform itself into a vanguard Marxist-Leninist party, or a revolutionary party directed to youth and blacks, or a "movement for a democratic society" that could carry the program of participatory democracy into the unions, community organizing, and the professions but, at the same time, maintain a decentralized structure. For anyone who would listen, Murray Bookchin's passionate pamphlet, "Listen Marxist," written in the heat of the controversy, provided readers with a grim reminder of the legacy of the Marxist-Leninist left, not only in the United States but in Spain and Russia itself. Bookchin suggested that the anarchist organizational form—the federation of independent groups, which retained their autonomy—was most appropriate to a political formation that respected the tenets of participatory democracy. Bookchin reflected the viewpoint of a number of the relevant discussants but, in the cauldron of ideological fire, was largely ignored.

The breakup of SDS in 1970 was both a symptom of and a tremendous force in the collapse of the New Left. Excepting the feminist and ecology movements, which had yet to peak, other movements were clearly in trouble. Massive demonstrations against the war may have forced a president from office, but the new administration of Richard Nixon had responded to certain defeat on the battlefield by widening the war. The killings of anti-war student protesters at Kent State in 1970 were a severe warning that the Nixon administration was in no mood for tolerance, even of whites. When Nixon, in the wake of massive resistance by draftees and objectors, abolished the draft, the protests were visibly weakened. And the black freedom movement, whose civil rights wing was already co-opted by the legalistic hopes surrounding the Voting and Civil Rights acts, was further disarmed when, after Martin Luther King's assassination, it failed to address the long-festering deterioration of black living standards resulting from the deindustrialization of most major northern cities, the already evident abject failure of *Brown v Board of Education* to remedy de facto discrimination in schools, and the obdurate refusal of organized labor to address its own racism. At the nadir of the mass street expressions of the movements after 1973, various formations scrambled to preserve what they had already achieved and, fearing that efforts to build a coherent ideological and political left would anger their potential allies at a moment of advancing conservatism, tended to build coalitions with elements of the Democratic Party. Thus, after a nanosecond's flirtation with third-party electoral politics and something more than a flirtation with Leninist vanguardism, the left has mainly been inclined since the 1980s to revert to single-issue politics represented, for example, by the current anti–Iraq war coalitions, by local-level struggles such as fights against urban redevelopment, and by social movements such as the black freedom movement and feminism, which are on the defensive in the wake of right-wing assaults on their achievements during the 1955–1975 period.

It may be superfluous to remark that there is the rising anger concerning many of the Bush administration's policies: demonstrations against what has become an unpopular Iraq war; the impatience of large sections of Americans with the administration's drift toward barbarism; the looming economic crisis, including gas inflation and the resumption of mass layoffs by leading industrial and financial corporations; the administration's palpable incompetence and class/race bias during the Hurricane Katrina debacle; the impending bursting of the housing bubble that has made even the most blinky-eyed neoliberals nervous; and the absolute paralysis of the center-right Democratic Party, which seems unable to remember what political opposition is. These symptoms of a growing political crisis have yet to inspire the left to seek a voice that may spur a new wave of opposition that would clearly articulate a series of alternatives and begin a discussion of what a new society might look like. With social movements at or near a standstill, and Organized Labor in decline and seriously divided, the problem of building an alternative left—particularly with regard to its organizational aspects—may appear to be merely an academic, even utopian, exercise. On the contrary, I want to suggest that this issue takes on urgency today precisely because the so-called objective conditions are ripe. If they have a utopian dimension, it is no more accidental than that of any proposal for fundamental structural change in the present political environment, when most radicals find themselves constrained to fight for something less than increments.

In referring to "objective conditions," I do not mean to repeat the mechanistic formulae of the Old Left: economic crisis, war, and a certain degree of disarray among sections of the ruling class. Among these conditions are what in the traditional rhetoric one might term "subjective"—that is, the effects of the interventions of specific groups and individuals: considerable evidence of popular disaffection with the war and renewed activity, exemplified by Cindi Sheehan's dramatic and media-savvy summer 2005 encampment at Bush's ranch and the astonishing outpouring of support, despite *New York Times* columnist Frank Rich's rue that "slick left-wing operatives" had succeeded in making her protest into a "circus"; the open, unprecedented acknowledgment by labor leaders and their intellectual acolytes that the unions are in crisis, even if their solutions are largely administrative; and the growing recognition in wide circles of the black freedom movement that the legal framework of civil rights established since *Brown* and the Voting Rights legislation do not equality or even freedom make. In fact, in the aftermath of Katrina some agreed with New York Congress member Charles Rangel that federal neglect was a reminder that some conditions have changed little in the past forty years. And, miracle of miracles, some journalists have discovered that class plays an important role in American politics and culture.

Radical Steps and Missteps

For almost a century, Sombart's theory of American Exceptionalism, combined with its implication of the "end of ideology" ("end" because America is simply not a class society on the European model), has remained a major argument for ex-radicals who, in different generations, have joined the liberal party cum New Deal Democrats or have moved further to the right. Writers such as Arthur Schlesinger Jr., Daniel Bell, and Seymour Martin Lipset have barely embellished Sombart's theory in their claim that the highest possible progressive aspiration is incremental reform within a virtually permanent capitalist system whose framework of liberal-democratic political institutions is perfectly adequate to address the remaining, albeit residual, cultural and social problems. Thus, according to this view, traditional European forms—labor and socialist parties and radical, let alone revolutionary, ideology—did not form because they were unnecessary. Underlying this perspective is the tacit assumption that the system is sound and increasingly egalitarian, at least open to mass social pressure or sufficiently democratic to accommodate and respond to dissent. Many leftists—people who call themselves socialists, anarchists, communists—function, in practical terms, as part of the liberal party. Irving Howe goes so far as to refuse the idea that capitalism is wracked by structural contradictions; thus democratic socialism, according to Howe, is an ethical ideal whose possibility of realization is dim but which provides a "margin of hope" for some important changes. Howe never went the way of his contemporaries Daniel Bell and Irving Kristol in embracing the main lines of neoconservatism, but these arguments are more than justifications for individuals to move to the center or to the right.[5]

I want to suggest that American Exceptionalism is a powerful ideology that has become integral to the American political landscape and has influenced the left to confine its activity to incremental remedies for what otherwise would be recognized as systemic contradictions. Its material basis at the level of subjectivity is the pervasive perception of the Democratic Party as the party of working people, which emerged when it adopted populism during the campaigns of William Jennings Bryan and Woodrow Wilson and which was echoed in the shift within the labor movement, first made by AFL president Samuel Gompers when the Federation supported Bryan in 1908 and Wilson in 1912. The decisive break came during the New Deal when socialists and some communists alike enthusiastically embraced the Roosevelt coalition, even before the social welfare state policies of the "second New Deal" emerged in 1936. That the labor movement and major radical detachments were "integrated" into an explicit acceptance of the capitalist system and of the Democratic Party was not inevitable. This outcome was conditioned by the ideology of exceptionalism, according to which class consciousness was permanently thwarted by the opportunity structure of American capitalism; the American left's response to the rise of fascism and its belief that Roosevelt and a progressive wing of capital would join a grand alliance to oppose Hitler, Mussolini, and Franco; the real, albeit temporary, benefits that workers, farmers, and others made destitute by economic depression would derive from Roosevelt's social welfare programs; and a profound misunderstanding of the contradictory nature of the Labor Relations Act, which the left was loathe to criticize, let alone oppose. To be sure, unions gained in membership and collective bargaining power during the first decades after the passage of the labor relations law. While the Wagner Act marked an historic shift from government hostility to recognition of labor's right to organize and make demands on employers, and to open support of the "right of workers to form unions of their own choosing," Labor has since submitted itself to a regime of regulation that, during decades of court rulings and legislative action on behalf of capital, effectively repealed the Act.

The New Deal, whose legacy was preserved, in part, by the Warren Court, proved to be an episode in an otherwise unbroken two centuries of race and class oppression, but it retains huge force as a sustaining myth of the liberal party. In any case, labor and the main forces of the left remain, against all historical evidence, firmly tied to a Democratic Party that has long abandoned them; even the slogans that animated the party until Kennedy's enunciation of a "New Frontier" or Johnson's "Great Society" have disappeared. Still, at the political level, most of the left (labor, organizers of social movements, the intelligentsia) reject the idea of forming a new electoral vehicle, let alone a radical, ideologically alternative political organization.

This was not always the case. Between 1900 and 1917, the Socialist Party (SP) grew to over 100,000 members. By 1912, when Eugene Debs received 6 percent of the popular vote, its electoral constituency had reached nearly a million, and it exceeded that number in the 1920 election. In its heyday and thereafter, the Socialist Party was opposed to supporting candidates of the two capitalist parties. It elected thousands of local officials, including mayors and council members, state legislators, and two US Congress members who were expelled in 1917 for opposing America's entry into the war. The party was nearly fatally wounded when two-thirds of its membership bolted to heed Lenin's call to form a Communist Party linked to the international revolutionary movement. The Communist Party's membership grew to about 100,000 during World War II, but more to the point, Communists and other socialists led unions with more than a third of the CIO membership and many locals of the AFL.[6]

The CP was influential in many sectors of American society, at both the national and local levels. In New York, the communist-influenced Teachers Union became a major ideological force in public education. Its activists were among the main organizers of a mass tenants movement and were key participants in the growing black freedom movement. The party's intervention in cinema, music, and literature later became one of the hallmarks of the McCarthyite counteroffensive, in part because it was immensely influential. Novelists Theodore Dreiser and James T. Farrell (who later defected to the trotskyists), playwrights Clifford Odets and Irwin Shaw, composers Aaron Copland and Wallingford Reigger, and painters Max Weber and the Soyer Brothers were only the most prominent of a legion of artists who were instrumental on the cultural front.

While the CP's electoral strength was negligible except in New York City and California, many of its members ran as Democrats or American Labor Party candidates and won public office. This aspect of the CP's strategy was extremely dubious. In fact, in contrast to socialists and anarchists, who, for the most part, wore their politics on their sleeves, the CP undercut its influence by its Popular Front policies, one feature of which was to send cadres into movements and parties without revealing their affiliations or even their fundamental views.[7]

From 1900 to about 1970 there was a visible left press. In the first decades of the twentieth century, the SP had several daily newspapers in cities where it had substantial membership, especially in the Northeast and Midwest; the *Appeal to Reason,* for example, an independent nationwide socialist weekly with 700,000 in sales and several million readers, came out of Girard, Kansas. And from the 1930s through the 1950s the Communists published the *Daily Worker,* which periodically had several supplements, especially in Chicago and Detroit, and the *Peoples World* on the West Coast. These papers were often the main form of open Communist participation in national and local politics and were a key ideological link for party activists who, in the main, were immersed in practical tasks and had little or no other intellectual activity. In New York City the left-liberal *PM* and its successors, the *Compass* and the *Star,* lasted for more than a decade but folded in the mid-1950s due to lack of finances and prohibitive costs. And the independent left weekly *The National Guardian* was launched during Henry Wallace's 1948 Progressive Party presidential campaign and was able to outlive its origins: Although its paid circulation never exceeded 35,000, it became an influential voice for the New Left in the late-1960s.

In retrospect, one of the great political misfortunes of late-twentieth-century America was the failure, nay, refusal of the New Left—which by 1969 had grown to popular proportions—to form a coherent radical democratic political organization that proposed the fundamental transformation of capitalism, engaged in serious theory and ideological practice, and could take a leading role in the analysis of and struggles around contemporary political and cultural questions. Although the SDS undertook some of these tasks, the organizations that arose after its demise were little more than parodies of the Marxist-Leninist parties they attempted to emulate. In fact, only the Weather Underground made an effort to rethink the traditional party form that had arisen in the shadow of the Bolshevik ascent to power in Russia, proposed new organizational strategies, or, indeed, grappled with fundamental ideological questions that had been addressed by earlier revolutionaries. Nor were the New Left's members particularly concerned to address the specificity of the United States, its history, its class formations, or its economic, political, and cultural institutions. Instead, armed with the *Little Red Book* of Mao's timeless homilies and with Stalin's *Marxism and the National Question*—and in the case of the Revolutionary Communist Party (RCP), "Dialectical and Historical Materialism," a section of *The History of the Communist Party of the Soviet Union (Bolshevik)*—they thereby bypassed the grueling work of rethinking. All of them, including the Weather people, adopted one version of vanguardism or another and accepted the dominant interpretations of Lenin's writings as biblical texts to be followed like an evangelical cookbook. From the ashes of SDS rose two party formations, the October League and the RCP, both of which imagined themselves as vanguards and soon after their birth morphed into "parties" complete with central committees and political bureaus even though they remained relatively small. Each had a press with extremely limited outreach and copied the old CP strategy of intervening in the trade unions by sending their mostly young cadres into auto, steel, and other basic industries to recruit workers into the party and hopefully influence the unions. With only a handful of exceptions—such as the RCP's work in postal unions and the work of maoists in Ed Sadlowski's insurgent campaign for the presidency of the Steelworkers, in Jesse Jackson's presidential bids of 1984 and 1988, and in the fight to save a General Motors plant in Southern California—these interventions were not accompanied by efforts to conduct public education around their ideas. In most instances, the intervenors functioned as rank-and-file militants rather than publicly advancing their ideological perspectives, and in a few years most of the them quit their factory jobs or were laid off, whereupon they returned to graduate school. Thirty-five years later, only the RCP remains a propaganda machine; like some of the other sects, particularly the erstwhile Trotskyist/Maoist Workers World Party, it has sponsored front organizations to give its member some leverage and recruiting space within the anti-war movement.

Whereas the Marxist-Leninist formations displayed a remarkable poverty of imagination, for a time the Weather Underground provided enough revolutionary romanticism to excite a significant fraction of young radicals. Invoking, alternately, images of Bonnie and Clyde, the James Brothers, and the Bolsheviks during the Tsarist tyranny, Weather elevated underground resistance—a product of a conclusion they had reached with the Black Panthers that the United States had embarked on the early phase of fascism—to a new principle. Actually the Weather people never organized a formal party. In some respects they resembled the Narodniks (Friends of the People) who came under Lenin's surgical scrutiny at the turn of the twentieth century. They believed the revolutionary process began with an educational gesture that would show the masses of youth the vulnerability of the system, so they engaged in some acts of violence against property (with some tragic, unintended loss of human life), tried to incite uprisings among high school students in working-class (often black) districts, and admonished the rest of the left to follow their example. But since the state viewed them as criminals, they were hunted down by federal authorities for armed bank robbery, and in time, many Weather fugitives surfaced and turned themselves in.

A trained academic librarian, Hal Draper was the author of several scholarly books on the history of marxism as well as a tireless champion of a radical version of democratic socialism. For our purposes it is important to take note only of his efforts on behalf of the Berkeley Free Speech Movement (FSM) of 1964 and his attempt to transform it into the base for a new self-conscious democratic socialist formation. Draper had been a member of the Independent Socialist League (ISL), which, under the tutelage of the Communist-turned-Trotskyist Max Shachtman, refused to characterize the Soviet Union as a "workers'" state. The ISL debated terms such as "bureaucratic collectivism" and "state capitalism" but insisted, unlike the SWP from which it had split, that the Soviet Union was not socialist in any way. Thus, it responded to the two-camp political divisions engendered by the Cold War by proposing a "third camp" that explicitly rejected the proposition, advanced by most noncommunist left intellectuals, that one must "choose the West," however distasteful that might appear, or render "critical support" to the Soviet Union on the basis of its abolition of private productive property. Draper broke with Shachtman over the decision to abandon the third camp and dissolve the organization into the Socialist Party, which, by the 1950s, was pro-Western. But as many independent radicals discovered, in a bipolar world there was little room for political reason. In the late 1960s Draper founded the Independent Socialists (IS), a loose federation of like-minded intellectuals and activists, some of whom were former ISL members, but most of whom were younger people who had cut their political teeth on the doctrines of the New Left. Renouncing some of its Bolshevik-Leninist origins, IS remained a radical democratic socialist movement that, like its predecessor, avoided forming a sectarian vanguard party. In the late 1960s, IS managed to attract some of the best veterans of the FSM, SDS, and white supporters of the black freedom struggles. But it could not avoid falling into some of the characteristic pitfalls of a Marxist sect.[8]

In the early 1970s, when Draper's direct influence had receded, IS revived the practice of sending young intellectuals into important trade unions. But the IS-ers were much more intelligent than most of the others. They made Detroit a national concentration of union activity, especially unions in the trucking and auto industries, where the League of Revolutionary Black Workers had recently given the UAW leadership many sleepless nights; and they displayed a degree of patience (not often found among radicals who expected the revolution to be just around the corner), so that by the early 1980s the organization had successfully organized a viable caucus within the Teamsters Union. This was the Teamsters for a Democratic Union (TDU), which focused narrowly on the two closely connected problems facing working teamsters—namely, the deterioration of its contract and the autocratic and corrupt nature of the union leadership. By linking the problem of union democracy with bread-and-butter issues, and by assiduously avoiding both "divisive" larger issues such as war, abortion, and other social questions, on the one hand, and problems of political ideology, on the other, the TDU built alliances with some breakaway mainstream Teamster locals and became a genuine force in reforming the union. By 1995 it had spearheaded the election to the national Teamster presidency of Ron Carey, a Queens, New York, leader of a major local of the United Parcel Service (UPS), the biggest employer in the industry. With the TDU's assistance, in 1997 the Carey administration organized a national strike against UPS over the issue of the two-tier wage system and won an impressive victory, but then Carey went down over financial scandals and the old guard returned to power under Jimmy Hoffa's son, James P. However, TDU survives as the leading force within a minority caucus that still leads some of the union's large Midwest and Southern locals, among others. Building on a long dissident tradition in the Detroit region, IS members played an important role in some important UAW locals in Detroit and New Jersey, although IS itself was not able to build a credible national movement.[9]

The true inheritor of IS, Solidarity, has carried on the best aspects of its work—mainly, fighting to organize rank-and-file caucuses capable of winning leadership in unions such as New York's Transport Workers Local 100, some telephone locals of the Communications Workers, and others. Solidarity's strategy remains essentially syndicalist—that is, radically trade unionist. Its members within the caucuses advocate democratic unionism, direct-action methods of struggle, and transparency in the conduct of collective bargaining and grievance administration, but they do not influence workers' political decisions/ tendencies outside the trade union framework. Among the best features of Solidarity's activities is the work of some of its long-time activists, particularly ex-SDS member Kim Moody, who in the early 1980s founded the monthly newspaper *Labor Notes*, arguably the best labor paper in the United States. While the paper has hewed fairly rigorously to the politics of radical trade unionism, recently it has moved slightly toward a broader conception of its purview.

The first new postwar socialist organization of relatively large size formed when a substantial chunk of members of the Socialist Party split from the parent organization to organize the Democratic Socialist Organizing Committee (DSOC) in 1972. The move was initiated by writer Michael Harrington, who disagreed with the Socialist Party's traditional refusal to engage in fusion politics by supporting Democrats—he argued that in so doing the SP had condemned itself to being a sect—and determined to make socialist ideas relevant to practical electoral politics. However, for Harrington there was no question of forming a mass socialist party, either in the immediate aftermath of the split or at any time in the future. DSOC was not a movement in the tradition of American socialism; rather, it patterned itself after the Communist Party's popular front policy of the fascist era. As Harrington and his colleague Irving Howe put it, DSOC's program would be the "popular front without Stalinism." Within this configuration socialists would become the "left wing of the possible."[10]

Other tendencies stepped into the political vacuum left by the demise of the New Left. In 1974, two prominent New Leftists—*Socialist Revolution* editor James Weinstein and historian and anti–Vietnam war activist Staughton Lynd—helped organize the New American Movement (NAM), whose aim was to refound the democratic socialist and radical project on specifically American grounds. The name itself signified its orientation: It would be "new" in the sense of C. Wright Mills's admonition not to get bogged down in the debates of the past; "American" in its quest to address the specificity of our own situation; and a "movement" in that it was not a party of either the social-democratic (i.e., electoral) or the Leninist variety, nor an association that enrolled members who agreed with its principles but did not intend to be active. From the start, NAM sought to revive the Muste project: to align a significant fraction of the New Left with a parallel group of "old" leftists who had been disaffected from the Stalinist and Trotskyist orthodoxies but who possessed long political experience and ideological sophistication that would be valuable for a movement composed, primarily, of younger people. Among the early recruits was Dorothy Healey, who had been the longtime chair of the CP's Southern California district and had recently resigned from the party. Healey's adherence to NAM symbolized the intention of bringing the old into the new, but she was among the few who took this step.

Although the two founders abandoned the organization shortly after its first convention, during NAM's almost nine years of life it managed to recruit some 1,500 members, a relatively high proportion of whom were activists. With some twenty-five chapters, NAM distinguished itself from many other formations by emphasizing the educational and cultural development of its own members as well as of nonaffiliated leftists. In several cities it ran rather successful socialist schools, which offered courses in political economy, politics, international relations, and cultural subjects, and which occasionally sponsored weekend children's activities. NAM members were prominent in some professions, particularly health care and social work, and some were officers or staff members of unions, mainly in the public sector. Prior to its annual conventions, NAM offered an intensive week-long institute on marxism, weighted particularly toward the work of Antonio Gramsci. But plagued by perennial financial problems, and facing the virtual "retirement" of a considerable portion of its activists who were anxious to get on with their careers, a sharply divided NAM national committee decided to merge with DSOC in 1983. The new organization was christened the Democratic Socialists of America (DSA) and was led by Harrington.

DSOC was much larger than NAM; at the time of the merger in the spring of 1983, it claimed nearly 5,000 members, among them trade union leaders of considerable stature. Harrington was a genius at collecting notables, but the organization had only a handful of functioning locals. Harrington ruminated that since socialism was not on the agenda of American politics, DSOC had to rely on "smoke and mirrors" to present a semblance of relevance and showed little interest in problems of organization. DSOC's relevance, he thought, was to be a catalyst in the formation of a significant left wing within the Democratic Party, based chiefly on the progressive trade unions. DSOC's main activities were twofold: working within the Democratic Party on the road to what Max Shachtman, Harrington's old mentor, called "political realignment," and operating as an informal hiring hall for progressive union staffs. DSA departed from this formula only slightly. After Harrington's death from cancer in 1990, the organization went into steep decline, for despite his formidable political and intellectual talents Harrington had been indifferent to the processes of internal political education and public socialist propaganda. His strategy strictly precluded utopian or radical thinking as a political act. As a result, DSA was dull and uninspiring to many who were becoming radicals.

What Is Political Opposition?

The idea of a party system was initially controversial to many of the leading lights of the American Revolution. For example, George Washington may have refused to accept the mantle of royalty but, as Richard Hofstadter has shown, he saw the presidency in the imperial model. John Adams and Alexander Hamilton insisted that a strong, centralized national government was necessary both to protect the fledgling United States from its foreign enemies and to facilitate national economic development and preferred to create a government that ruled without significant opposition. It fell to the agrarians and artisans, led by Thomas Jefferson, to propose a party system that could ensure that the executive branch would not become a self-perpetuating aristocracy and that sovereignty would remain in the Congress, which, however imperfect (universal manhood suffrage was not enacted until 1828 and black slaves and women were completely excluded), remains the most representative institution of national government.[11]

If the idea of a systemic opposition to established authority was largely won by 1800, when Jefferson defeated Adams, it had to be a *legitimate* opposition. That is, against Jefferson's earlier statement that when the people "shall grow weary of the existing government they can exercise their constitutional right of amending it, or their revolutionary right to dismember or overthrow it," the opposition was now sworn to uphold the constitution, especially its declaration of individual liberties such as free speech, the collective right to assembly (to protest existing policies and laws), and private property rights. The term "legitimate opposition" has pervaded party systems in North America and most of Western Europe since the inception of constitutional democracy. The opposition is legitimate if, and only if, it remains loyal to the precepts of liberal democracy and to its constitution, whether formally installed or not. "The rule of law" is, by tacit political consent, understood to be the ultimate constraint upon political action; the opposition party may wish to change the law but pledges to do so within the principles and procedures established by the constitution.

Indeed, the Alien and Sedition Acts, passed by Congress during the Adams presidency and under the influence of Hamilton, attempted to define the concept of opposition itself as seditious and "alien"—that is, imported from France. Jefferson, the drafter of the Declaration of Independence, was elected on the idea that a legitimate opposition was consistent with the ideals of the revolution because its aims were well within constitutional legality. His Democratic Republican Party understood that power was never permanent, except the power inherent in the precepts of liberal capitalist democracy. Under these rules, the workingmen's parties created during the regime of Andrew Jackson worked for local reforms such as free public education, limitations on the working day, and other legitimate demands. None adopted the revolutionary aims of the various political formations in Europe, although some were sympathetic to Robert Owens's utopian socialist experiments in the United States. It was not until the American Federation of Labor drafted its constitution that the idea that unions were constituted to engage in a "class struggle" to secure a better living standard and working conditions was promoted. Without declaring revolutionary aims, a major labor organization enunciated the marxian concept of irreconcilable antagonism between labor and capital.

In 1848 Karl Marx and Frederich Engels drafted a "Manifesto of the Communist Party" for the Communist League, first a German workingmen's association, later an international organization, and, as Engels says in his 1888 preface to the English edition, "unavoidably a secret society." We commonly refer to the document as *The Communist Manifesto,* but it is important to remember that its authors wrote it as the statement of a political party. Clearly, they were not interested in writing a program for a "legitimate" opposition to prevailing authority since "*the immediate aim* of the communists is the same as that of all proletarian parties; formation of the proletariat into a class, overthrow of the bourgeois supremacy, conquest of political power by the proletariat" (emphasis mine). They continue: "The distinguishing feature of communism is not the abolition of property generally but the abolition of bourgeois property. But modern bourgeois private property is the final and most complete expression of the system of producing and appropriating products that is based on class antagonisms, the exploitation of the many by the few."[12] No political opposition within the context of liberal capitalist democracy that was serious about such aims could long expect to be tolerated by the ruling order for which the protection of bourgeois property is always an incontrovertible premise. When, periodically, communists and revolutionary socialists are indicted, stand trial, and are convicted of sedition, conspiracy, and other state crimes, the prosecutors are often liberal democrats, members of an officialdom that fervently believes that with the establishment of constitutional rights the right to revolution must be permanently laid to rest and that the exercise—even advocacy—of this right may stand outside the purview of accepted definitions of civic freedoms.

The imperatives of liberal democracy have bedeviled European Marxists since, in the aftermath of the suspension of the anti-socialist laws in Germany, they formed social-democratic parties. While proclaiming their revolutionary aims, in the interest of winning necessary reforms for their primary working-class constituencies after 1870 the social democrats decided to participate in parliamentary elections. Between 1875 and 1914 they became so powerful that at the outbreak of the war they held the balance of power in some countries in Western Europe. But success within the context of bourgeois democracy was fraught with problems, at least from the perspective of the social-democrats' revolutionary pretensions.

Engels's allusion to one such problem might help explain the long record of socialist consent to the rule of law: A specter of communism might have haunted nineteenth-century Europe, but on the ground was the real tyranny—of absolutist and reactionary states in France before and after the Paris Commune, of Tsarist dictatorship in Russia, and of Germany's anti-socialist laws—that greeted social democracy and the organizations and doctrine of revolutionary marxism with exile and imprisonment. To achieve the status of legitimate opposition, to enjoy the privileges of ordinary civil liberties, was indeed a great achievement not to be sneered at. If most social democrats recognized the fragility of their newly won rights at the turn of the twentieth century, many were hesitant to abandon them voluntarily. Thus, legitimacy and its obligations became habitual for many social democrats and their parties, a habituation abetted by real reforms that they and the workers' movements won within parliament and at the workplace.

In 1899 a major German party leader, Eduard Bernstein, published *Evolutionary Socialism*, a virtual reformist manifesto.

The major thesis of the book was that the working class and its party were destined to transform capitalism, not by revolution but by the cumulative effects of their successful struggles for reform. His motto, "the final goal, whatever it may be, is nothing; the movement is everything," signified what he noted had already occurred: "Revolutionary socialism" was already an empty phrase, a slogan relegated to speeches and pamphlets. In practice, revolution had been rendered unnecessary by the victories achieved through the parliamentary process and by trade union action.

Although most of the major party theoreticians and leaders—notably Rosa Luxemburg, Karl Kautsky, and August Bebel—soundly refuted Bernstein's position, the issue remains ideologically and theoretically viable. The labor and socialist movements' impressive struggles to achieve social insurance, legally sanctioned shorter working hours, child labor legislation, and many other reforms *within the prevailing system of bourgeois property relations* had, in effect, pushed the aim of transforming capitalism root and branch into the background. And in the process of engaging in parliamentary struggle, socialists had developed loyalty to liberal democratic institutions. Bernstein argued, following the work of Rudolph Hilferding, that capitalism had entered a phase of high-level organization that would preclude systemic crises, and that one could expect gradually to exact concessions from capital without resort to the measures taken during the Paris Commune or the 1848 French, German, and Italian revolutions. Relying on Marx's own arguments, Luxemburg demonstrated that the inherent tendency of capitalist overproduction and falling profit rates would lead to crises; and Lenin advanced the view that war was both an expression and a displacement of the crisis tendencies of the system. In *Social Reform or Revolution,* her famous refutation of Bernstein's theses, Luxemburg did not renounce reform struggles but emphasized their temporary nature; under no circumstances could the working class expect economic security and permanently rising living standards as long as capital ruled.

But the social democrats' successes within the framework of parliamentary liberal democracy were simply too impressive for many to accept the proposition of revolutionary intransigence. By the dawn of World War I, it was plain to many trade unionists and socialist parliamentarians that advanced capitalism, as contrasted to its competitive, cutthroat predecessor, had produced a large economic surplus that was available to the workers and their parties—if they maintained a high level of militancy and political will. While Bernstein's views may have been scorned by marxist orthodoxy, they seemed to resemble social and political reality more than dire predictions of impending systemic crisis. Moreover, what may be described as the *institutionalization* of social democracy—that is, its correspondence to the Weberian model of bureaucratization—made it likely that labor and socialist parties would become integrated into their own national frameworks and that the material interests of the labor movement, intellectuals, and the middle strata that had been attracted to social democracy could be fulfilled within, and not necessarily against, the prevailing social and political order. In his classic work, *Political Parties,* Robert Michels argued that in spite of their democratic professions, socialist parties had become hierarchical and autocratic organizations. Through its control over the party press and internal communications, and through its role in representing the party's program in parliament and in the popular media, the top leadership exercised control over the party's rank and file and became progressively less in touch with their needs.

Seeking to protect their material and political gains, but also having assimilated nationalist aspirations, in 1914 most socialist and workers parties with parliamentary representation voted war credits to their respective governments. These "renegade" acts led Lenin and Luxemburg to conclude that the forty-year experiment in parliamentary socialism was seriously flawed and had to be abandoned. Lenin theorized that World War I was a marker of the general crisis of the system. In his 1916 pamphlet "Imperialism," Lenin theorized that capitalist collapse would begin "at the weakest link of the imperialist chain," and he predicted that the outcome of the war would be a prolonged period of world revolution that would begin among the masses of the defeated countries, including Russia, which, although ostensibly on the winning side, was actually defeated by Germany. Indeed, when, upon wresting power from the liberal Democratic Kerensky government, the Bolsheviks had to sue for peace with Germany before the General Armistice of 1918, his view proved prescient. By 1919 Russia and Hungary had communist governments and a Bavarian Soviet Republic was declared. But the German revolution ended when the social-democratic government ordered the murder of Rosa Luxemburg and Karl Leibnicht, whose Spartacist League had executed a short-lived uprising to overthrow the government.[13]

The revolutionary period having been exhausted—the Hungarian communist regime lasted just 133 days, the Bavarian Soviet fell apart even more quickly, and the Italian factory occupations did not swell to revolutionary activity—in 1920 Lenin announced a new phase of relative capitalist "stabilization" and advised communists to dig in and take advantage of democratic institutions in the leading capitalist states by joining with established unions and other workers' parties in the struggles for reform. Needless to say, the social democrats were not eager to accept the Communist offers for a united front in actions against capital and the state. The 1920s were a decade of increasing isolation of the revolutionary forces even where, as in Germany, they succeeded in building a mass working-class base.[14]

From the perspective of the worldview articulated by Marx and Engels in the *Manifesto of the Communist Party,* the movement for fundamental social change has been on the defensive in the advanced capitalist societies for more than three-quarters of a century and can only really be seen in the extraordinary movements for national independence in the colonial and semi-colonial nations. In fact, the cleavage between social reform and revolution has widened, and while revolutionary ideas continue to serve as inspiration, the everyday activities of the parties and trade unions are devoted exclusively to reform of the existing system. The social-democratic parties in the most advanced capitalist countries have settled into a pattern according to which the party consists chiefly in its parliamentary delegation and the campaign apparatuses created to win elective offices. In fact, after World War II the Socialist and Social-Democratic parties resolved, at their party congresses, to permanently adopt the role of legitimate opposition when not in power and to seek to become parties of government, within the framework of capitalism. Even the left wing of, say, the British Labor Party, or the French Socialists, or the French and Italian Communist parties themselves hesitate at the prospect of revolution or even proposals for fundamental change. They have flirted with ideas and programs of workers' control, but when they have had the power to nationalize industries it invariably has been under a regime of hierarchical management. The trade unions have become more autonomous even when, as in the case of the British Labor Party, they remain affiliated. In some instances the relative distance between unions and the party has been advantageous to workers who are inclined to engage in direct action against capital. But it is also a sign of the consequence of the transition from opposition to parties of "government." As parties of government, the socialists are responsible for administering the institutions of the capitalist state. And within this perspective, it places the party, as administrator, in potential conflict with labor.

As Carl Schorske has brilliantly chronicled, German social democracy between 1905 and 1917 constituted a "state within a state." The party was home for the overwhelming majority of its members and a considerable part of its constituency as well. For the parliamentary delegation and trade unions, a third wing existed that provided a wide range of education and cultural life to its adherents. Schorske shows that this all-enveloping series of activities and social relationships may have isolated the party's rank and file from the rest of the German population and, for this reason, had some dire consequences. However, establishing, for adults and youth alike, a culture of education, art, and sports counter to the prevailing capitalist cultural and educational institutions was generally recognized as an important contribution to the development of class consciousness. But with the growing reliance on parliamentary reforms—a vital element in the transformation of social democracy into a legitimate opposition—the ideological element in social democracy receded. The parties' educational, sports, and cultural institutions—upon which the traditional social-democratic and communist parties relied for raising the intellectual and cultural level of leaders and activists in the party organizations, unions, and social movements and for the development of cadres—have been reduced or have disappeared.[15]

Today, European socialism, if that term is still appropriate, is a series of government parties that, like the Democrats in the United States, have difficulty, when out of power, assuming the role of even a legitimate opposition. In consequence of the narrowing of differences between the center-left (the mainstream

social democrats) and the conservatives, the parties are beginning to come apart at the seams. In recent years, German
social democracy has experienced a severe split—a result of its
leadership's enthusiasm for surrendering some of the crucial
social welfare gains of the last sixty years and its compliance
with the job-cutting program of capital. The new party of the
left includes a fraction of trade union militants, left intellectuals, and the former East German Communist Party, now
called the Party of Democratic Socialism. As previously noted,
the Italian Communists have split and its left wing is steadily
gaining ground. And, after fifteen years of holding government
power and six years as the putative opposition, the French
Socialists are deeply divided and the once-moribund Communists—whose alliance with the Socialists-in-power nearly
destroyed them—are experiencing something of a revival. These
divisions are symptomatic of the decay of social democracy as
it mutated over the past sixty years. For the mainstream of
European socialism, even in the Scandinavian countries, can
no longer be described as parties of social reform. Their survival
is due much more to the widespread fear of the rise of the New
Right than to its own social and economic program. While they
have differed sharply with the policies of George W. Bush on
some issues of global politics, socialists have become parties
of government who differ from the conservatives only in matters of emphasis and timing, and who exhibit characteristics
of parties of order when extraparliamentary movements take
to the streets.

By the1960s it was apparent to many intellectuals, young
workers, and political activists that the main political parties
of the left were bankrupt. The rise of a New Left in all Western
nations was as dramatic as it was short-lived. The French May
of 1968, the Italian Hot Autumn the following year, and the
massive anti-war demonstrations and civil rights struggles
in the United States during the same period were collective
expressions of a new burst of anti-establishment, anti-parlia-
mentary, and anti-capitalist political will. The mutation of the
revolutionary socialist and communist movements into parties
of reform and of government not only produced widespread
disaffection among intellectuals and activists from the "left"
parties but spawned a series of "new" social movements that
consciously spurn the concept of "party" itself.

The exception, the global phenomenon of Green parties, may be understood within the framework of the revolt of the ecology movement against the social-democratic mainstream rather than as an attempt to form a new radical party. That project was largely defeated in the 1990s when, in an exemplary internal struggle, the German Greens divided over the question of parliamentary and extraparliamentary perspectives. Founded in the 1970s as a movement/party dedicated to direct action, in a country where electoral divisions between the center-left and right were extremely close, the "realies" (Greens dedicated to parliamentary politics) won the internal battle and soon grasped the chance to affect the balance of power. After winning as much as 10 percent of the vote in federal elections and elective office in many municipalities, the Greens eventually helped their coalition partner, the Social Democrats, to regain national power and accepted cabinet positions, including the powerful foreign ministry. However, in most countries, including the United States, the 1970s saw the feminist, ecology, and a considerable fraction of the black freedom movements distance themselves from the parties of the center and left in order to retain their freedom of action even while they continued to influence their policies. Then came the Reagan revolution. The leadership of these movements began to falter, nearly all of them reevaluated their stances, and, in most cases, they enlisted in electoral, coalition politics subsumed under an increasingly center-right Democratic Party that tempered their radical will.[16]

Party and Class

Among the fundamental concepts of historical materialism is what Karl Korsch terms "the principle of historical specification." According to Korsch, categories such as labor, capital, value, profit, and so on are subject to the historically specific context within which they function. For this reason, the significations of these categories change as well. In the debate about the role of the party—questions of its relation to revolutionary class consciousness, problems of organization, and issues of strategy and tactics—there are few, if any, principles that transcend conditions of time and place. For example, Lenin's major writings on political organization were produced under the Tsarist tyranny when social-democratic parties and trade unions were illegal and strikes were banned. Both Lenin and his adversaries, for example, assumed, at the turn of the century, that capitalism had reached a state of crisis—it was both on the brink of profound economic upheaval and on an almost inevitable trajectory toward war—and that the rise of the labor and socialist movements presented "objective" possibilities for revolutionary action.[17]

Against two tendencies within the Russian movement—the "economists" who advocated almost exclusive attention to trade union struggles, and those who favored a decentralized party or at least a weak center—Lenin argued, on the one hand, for politics and for political organization and, on the other, for a strong party center. In his polemic against the views of Vladimir Akimov and other proto-syndicalists, he stressed the significance of specifically political struggles, including those in the Duma (parliament) where, periodically, the government opted to initiate representative assemblies. Moreover, he argued against the expressed as well as the implicit position of large sections of the party that the working class, in the course of struggles around elementary needs, would achieve revolutionary class consciousness. Lenin's argument against Martov for strict centralization is based, largely, on the fact that the workers' movement was obliged to operate underground, where the violation of secrecy was often an invitation to the police. He views both tendencies as worshipful of the spontaneity of the masses, with a strong affinity for anarchism.[18]

For Lenin, following his theoretical mentor Karl Kautsky, the working class can achieve trade union consciousness only in the course of its struggles for economic justice; revolutionary class consciousness must be brought to the working class "from the outside," specifically from intellectuals organized in revolutionary parties as professional revolutionaries. It is they who provide education for the most "advanced" working-class leaders, recruiting them into the ranks of social democracy and into the center. But for Lenin, as for other contemporary revolutionaries, there is never any doubt that ultimately the task of working-class emancipation falls on the most class-conscious contingent of the workers themselves:

Firstly, the active elements of the Social-Democratic work-ing-class party will include not only the organizations of the revolutionaries, but *a whole number* of workers' organizations recognized as party organizations. Secondly, how, and by what logic, does the fact that we are a party of a class warrant the conclusion that it is unnecessary to make a distinction between those who *belong* to the party and those who associate them-selves with it? Just the contrary: precisely because there are differences in consciousness and degree of activity, a distinc-tion must be made of proximity to the Party. We are a party of a class, and therefore almost the entire class ... should act under the leadership of our party. But it would be ... tailism to think that the entire class, or almost the entire class, can ever rise, under capitalism, to the level of consciousness and activity of its vanguard, of its Social-Democratic Party. No sensible Social-Democrat has ever doubted that under capitalism even the trade union organizations ... are incapable of embracing the entire, or almost the entire, working class. To forget the distinction between the vanguard and the whole of the masses gravitating towards it, to forget the vanguard's constant duty of raising ever wider sections to its own advanced level, means simply to deceive oneself, to shut one's eyes to the immensity of our tasks, and to narrow down these tasks.[19]

It fell to Rosa Luxemburg to reply to Lenin's stringent con-ception of Russian Social Democracy. But it was not only as a marxist theorist that Luxemburg claimed authority to speak. As a founder and leader of one of the two Polish Social-Democratic parties, which at the time were closely associated with the Rus-sian party owing to Poland's annexation by the Tsarist regime, she was vitally interested in developments within the Russian party. Noting that "[t]here is no doubt that, in general a strong tendency toward centralism is inherent in Social Democracy" since it "grows in the economic soil of capitalism, which itself tends towards centralism," she maintains that Social Democ-racy is "called upon to represent within the framework of a given state, the totality of the interests of the proletariat as a class, opposed to all partial and group interests. Therefore," she concludes, "it follows that Social Democracy has the natural aspiration of welding together all national, religious, and profes-sional groups of the working class into a unified party."[20]

So far, she agrees with Lenin's general argument for cen-tralism. But Luxemburg departs from Lenin on two points:

She characterizes as "conservative" his idea that the party center has the right and duty to intervene on a *tactical level* on all matters local as well as national and believes that it might result in stifling "innovations" that can arise only in the course of actual struggles; and she vehemently disagrees with the Kautsky/Lenin thesis about how revolutionary class consciousness occurs. Note that the concept of "spontaneity" has remained ambiguous in these debates. For example, in her article "Organizational Questions of Russian Social Democracy," Rosa Luxemburg advances a thesis that cannot easily be described as a statement in favor of spontaneity.

While acknowledging the importance of the party's role in political education, cultural development, and agitation, Luxemburg holds that social-democratic action

> grows historically out of the elementary class struggle. It thus moves in the dialectical contradiction that here the proletarian army is first recruited in the struggle itself and only in the struggle does it become aware of the objectives of the struggle. Here organization, enlightenment, and struggle are not separated mechanically, and also temporarily, different moments as in the case of the Blanquist movement [a conspiratorial organization prominent during the 1830 French rebellion]. Here they are only different sides of the same process. On the one hand, apart from the general principle of the struggle, there is no ready-made pre-established detailed set of tactics which a central committee can teach its Social Democratic membership as if they were an army of recruits. On the other hand, the process of the struggle, which creates the organization, leads to a continual fluctuation of the sphere of influence of Social Democracy.[21]

Although both agree that the party is nothing other than an organization of the workers' movement—because, as the movement's most theoretically prepared force, it can grasp the relationship of sectoral struggles to the totality—Luxemburg's refusal of the concept of tactical centralism is by no means identical to Lenin's attribution of bowing to "spontaneity" to his opponents. Revolutionary socialist parties tend toward centralism; that is, they attempt to "weld together" disparate elements, to overcome the "atomization" of various sectors of the workers' movement so that, in Luxemburg's own words, the party "can be nothing but the imperative summation of the will and the fighting vanguard of the working class as opposed to its individual groups and members." According to Luxemburg this is, so to speak, a "self-centralism of the leading stratum of the proletariat; it is the rule of the majority within its own party organization."[22]

In these passages there is a striking convergence as well as difference between Lenin and Luxemburg. Both agree to the propositions that (1) the party is necessary and is a vanguard of the working class composed chiefly of revolutionary workers and intellectuals; (2) it requires centralism to fulfill its tasks, chief among which is the job of (3) welding together disparate elements to exercise unified political will. But the argument is in the implications of terms such as "centralism" and "vanguard." Lenin's conception of the party's centralism was one of "control," both of its own ranks as well as of the course of the struggle; Luxemburg speaks of "self-centralism" and rejects the idea that the party brings revolutionary class consciousness to the workers from the "outside." Instead, it is part of the struggle and subject to fluctuations in its influence because the struggle is, in many respects, unpredictable. Lenin writes from the perspective of a revolutionary elite, which, because of its advanced consciousness and political education, has earned the right to lead in matters of strategy and tactics as well as general orientation. On the other hand, Luxemburg believes the vanguard is forged in the course of struggle and that leadership in the day-to-day battles emerges from the ground up.

Thus, according to Luxemburg, the party is a tendency within the class struggle whose influence, let alone leadership, can only be earned, not assumed on the basis of its mastery of the marxist science of revolution. However, in the immediate aftermath of the Bolshevik Revolution, the Leninist conception of the party and its vanguard role overcame the Luxemburgist objections (objections advanced, among others, by the Council Communist group, which included Korsch, a German communist who served in the Bundestag as representative of the dissident Communist Workers Party [KAPD], and the Dutch left-socialists, notably the astronomer Anton Pannekoek and Herman Gorter), a fact attributable to the command exercised by the Communist International led by the Bolsheviks. Writing under the pseudonym "J. Harper" against Leninist ideas of centralized control, Pannekoek advanced Luxemburgist conceptions of the party when he argued that parliamentary struggle was subordinate to the party's extraparliamentary roles of encouraging workers to undertake direct industrial action, exposing the class collaborationist role of postwar social democracy, and promoting working-class international solidarity against capital.

Armed with their dire assessments of the degeneration of the Communist parties into cabals of bureaucratic centralism, and with an analysis of the Soviet Union as a new form of tyranny, by the 1930s the "left" communists, although still marxist in their political and theoretical orientation, renounced party formations and all forms of political centralization as instances of groups of intellectuals and bureaucrats who imposed "dictatorship over the proletariat" and not alongside it. In Gorter's words, parties tend to "dominate the masses."[23] The left communists became known as council communists when they decisively rejected Marx and Lenin's conception of the "transitional state." Pannekoek published his political magnum opus, *Workers Councils,* which comes close to associationism in its argument against political centralism, at the level both of political organization and of the state form itself, and in its description of how associations of workers' councils might collectively control production and the distribution of goods, conceived as use rather than exchange values in the capitalist sense, and self-manage society as a whole. Pannekoek's thesis is that the Paris Commune, the Russian and German Soviets, the Italian occupations, and the workers' rebellions in other countries had already shown that they were capable of conceiving of a society without hierarchy and that, without party control, they would be able to invent new forms of self-management.

Thus the workers' councils brought to theoretical fruition Luxemburg's worst fears concerning parties that control their members and, through power within workers' organizations, the working class itself. The organizations the council communists maintained until the mid-1940s were brought together by the regular publication of *International Council Correspondence,* followed by the journal *New Essays,* which was published in several languages. Like the historical socialist and communist movements, the press remained their ideological center, while the groups that adhered to their politics constituted a loose federation that met periodically but had no binding power to decide anything for the groups. Thus, although intellectually Marxists—their economic and political analysis followed closely the critical perspective of Marx himself rather than the second or third international orthodoxies—they came to adhere to the anarchists' federated principle of political organization. But most of the ICC groups opposed World War II, characterizing it as an unprincipled struggle between two rival authoritarian camps. Under the overwhelming weight of the bipolar world that followed the war, they met the fate of other third-camp movements—they disappeared.

The Party in a Nonrevolutionary Era

We have already noted that, the Russian Revolution aside, by 1919–1920 popular uprisings, sometimes in the form of seizures of state power, and sometimes in the form of mass strikes, especially in Italy and the United States, were spent. The 1920s were years of retreat for the workers' movement. In Germany and the United Kingdom, where the bourgeoisie was weak, socialist parties were able to win governmental power in coalition with more centrist formations, but were unable to sustain it in the wake of weak economies. A socialist government that presides over mass unemployment is not likely to inspire confidence. The United States, triumphant in the war, entered a fifteen-year period of reaction as the labor and radical movements were nearly decimated by a combination of employer and police power and by the perfidy of the conservative, craft-minded AFL.

In Eastern and Southern Europe, fascist and proto-fascist military regimes took power. And two luminaries of the newly formed international communist movement, Georg Lukács and Antonio Gramsci, exemplified the fate of the revolutionary intellectuals in countries seized by counterrevolutionary force. Lukács, a leading Hungarian intellectual who had joined the Communist Party, served as minister of culture in the Hungarian Soviet Republic of 1919. When the government collapsed, he was forced into exile and settled for a decade in Vienna, where, in sharp contrast to his largely literary past, he worked for a decade as a full-time revolutionary. Gramsci, an editor of a newspaper, a major figure in the Turin factory occupations of 1920, and, later, the general secretary of the Italian Communist Party, was imprisoned by Mussolini's fascist regime in 1926 and died in prison eleven years later.

These personal circumstances, combined with the ebbing of the revolutionary movement, became the occasion for two of the more original and discerning reflections on problems of political organization in a nonrevolutionary period. Precisely because of the particular character of the interwar period, it became possible to consider these issues with a degree of reflexivity missing in the earlier debates. (Recall that Lenin and Luxemburg were fully confident that the urgency of issues of party organization were directly related to the fact that, in their judgment, the first two decades of the twentieth century constituted a revolutionary situation when the class war would imminently take the form of an assault on the capitalist state.) The questions for Lukács and Gramsci were: In a period of relative capitalist stabilization, what are the forms of praxis for revolutionary forces? What is the relation of theory to practice? Is it possible to build the movement such that it avoids the formation of a tight bureaucratic leadership?[24]

Every essay in Lukács's *History and Class Consciousness* (*HCC*) (1923) was written from Vienna in the context of his period of work as a leader of the illegal Hungarian Communist Party. But the fact that this world-famous philosopher and literary critic devoted himself to practical politics for a decade has been lost on many of his readers, who tend to study this writing as an instance of Marxist scholarship. Although Lukács is an exemplary scholar, *HCC* must be understood as a contribution to political theory. Without the perspective of the economic and political situation in Europe, *HCC* becomes, in some respects, unintelligible. Or put more generously, when seen in an essentially apolitical way, the central arguments of even the most philosophical essays can be grasped only partially. Yet the essays in *HCC*, *Lenin* (1924), and Lukács's second collection from this period, *Tactics and Ethics* (1968–1972), contain some of the more valuable reflections on the problems of political organization in a nonrevolutionary period. Many readers of *HCC* (which was reissued in German in 1967 and first appeared in English four years later) are inevitably drawn to two essays in particular: "What Is Orthodox Marxism?" in which Lukács defends the materialist dialectic, especially the concept of the totality and its corollary, the indissoluble relation of the subject and object as constitutive of the totality; and the magisterial "Reification and the Consciousness of the Proletariat," actually an elaboration of the same themes, with particular emphases on the philosophical underpinning of the subject/object split in everyday life and the objective basis of this split in the universalization of the commodity-form in capitalist society. Lukács's conception of reification, derived from his reading of Marx's *Capital* (but owing its elaboration to Georg Simmel), is that in a capitalist system dominated by commodity production and exchange, relations between people take on the appearance of relations between things. That is, subjectivity is subsumed under reified objects. Read in the context of the debates over political organizations rather than as an occasional work of philosophical reflection, Lukács's work provides a "scientific" and philosophical basis for Lenin's claim that revolutionary class consciousness cannot arise from the workers' struggle. For Lukács that struggle is always conditioned by (a) a rationalization in which every aspect of human activity can be calculated and classified into "specialized systems," (b) "the fragmentation of human production [which] necessarily entails fragmentation of its subject," (c) the division of labor, and (d) the hierarchies produced by the occupational structure of the labor market. But at the core of the argument is his claim that, under the domination of capital, workers see themselves as fragmented objects rather than as subjects of the historical process.[25]

Consciousness, therefore, is not lodged in perception or individual understanding. The perception and understanding are determined by the logic of capital, but, read in isolation, "Reification" might be interpreted as an argument for either voluntarism, the doctrine according to which even adverse objective circumstances can be overcome by revolutionary will, or fatalism, the concept that the capitalist crisis will, under its own weight, lead to the system's self-destruction. Lukács's theory of political organization refutes these antinomies. Argued in philosophical terms, even in "Reification" Lukács provides the basis for a methodology of political organization. Beyond political discourse itself, Lukács sees the root of contemporary conceptions of the subject/object split in Kantian ethics. He addresses Kant, not only because Kant's three *Critiques* dominated German and French philosophy for almost a century after Hegel's death in 1831, but also because Kantian ideas had permeated some of the leading figures of international socialism—notably Bernstein; Max Adler, the leader of Austrian social democracy; and some of the Russian intelligentsia as well. In Lukács's view, unless a sound philosophical basis is established for the objective possibility of revolutionary class consciousness, efforts to make change are likely to founder on the twin fallacies of objectivism and voluntarism. The task, in his view, is to provide a structural basis for explaining both the reproduction of bourgeois consciousness within the proletariat in the wake of crises and war and the objective possibility of class consciousness.

Condemning what he calls the "contemplative attitude" toward social reality, in which the "thing-in-itself" is not available to consciousness, he argues:

> [I]n order to overcome the irrationality of the question of the thing-in-itself it is not enough that the attempt should be made to transcend the contemplative attitude. When the question is formulated more concretely it turns out that the essence of praxis consists in annulling *that indifference of form towards content that we found in the problem of the thing-in-itself.* Thus praxis can only be established as a philosophical principle if, at the same time, a conception of form can be found whose basis and validity no longer rest on that pure rationality and that freedom from every definition of content. In so far as the principle of praxis is the prescription for changing reality, it must be tailored to the concrete material substratum of action if it is to impinge upon it to any effect.[26]

These concepts underlie Lukács's major statement on the party, "Towards a Methodology of the Problem of Organization," the last chapter of *HCC.* Here, Lukács advances a bold definition: Organization is "at once the form of mediation between theory and practice"[27] and, more generally, "the concrete mediation between man and history—this is the decisive characteristic of the organization now being born."[28] In these passages Lukács stresses the fallacies of the inherent hierarchy present in many workers' parties, which overestimate the importance of the individual—that is, the leader and his activity—and the complementary "fatalistic" passivity and subordination of the masses. Both tendencies lead to bureaucratization of the party and thwart the development of a movement that promotes "real active participation" of members in every event, in the full scope of party life.

The idea of organization as the "concrete mediation between man and history" is closely linked to the problems of fragmentation and rationalization raised in "Reification." Every struggle is necessarily partial: Workers employed by a single capitalist enterprise or in a single industry fight for higher wages (or, most recently, against wage cuts) or for better working conditions; tenants oppose landlords' demands for more rent; communities fight developers seeking to gentrify their neighborhoods or destroy natural systems for commercial uses; blacks and other oppressed minorities fight for civil rights and women for sexual and gender equality. The party is, in the first place, the mediation between these struggles and the fight against capital. For example, it must show the class dimension in the struggle for abortion rights and the sexual dimension of labor struggles. Second, the party indicates the principles for a better life that are inherent in these struggles and why this aspiration is frustrated by the priorities of employer, landlord, developer, government officials, and (white) men. Third, does the party expose the role of the state in these struggles? Whose side is it on? What are the necessary tasks regarding legislation, and what are the costs of legal solutions versus direct action? We will return to some of these questions in the next and final section.

Antonio Gramsci developed his political theory while in a fascist prison. His captivity was the outcome of the success of the counterrevolution against the 1920 Turin factory occupations and his founding of the Communist Party with other left-Socialists who had heeded the call of the CI to form revolutionary parties linked to the international. Since 1924 Gramsci had been general secretary of the party. Since its founding in 1920, he had conducted a fierce ideological struggle against the "left" Communists led by Amadeo Bordiga, who had actually called the meeting to form the party. Arrested in 1926 under suspicion of participating in a plot to assassinate Mussolini, by 1929 Gramsci was tried by his fascist captors for attempting an armed insurrection and sentenced to twenty years in prison. Between 1929 and 1933, he wrote ten notebooks, five of which have been edited and translated into English by Joseph Buttigeg. Under the watchful eye of the censor, Gramsci was obliged to invent his own vocabulary—which consisted of euphemisms for conventional terms, but also graphic descriptions of them—and to smuggle the material out, which he succeeded in doing thanks to his friend, the economist Piero Sraffa, and his sister-in-law Tatiana. The immense scope of these works can be explained not only by the fact that he had been trained as a "traditional" intellectual and was familiar with many languages, the natural and human sciences, the arts, philosophy, sociological theory, and politics, but also by his conception of the movement as more than transformative of the nature of property—indeed, as a vehicle for the development of the full capacities of individuals. Like Lenin, Luxemburg, and Lukács, Gramsci held that the party was a fusion of the most class-conscious workers and revolutionary intellectuals. To make sure it did not degenerate into the private preserve of the latter, the party had to develop a broad-ranging educational program both for its own cadres and for the "masses," not only in the scientific aspects of Marxism but in the whole range of literary and philosophical works that mark the Enlightenment as well. The key task of party education was to help develop critical self-consciousness:

> Critical self-consciousness means, historically and politically, the creation of an elite [i.e., a politically specialized group] of intellectuals. A human mass does not "distinguish" itself, does not become independent in its own right without, in the widest sense, organizing itself; and there is no organization without intellectuals, that is, without organizers and leaders, in other words, without the theoretical aspect of the theory-practice nexus being distinguished concretely by the existence of a group of people "specialised" in conceptual and philosophical elaboration of ideas. But the process of creating intellectuals is long, difficult, full of contradictions, advances and retreats, dispersals and regroupings in which the loyalty of the masses is sorely tried.[29]

Gramsci then stresses that this task is tied to the dialectic between intellectuals and masses, in which the latter develops to a "higher level of culture" and whose influence on intellectuals is decisive for their own development. In turn, the intellectuals, "organically" linked to the subaltern classes, conduct a struggle to impose a new common sense within civil society.

The importance of the development of intellectuals becomes clearer when we consider one of Gramsci's more celebrated formulations. Consistent with the principle of historical specification, Gramsci argues that there are two aspects to the struggle for social transformation: the war of maneuver, in which the revolutionary movement, of which the party (after Machiavelli, "The Modern Prince") is its leading detachment, undertakes the assault on the state; and the war of position, the period when the possibility of revolution has been foreclosed to the proletariat and its allies. The moment of the war of position is characterized by two extremely important party activities, both of which fall largely, if not exclusively, on intellectuals. Stating that every class in history seeking power must prevail at the ideological as well as the military/political level, Gramsci claims that the possibility of winning a war of maneuver depends both on the level of organization and the strength of the movement and, crucially, on the capacity of the workers' movement and its intellectuals to impose a new "common sense" on society as a whole. By "common sense" Gramsci connotes a disaggregated collection of myths, deeds, and superstitions that constitute bourgeois hegemony and that are in dialectical tension with "good sense." As long as the constellation of ruling ideas prevail, every struggle will remain local, fragmented, and even perceived by the workers and other subalterns in terms of those hegemonic ideas. For Gramsci, critical understanding presupposes a struggle of "political hegemonies" pulling in opposite directions. Where there is no contest of hegemonies, the ruling common sense will inevitably undermine the significance of what might otherwise become a generalized battle. One of the main tasks of the war of position is to create a new common sense.

One American example may illustrate what a counterhegemonic "good sense" might be. In the heat of the great industrial union upsurge of the 1930s and 1940s, the communist composer and lyricist Earl Robinson wrote the song "Joe Hill" as an attempt to displace the bourgeois myth of individualism with a myth of collective action mediated by Joe Hill, the IWW organizer. Joe Hill was, in Robinson's phrase, "framed on a murder charge" and executed. But as the song goes, Joe Hill "never died.... Wherever workingmen [*sic*] are out on strike, that's where you'll find Joe Hill." So without using the term, for Gramsci, as for Lukács, the party organization is a mediation between theory and practice, between "man" and history. It must challenge the prevailing common sense at every level: the trajectory of the economy and its effects on class structure; the analysis of the political situation; the articulation of a social and cultural ethics on questions of sexuality, issues of law, education, and artistic representation; the interpretation of history; and the problems of science and technology, both their theoretical implications and their practical applications. In short, unlike the modern social democratic dictum that the limit of political intervention is the material interests of class, defined narrowly as economic and welfare issues and, of course, civil liberties, the party organization must be capable of intervening on the widest range of economic, political, social, and cultural questions. Prior to any set of specific tactics, its fundamental role is to weld together the fragments of the working class through the interpretation and dissemination of the significance of particular, sectoral struggles in relation to the totality. So the struggle for political and cultural hegemony is a cardinal strategic task during the nonrevolutionary period.[30]

In order for a struggle of this magnitude to be conducted, Gramsci argues, the corps of "intellectuals" must be expanded; but since there are simply not enough traditional intellectuals (and, in any case, one would not want to create an elite in the old sense), raising the level of culture in the "widest" meaning of the term becomes crucial. Here lies the importance of theoretical and philosophical education. Declaring that everyone is a (spontaneous) philosopher and also a politician, Gramsci argues that the task of the "organic" intellectuals is to fuse this spontaneous wisdom with historical materialism. He transforms the concept of elite to mean those who engage in the counterhegemonic activities of education, propaganda, and theorizing to produce a new "common sense," and not only as a specialized professional activity. The class develops "organic" intellectuals; some are recruited from the traditional intellectuals who are trained to serve the crown or, after the English and French Revolutions, the bourgeoisie. As the strength of the subalterns (including the proletariat) grows, so too does the number of intellectuals who come over to the movement. But throughout the *Prison Notebooks,* it is clear that Gramsci expects the ranks of organic intellectuals to swell by recruiting a new type of intellectual from the rank and file as a result of the party's educational and cultural efforts.

Is a Radical Party Possible in the United States?

What are the prospects for the emergence of a "party" in the United States capable of mediating between the existing labor and social movements and history? In order to address this question we need first to make a sober assessment of the specific features of the economic and political situation within the United States and its relation to global capitalism. Within this assessment we ask: What are the conditions of the labor and social movements? And finally, what, in general, is the prevailing "common sense," both within the movements and in the population as a whole? Then, and only then, can we make organizational proposals.

It is no secret that the US national economy has been seriously weakened over the past quarter-century by massive deindustrialization in many of our largest cities and by the emergence, through globalization, of new players in the world economy. Labor-destroying technological change has reduced labor forces in many major industries, while new "tech" knowledge industries have failed to make up for the losses. Reinvestment in US-based industries has declined relatively, even in the crucial energy sector, and global investment by finance capital has increased. Real wages have declined during this period by nearly 25 percent, and official poverty has increased, but many who are not officially poor struggle to make ends meet. Further, we have experienced a radical restructuring of the labor market: "Jobs," a term that once implied a degree of permanence, have increasingly been replaced by temporary, contingent, and part-time "work." And while the official level of unemployment hovers around 5 percent, the hidden joblessness—premature retirements, people forced out of the labor force, job scarcity for first-time job seekers, part-timers counted as full time by official statistics—brings our real rates closer to the double digits of Western Europe.

At a time when global warming or, more precisely, abrupt climate change threatens life on the planet, US rail and air transportation industries are experiencing a huge crisis, even as the federal government pours hundreds of billions of dollars into the highway program. Among the chief targets of deregulation in the 1980s, airlines have been a net loser in the much-praised free market innovations of the Democrats, who controlled Congress until 1994, as well as in successive Republican administrations. Several airlines have declared bankruptcy, degraded their service, and cancelled contractual mandates for pensions and other benefits, even as they have demanded, and received, substantial wage concessions from unionized workers. Biased without forethought toward autos and trucks, federal investment in rail has been reduced to a trickle as railroads attempt to stay afloat by raising ticket fares and freight rates. Skilled rail employees have been laid off, and Amtrak has announced further cuts in service. And the American auto industry, once the envy of the world, has been plunged into near-depression by global price competition, the poor quality of its products, and short-sighted and self-destructive corporate planning. The transportation industries alone affect a quarter of the economy and millions of jobs. General Motors has announced a 25 percent cut in jobs over the next three years, and the prospects for Ford are no better.

Meanwhile, domestic and global manufacturers of electronic equipment and computer hardware have merged under stress from relative shrinkage of sales and technological innovation, have engaged in extensive outsourcing, and have reduced workforces, shattering the classic neoliberal dismissal of the crisis in intermediate technology industries such as auto, steel, and electrical products. Remember the mantra? "Not to worry. These are Rust-belt industries. The Sunbelt industries will more than make up for the losses. All displaced workers need is retraining for these hi-tech jobs." But the fact is, with the exception of China and India, which have embarked on a contemporary version of primitive capitalist accumulation by means of what David Harvey terms "dispossession" (for instance, 150 million Chinese have been driven from the countryside into the cities), global capitalism is in a state of stagnation and decline.

But what is the state of the unions and the social movements? How have they responded to the veritable cascade of economic, environmental, and political crises brought about by daily revelations that, as Marx and Engels remarked in the *Manifesto*, the bourgeoisie can no longer meet the needs of the immense majority of people? (We need not rehearse in detail the appalling levels of US education and health care, let alone the chronic shortage of affordable housing.) How did the left and the labor movement respond to Hurricane Katrina? Apart from joining in private relief efforts and criticizing the slow response of the Bush administration, not a single public voice of any consequence was raised to point out that privatization of relief services was a symptom of the systematic destruction of federal civil service in the diplomatic, intelligence, and technical areas and that one of its most competent branches, the Army Corps of Engineers (as well as many state and local engineering departments), had been seriously weakened before the hurricane by the billion-dollar contracts handed to Halliburton and Bechtel and other private construction firms. Where is the voice that places the blame squarely on capitalism itself, on its evident incapacity to engage in planning beyond the interests of the individual firm? While economist Joseph Steiglitz can show the limits of market ideology, and while Paul Krugman insists that the Bush administration is to blame for countless economic woes, not the least of which is the mounting debt due to war expenditures and balance-of-payments deficits, few analyses link the current situation with the history of neoliberal economic policy and with the self-interested faith in the market to solve most problems.

How has the left and the labor movement addressed the steady bleeding of good jobs, the incessant corporate demands for wage and benefit cuts to make them profitable, the pattern of concessionary bargaining that has spread like an epidemic throughout the labor movement? Can we say that any significant force within the labor movement has been able to mount a campaign against concessionary bargaining, whereby the union becomes the instrument of the employers' program? And when a union of Northwest mechanics dares to withhold its labor rather than grant yet another round of wage and benefit concessions, and, with few exceptions, notably the UAW and UNITE HERE, the rest of the airline unions and the AFL-CIO and its rival federation snub the strike, where are the voices of solidarity that take a public platform to criticize the parochialism of the unions, especially in the airline industry, that cross picket lines and condemn the mechanics for their resistance? While the courageous labor periodical *Labor Notes* has raised these issues, it is only putatively an ideological organ of a fragmented and largely incipient radical wing of organized labor. Since there is no "party" with members broadly distributed in the unions and with a presence in the public sphere to take up these issues, and since there is no intellectual and political force to attempt to weld movements of resistance and to link them to history, we are now confronted with a working class that is ideologically and politically defenseless because bourgeois hegemony—particularly the fatalism that has accompanied the huge shifts in the economy—is virtually uncontested. In this case, and in many others over the last quarter-century, some workers have identified their interests with those of their "own" corporation, a de facto instance of corporatism. Of course, many are discontented with these alignments but have no vehicle to contest the dominant leadership. Finally, as left-liberals bemoan the absence of political opposition, they remain in thrall to the old "common sense" that the two-party system—and the current electoral swindle—is the only game in town and convince themselves that it is folly to imagine alternatives.

Only those who are in the grip of political myopia would suggest that a party formation is on the immediate agenda. Given the concrete historical circumstances whereby, for example, a large portion of radical activists are self-described "anarchists," many in the movements remain in thrall to the "lessons" of the history of international socialism and communism (namely, that the party as a form has been discredited), and the left, broadly conceived, has not seriously debated radical, let alone revolutionary, political theory for decades, one might propose to form an organization that would attempt to mediate among theory and practice, humans, and history. In practice, it would initially have three principal tasks:

1. *To bring together those who are already discontented with the current state of things.* Movements remain

fragmented, locked into single issues, and avoid integrating their specific political foci with a broader vision of a new society. Among the early tasks, then, are the development of a public presence, largely through the creation of a left press, and the formation in every large city of groups that dedicate themselves to forming study groups; to intervening, where appropriate, in local struggles; and to contributing to larger projects such as those outlined below.

2. *To initiate a broad discussion of the central problems of social and political theory, situated in the actuality of global as well as national situations.* We have barely come to terms with the significance of the reemergence of a Latin American left, once solemnly buried by ex-radicals who went over to centrist governments in Mexico, Brazil, and Venezuela, among others. How, then, to account for the virtual collapse of European social democracy and American liberalism? Perhaps most important, will the left take up the critique of liberal democratic institutions advanced by, among others, Benjamin Barber, Grant McConnell, Robert Dahl, and Robert Wiebe, each of whom has written persuasively that democracy has become largely an illusion in the United States? If so, what are the prospects for electoralism in what otherwise might be viewed as a stacked deck? And, of course, we need to revisit the question of the state and what Althusser termed its "ideological apparatuses." Is it really possible to reform the state so that it becomes an expression and instrument of popular power? Or, as others have claimed, must the state itself be uprooted? The World Social Forum raises crucial issues, among them the project of reinvigorating civil society—the space between the economy and the institutions of political rule. The question is: Can we envision radical social change in which the underlying population actually takes hold of the economy and invents forms of coordination that address common problems without creating a series of repressive state apparatuses and a whole new social formation of "organic" intellectuals (including self-described "activists," many of whom are already intellectuals without acknowledging it)?

3. *To discover what forms a left political organization might take under the concrete, historically situated circumstances of the American movements.* This means revisiting the history of the left, especially the American left, as well as developing an adequate theory of our own situation. Issues such as the role of a center and how to ensure that funds and other resources are available for education, publications, and so on, should be discussed.

A left political organization may or may not be a "mass" party of hundreds of thousands, but from the standpoint of the totality it would articulate the demands of millions. It would seek its membership among the leaders and rank-and-file activists of trade unions, women's organizations, environmental and ecology movements, various factions of the freedom movements for blacks, Latinos, Asian-Americans, and other oppressed peoples, and the anti-war and global justice movements—and its most important roles might be to link the various forms of discontent experienced by these groups and to begin to make connections between what seem to be a series of unrelated events and sectoral struggles. In liberal democratic societies such as the United States, the organization can expect to win substantial support from the electorate, especially at the local level.

To accomplish these aims, the organization would assemble a small army of intellectuals—not only academics but also journalists, theoretically oriented trade unionists, and others—who would engage in the work required by the project of transforming capitalist social formations (including extensive propaganda activities and the sponsorship of schools of popular and advanced political education) and research institutes. A press will be essential for ideological intervention, and the organization would sponsor, through financial or organizational support, a series of independent left periodicals, especially daily and weekly newspapers and journals, all of which would take advantage of the vast potential audiences offered by the Internet.

All of the old arrangements are now in disarray. In much of Europe and Latin America, the ideological and political disintegration of the center/left parties has resulted in a revival of a series of left political formations whose relation to the old Russian question has been partially severed. It is time for the left in the United States to make a similar break.

Notes

1. Wini Breines, *Community and Organization in the New Left* (South Hadley, MA: Bergin and Garvey, 1982).

2. C. Wright Mills, "The New Left," in *Power, Politics, and* People, edited by Irving Louis Horowitz (New York: Oxford University Press, 1963).

3. For an explication of the idea of participatory democracy, the best SDS source is Tom Hayden et al., *The Port Huron Statement* (New York: SDS, 1962).

4. The irony of the populist anti-intellectualism of the New Left is that many of its protagonists were themselves trained intellectuals. Anti-intellectualism outlived its initial populist moment; it pervades the "activist" left to this day.

5. Daniel Bell, *The End of Ideology* (Glencoe: The Free Press, 1960); Irving Howe, *A Margin of Hope* (New York: Harcourt Brace and Jovanovich, 1982).

6. On the Socialist Party, see James Weinstein, *The Decline of Socialism 1912–1925* (New Brunswick: Rutgers University Press, 1984); and David Shannon, *The Socialist Party of America* (Chicago: Quadrangle Press, 1967). On the Communist Party, see Frasier M. Ottanelli, *The Communist Party of the United States* (New Brunswick: Rutgers University Press, 1991). Irving Howe and B. J. Widick's *The American Communist Party* (New York: Praeger Publishers, 1957) is a wholesale indictment of the CP by two fervent left anti-communists who make no pretense at dispassion.

7. The best history of the CP's popular front cultural policies is Michael Denning, *The Cultural Front* (New York: Verso Books, 1998); on Foster and the 1932 presidential campaign, see Edward Johanningsmeier, *Forging American Communism: A Life of William Z. Foster* (Princeton: Princeton University Press, 1994).

8. Hal Draper, *Karl Marx's Theory of Revolution* (New York: Monthly Review Press, 1989).

9. Dan LaBotz, *Rank and File Rebellion* (New York: Verso Books, 1990).

10. I cite this phrase on the basis of speeches by, and conversations with, Michael Harrington.

11. Richard Hofstadter, *The Idea of a Party System* (Berkeley: University of California Press, 1968).

12. Karl Marx and Frederich Engels, "The Manifesto of the Communist Party," in *Marx and Engels: Basic Writings on Politics and Philosophy,* edited by Lewis Feuer (New York: Anchor Books, 1989).

13. V. I. Lenin, "Imperialism: The Highest Stage of Capitalism," *Little Lenin Library* (New York: International Publishers, 1929).

14. V. I. Lenin, "Left-Wing Communism: An Infantile Disorder," *Little Lenin Library* (New York: International Publishers, 1929).

15. Carl E. Schorske, *German Social Democracy 1905–1917* (Cambridge, MA: Harvard University Press, 1954).

16. On the French May, see George Katsiaficas, *The Imagination of the New Left: A Global Analysis of 1968* (Boston: South End Press, 1987), ch. 3.

17. Karl Korsch, *Karl Marx* (New York: Russell & Russell, 1961), ch. 1.

18. On the economists, see V. I. Lenin, "What Is to Be Done?" *Little Lenin Library* (New York: International Publishers, 1929); on centralization, see V. I. Lenin, "One Step Forward, Two Steps Back," *Little Lenin Library* (New York: International Publishers, 1929). On Lenin's misrepresentation of the economists' position, see Jonathan Frankel, *Vladimir Akimov and the Dilemma of Russian Marxism* (Cambridge, UK: Cambridge University Press, 1969).

19. Lenin, *What Is to Be Done*, p. 7.

20. Rosa Luxemburg, "Organizational Questions of Social Democracy," in *Political Writings of Rosa Luxemburg*, edited by Dick Howard (New York: Monthly Review Press), p. 287.

21. Ibid., pp. 289–290.

22. Ibid., p. 290.

23. See Herman Gorter, "Letter to Comrade Lenin," *The Workers' Dreadnought*, March 1921. The Councilists were prolific writers. A fairly comprehensive account of their view of communism is Anton Pannekoek, *Workers Councils*, introduction by Noam Chomsky (Oakland, CA: AK Press, 2003). See also Anton Pannekoek, "The Party and the Working Class" (1936), which is available online at http://www.marxists.org/archive/pannekoek/1936/party-working-class.htm. In addition, see the running commentary on the Communists and the Soviet Union in the 1930s and 1940s in *New Essays*, 5 vols. (Westport, CT: Greenwood Press, 1971).

24. Georg Lukács, *History and Class Consciousness* (Cambridge, MA: MIT Press, 1971); Antonio Gramsci, *Selections from the Prison Notebooks*, introduction by Rodney Livingstone and Geoffrey Nowell-Smith (New York: International Publishers, 1971).

25. Lukács, *History and Class Consciousness*, pp. 88–92.

26. Ibid., pp. 125–126.

27. Ibid., p. 299.

28. Ibid., p. 318.

29. Gramsci, *Selections*, p. 334.

30. Due in large measure to the legacy of the absolutist states of continental Europe, after the death of Engels social democracy tended to insist on the strict separation of the private and the public and to renounce intervention into cultural and social life. This led most of these parties to renounce the dictum that the socialist revolution was about the transformation of economic and political relations that would create a "new" individual whose cultural and social development would be the basis of the "free association of producers." Perhaps the most articulate statement of the need for the separation is found in Hannah Arendt's *The Human Condition*.

◇

3

Burdens of the Past, and Where Is the Contemporary Agency?

Opposition Without Alternatives

This is a time when the fight for America's future and that of the globe is, preeminently, between a dominant worldview that proclaims that free enterprise and the market are forces of nature, that human beings are inherently conservative, and naturally aggressive, that the very idea of collective interests are chimerical, and that individuals, conceived as atoms, are the veritable building blocks of economic and political life—and an unarticulated alternative. There is no attempt to think in terms of social relations; all that exists are individuals. Each pursues his self-interest and cooperates with other humans only under emergency conditions such as war and "natural disasters." Otherwise, as Adam Smith reminded us, God will rationalize the welter of competing interests, but the human hand should refrain from interfering with commerce. The opposition rejects many of these tenets, as well as the paradoxical belief that what is, is fate. Yet for reasons that are discussed below, the left opposition has moved away from alternative worldviews; in fact, if not doctrinally, it has become pragmatic, a position that refuses to address issues of human nature and accepts without acknowledgment the presuppositions of liberal ideology or, in its most radical forms, will judge programs and policies only by their consequences.

After a decade of uncontested dominance over the economic and political landscape, the powers of transnational corpora-

109

tions, their satellite states, and their neoliberal ideologies are being discredited by events as well as by the popular suspicion that, in the wake of the repeal of the New Deal, most of us are getting a bum deal. In every advanced capitalist society the leading political forces have all but renounced the traditional promises to create a better life for the underlying population. In France and Italy there have been mass demonstrations against welfare cuts, but in the United States the people remain divided and relatively quiet. Each passing day reveals the extent of death and destruction in Iraq, in New Orleans, and elsewhere. We are becoming aware of the wages of neglect afflicting the poorest continents: Africa, Asia, and Latin America. Whole regions suffer hunger and disease, and there is little political will by the great powers to intervene. And flaunting its awesome military might, the US government cannot hide the deep flaws in its armor: corruption in high places, omnipresent administrative incompetence, and dogmatic refusal to address the festering ecological crisis. In Iraq, for example, the military has not been able to provide adequate armor even for its own troops, a misstep that has caused untold casualties. Meanwhile, capital can record one great success: Living standards are plummeting as workers and their unions in the advanced capitalist states, especially the United States, give up hard-won past gains.

Since they do not propose a different mode of life except to preserve some of the pieces of the welfare state, the worldwide opposition forces are not yet counterhegemonic. With the huge exception of the countries of Latin America, where the left is engaged in a struggle for economic as well as political power, they are stuck, in great measure, with the tactics of protest and resistance, and are burdened by a postmodern politics that is structurally unable to engage these ideological issues at the level of the totality because they don't believe in the totality, let alone the concepts of system and structure. While many are morally anti-capitalist, their conception of politics is parallel to pluralism. If there is a ruling class this recognition has little to do with what goes on in everyday struggles, typically directed against visible adversaries. Among some activists even the concept of alternatives is rejected in principle: Proposing alternatives to the current setup is intrinsically reformist since, using the example of the World Bank's reduction of "third world" debt after a decade of protests, such proposals are subject to co-optation.

Nor do the opposition forces, and many others engaged in "organizing," believe in the power of ideas, except those offered by muckraking and populist writers whose implicit message is that the problem standing in the way of social change is mass ignorance. They accept the prevailing common sense: People are moved by their perceived interests or their violated identities rather than by concepts. Thus exposing with overwhelming evidence the perfidy of big Capital and the corruption of large sections of the capitalist state is both the necessary and the sufficient condition to establish a new terrain of conscious political intervention. For this and other reasons, even when parties of the left—both center-left and radical—win electoral victories and assume governmental power, such as recently occurred in Latin America and Europe, they have been unable to offer a way out of the morass of war, unemployment and underemployment, and the alarming spread of hunger and disease. They may rebel against the imperative of meeting their country's debts to transnational banks and other lenders, but they are generally unwilling or unable to discuss, let alone implement, a whole new way of life that would, at least in principle, re-found production and civil society on a cooperative basis. Most of the left is still burdened by the past; it has not moved beyond the poetry of bygone days and therefore imagines that the main task is its restoration of some kind of mythic "golden age," whether the welfare state or some past revolution. Failing to comprehend that we live in a different "now," the left is unable to envision the "not yet"—that is, the project of radical futurity.

For example, in the largest country of Latin America, Brazil, decisive steps to alter the prevailing situation of mass unemployment and large-scale poverty are impeded by agreements with the World Bank and the International Monetary Fund that mandate fiscal restraint, require timely debt payments regardless of the consequences for social spending and other public goods, and oblige the state to stamp out grassroots urban and rural rebellions at the local level lest the rights of property be violated. In 2005 the Workers Party (PT) government responded to squatters affiliated with the landless movement by forcibly removing them. The fault lies partially in the presupposition of the PT victory itself. In order to defeat the center-right in the 2002 elections, the PT had to make alliances with centrists, forming a popular front that inevitably compromised its program of land redistribution, the development of workers' cooperatives to take over factories abandoned by capital, the introduction of a system of workplace councils in the private and public sectors, serious efforts at narrowing the gap between rich and poor, and the expansion of education and all types of public goods. These compromises estranged a wide section of the party's base, especially the social movements. Was the problem ultimately due to its aspiration for power over the liberal state? As we shall see, movements from below and liberal democratic states such as Venezuela—whose flexibility is enhanced by its huge oil reserves—offer, at best, different versions of state "socialism" and lack the radical imagination needed to generate the conditions for a change that can affect the everyday.

Even social movements such as those in Argentina, Bolivia, and Brazil presuppose, in some respects, capitalist social relations. Factory occupations by unemployed workers in Argentina and Brazil, and movements of landless peasants, seek to wrest the big land combines and institute cooperative or individual property, and propose to produce goods for their internal markets. In Bolivia the newly elected leftist president, Evo Morales, has promised to develop the country's largely untapped rich natural resources and has begun by nationalizing the natural gas companies and taken the first steps toward agrarian reform. In most of the newly installed regimes the governments are attempting radical reforms under conditions of populist political rule, which, for ideological reasons, they identify as "socialist." The question is: To whom are the populists accountable? Can the state create a framework for these reforms, or will the state bureaucracy and private capital be able to thwart the initiatives? That markets pose significant challenges to structural reform of property relations is evident. Nonetheless, the dramatic initiatives from below, especially in Chiapas and other Mexican regions and in Latin America, constitute an action-critique of the prevailing neoliberal government policies.

There are many reasons why in the United States a new political formation is needed—one capable of contesting capital's land grab; the assault on the great achievements of the working class and the advances by the black freedom movement and by feminists; the virtual monopoly over ideas enjoyed by capital and its neoliberal acolytes about economic and social reality; events such as Hurricane Katrina; and the continuation of the massive deindustrialization of America and its consequent orgy of wage and benefit cuts. (On November 29, 2005, Merck, one of the pharmaceutical giants, announced 7,000 layoffs in connection with its restructuring. Two days later Ford said it would lay off 7,500 workers and close five plants in the United States, Canada, and Mexico; by mid-January it increased the job elimination to 30,000 and the closure to fourteen plants in the next six years.) Corporate America has waged class warfare as well in the massive land grab from the workers to the wealthy represented by suburban and urban real estate development, which has displaced hundreds of thousands of working-class residents to make way for high-priced condominiums and expensive single-family homes. To which we must add the genuine rightist threat to legal abortion, and the burning questions associated with war, especially its relation to broader considerations of US–empire building and its effect on the critically diminished chance for domestic reforms. These issues cannot be adequately addressed by the left without an effort to capture intellectual as well as moral leadership.

Indeed, they cannot be effectively addressed ad hoc but require, simultaneously, attention to issues of ideology and alternatives. And they require organization. As Gramsci argued, struggles over specific issues are not enough to reverse bourgeois hegemony; a basic component of the struggle over power in nonrevolutionary times is the question of what forces control the popular conceptions of the future, and which proposals to address national problems and those of the world are taken seriously and which are consigned to the margins. Even if this is a moment when the prevailing conceptions are under fire and are met with widespread skepticism about their ability to meet popular needs (at least symptomatically), it does not follow that one or more alternative worldviews are bound to replace them.

The unprecedented outpouring of left and liberal organizations and activist interventions in American political life is heartening but not enough to engage, let alone reverse, the tide of neoliberal economics, the rapid erosion of civil liberties, and the dominance of conservative cultural ideology. Social movement activism has increased, not only against the Iraq war and other US foreign interventions, but also on issues such as gentrification, labor exploitation, and state repression of civil liberties, especially the growing practice of government electronic surveillance of individuals and organizations. Amidst palpable turbulence these organizations and movements have failed to come to terms with the fact that, in the absence of alternative conceptions around some of its assumptions, the old "common sense" is somewhat bloodied but remains unbowed and hegemonic. Its most important element is the air of *inevitability* that accompanies nearly every event. The idea that we can "do something"—that electoral choices, let alone demonstrations and mass rallies, can make a difference in the country's direction—is overwhelmed by a sense of despair shared by large sections of the putative political opposition, putative because it has failed to congeal in a concrete historical movement for change.

Changing the prevailing common sense to a situation where *good sense* prevails is not a mysterious process. It requires an organized political party that understands its tasks to include the development and propagation of new ideas through education, in the form of a broad campaign not only to develop and use new radical media but also to intervene in the prevalent media. The objective of education, of discussion, and of the development of ideas is to assist in bringing forth a new generation of highly informed, politically and ideologically competent intellectuals (including, in the wider sense, teachers, organizers, writers, and media producers). These people are the immediate agents for working in and educating workers, young radicals, and potential activists in radical politics and culture. It is arguable, for example, that the existence of a left-led countermovement to the American invasion of Iraq, even though its arguments embraced a distinct minority of the population, was doubtlessly partially responsible for the Bush administration's reversal of fortune. Public opinion polls in 2005 showed that the number of American military casualties were on many minds, accounting for shifts from majority approval to majority disapproval of the war, even among people who voted for Bush in 2004. Yet that figure is relatively modest compared to the number of deaths and injuries incurred during the early stages of the Vietnam war and during the first two years of the Korean war and World War II. Most Americans tolerated heavy losses during the latter two wars as "necessary" costs of what they believed to be a just cause. And during the anti-communist crusade, most, at first, were supportive of President Kennedy and President Johnson's military intervention in Southeast Asia; but when, after four years, it appeared that US troops were getting nowhere in their attempt to thwart the Vietnamese revolution, many began to act on their own discontents. By contrast, the anti–Vietnam war movement had a small army of educators as well as organizers to carry the weight. The opposition to the war took many forms: demonstrations, teach-ins on college campuses, talks and debates with administration officials at university and community forums (I myself debated the Johnson administration's assistant secretary of state for South Asian affairs at the University of Wisconsin), GI coffeehouses stationed near military bases, anti-draft actions, and strenuous efforts to persuade unions to take up the issue for debate, if not for immediate action.

In the early 1960s Vietnam war opponents led a lonely and apparently quixotic crusade. I remember chairing a 1964 outdoor anti–Vietnam war rally in Washington whose featured speaker was the writer James Baldwin. At most seventy-five hardy souls heard him, the pacifist leader A. J Muste, and other, lesser-known speakers. When SDS organized a Washington march against the war one year later, in 1965, even the organizers were startled by the 25,000 people who answered the call. Prior to the march, war protest consisted of the occasional picket line containing a dozen die-hard pacifists in front of the White House—a form of symbolic protest that was ignored by the press. Even when the first mass protest was assembled, liberal supporters of the war dismissed the significance of the event and smugly warned SDS that it was playing into the hands of the communists and the hawks who accused President Johnson of being "soft" on the communists. Then, too, there were the socialists and liberals who were doubtful about the war but opposed direct action because they feared its effect on the Democratic Party's domestic program and electoral chances. Some, such as Vice-President Hubert Humphrey, were openly hostile to the demonstration. Others, including socialist leader Michael Harrington and the Auto Workers' president, Walter

Reuther, applied back-channel pressure on the students to refrain from embarrassing the Johnson administration.

In his speech at the rally, SDS president Paul Potter called upon his listeners not only to "name the system" that caused the war but also to engage in anti-war activity. Instead of advocating moderation, this was a call to raise the stakes of opposition. Two years later, under pacifist and left organizational initiative, millions had joined the protest, signified by the 1967 demonstration at the Pentagon and the million-person march through New York streets, a minority of whom were prepared to engage in a different sort of politics; many concerned left-liberals became radical anti-capitalists, socialists, and communists. In 1967 Harrington and Reuther finally became war opponents, although they disdained the mass anti-war movement because of its policy of including all dissenting groups, even the communists. Others began to break their emotional ties to the Democratic Party, and to liberal ideology, but had no place to go. As we saw in Chapter 2 the New Left, which had momentarily captured the initiative within the anti-war movement, refused to take the next step toward a new political formation, even as, in 1966, some local activists (especially in California and New York City) began to experiment in independent electoral politics. Within five years of the SDS-sponsored march—signaled by the unfortunate events at the 1968 Democratic National Convention, during which mass arrests were made that had enduring effects; by the brutal police actions in 1970 at Kent State, where students were killed during an anti-war demonstration; and by Richard Nixon's abolition of the draft—even as most liberals joined the opposition, the anti-war movement was outflanked. Plagued by growing economic difficulties and by the war's unpopularity, the administration ended its military intervention, quietly.

Wars may concentrate and displace broader popular discontent. That the deposal of Saddam Hussein, his regime, and his armies in late 2003 did not end what Bush called the "military phase" of the Iraq war was deeply disappointing to many because they were told that the Baathists were unpopular and that American forces would be greeted with cheers and flowers in Baghdad and other cities by a fervently appreciative populace. As is well known, weapons of mass destruction were never discovered and, instead of introducing a period of peace and reconstruction, the end of the Baathist regime marked a new stage of the war. But it would be a mistake to assume that growing opposition to the Iraq war at home was simply an expression of popular disillusion with an increasingly messy US occupation. Many conservatives and liberals began to link evidence—tied to the incompetence and dishonesty of the Bush administration—that an assured military victory was turning into a guerilla-driven civil war that was destroying the country and killing tens of thousands of civilians as well as American and Iraqi soldiers. Whereas at first most Americans were prepared to support the administration's war aims, they were not prepared to be infantilized by lies and other deceptions. Discontent was overdetermined as well by the mounting domestic health care crisis, White House scandals involving high-level administration operatives, and the shaky economy. Since there are no serious national movements addressing our *general* crisis of political legitimacy, the focus on the war was not unexpected. What did not happen was a consistent and organized effort to link the war to the degradation of everyday life, to the erosion of politics, and to a conscious ruling-class program of less than benign neglect of basic human needs.

Without a sustained opposition that links every manifestation of discontent with the totality of transnational capitalism's assault on the ever-widening mass of humanity and on nature, and without consistent intervention at the ideological level (i.e., at the level of ideas), there is every reason to expect that, notwithstanding some deterioration in its hegemony, the prevailing power will regain its footing. Since the current left either is based on the received intellectual wisdom forged during the nineteenth and early-twentieth centuries or disdains intellectual wisdom altogether and functions, in the main, on its viscera—that is, *reacts to* the initiatives of Power—its leading slogan is "say no." But while the time-honored politics of refusal to participate in military adventures, in paid work, and in the rituals of social and political life such as elections retains a certain cultural appeal—especially among a significant core of young people who, calling themselves "anarchists," stimulated some of the most militant and highly visible protests against global capitalism in recent years—the fact is that this strategy, which had popular resonance in the 1960s and early 1970s among wide sections of the population, has met its historicity.

Opposition to the war and draft refusal among the young were stymied during the Nixon era by the advent of the "volunteer" army. And the "refusal to work" that accompanied the slacker moment and shop-floor rebellions against speed-up, managerial authority, and the sheer boredom of assembly-line production in the late 1960s and early 1970s, in both the United States and Western Europe, was predicated on a buoyant, late-1960s European economic recovery and US prosperity.

The "bohemian" moment of a revived civil society that sprouted up in many large cities had the unintended consequence of spawning a tide of gentrification in the 1980s. Beginning in the late 1960s we saw the emergence of a café culture in many American cities and towns, particularly as manifested in bookstores that sold radical books, posters, and artworks. And there was a small revolt against degraded jobs and careers that provided no work satisfaction. Against their will the bohemians became the advance guard of the real estate moguls. The counterculture foundered on the rock of rising urban rents and the shriveling of outlets for arts and politics in rapidly gentrified cities, reflecting the growing inequality between the rich and almost everyone else; the long wave of profound economic restructuring following Nixon's abrogation of the Bretton Woods agreement that stabilized world currency for almost thirty years; and, in the electoral arena, the relentless centrism of the Democrats and steep descent of Green parties—which in many respects were a movement of the remnants of the unwaged counterculture—almost everywhere, not just in the United States. Similarly, attempts to resurrect the leninist-type parties under nonrevolutionary conditions have resulted in their degeneration into sects, largely because of their dogmatism on questions of political theory and on political organization.

In the wake of one of the greatest concentrations of wealth and power in history are two nonviable propositions: that the liberal state can still be an arena of reform, and that civil society (which, Hegel observed, had devolved into the capitalist market) can be revived. A revived civil society is, in effect, a proposal for the radical decentralization of power, not chiefly for a return to civility. In the context of a struggle for urban space—the contemporary modern form of the historic land question that has animated revolutionary upsurge since the seventeenth century—the proposal for the creation of a noncommodified civil society, consisting of sites of conviviality and political discussion, requires political organization to realize it. Also required are concrete struggles to produce new physical and social space and to redefine the nature of local decision-making regarding services such as sanitation, schools, and housing so that neighborhoods and nongeographic social groups such as artists and writers are empowered. In this connection one might cite two examples: the community gardens movement in New York City, which, against the relentless efforts of real estate developers and the Guiliani administration, was able to hold its ground and win an agreement by its successor to preserve more than 600 gardens; and Critical Mass (CM), a worldwide movement of bicyclists to recapture urban space from automobiles and other motorized vehicles. Although it has made as many enemies as friends, CM has succeeded in many cities, along with other ecological efforts, in restricting the use of cars, forcing authorities to introduce "clean" fuels in buses and other mass transit facilities, and building bicycle lanes to protect cyclists from cars and trucks.

University and college classrooms are sometimes sources of critical thought that lead a fairly large contingent of students to seek out social movements or to gravitate toward the shards of the intellectual left, most of which is lodged in the academy. But sporadic mass actions of various kinds—not only anti-war protests but also demonstrations against university purchases of goods made by sweatshop labor, student support for farm workers at home and abroad, the struggle for union recognition by graduate student and adjuncts, and the comfort of a readily available radical literature—leave many of the newly radicalized in a state of permanent discontent. As noted earlier, a significant fraction have declared themselves anarchists and formed nonhierarchical collectives of bike riders and other crusaders for noncommodified urban space. Others join one of the several marxist-leninist sects or small democratic socialist organizations, usually for brief periods of time, while others find solace in solidarity groups such as those that support social movements and anti-authoritarian insurgencies in El Salvador, Chiapas, Nicaragua, and Haiti. Still others have recently been inspired by the Chavez government in Venezuela—not for his radical democratic practices but chiefly for his temerity in standing up to the Bush administration, and for his outrageous policy of redistributing some of the country's wealth to the poor, not only in Venezuela but in the United States as well.

Absent a visible and credible opposition, some conclude that a project of specifically American radicalism is too daunting and settle for the many opportunities to participate in the liberal bloc that, given its considerable financial and organizational resources and its relative political legitimacy, provides space for the politically committed, mainly in elections and issue organizing. However, the vast majority have no readily available outlets for their politics, either because they live far from the centers of geographically based political activity, remain unpersuaded by the appeals of the various groups proposing fundamental social change, or have a critique of liberalism that restrains their enthusiasm to heed the appeals of groups such as Move-On and other Internet listservs. Lacking a center around which to rally left and radical forces, after college most disappear into the everyday, find jobs, raise families, and confine their political thought to the kitchen table. Meanwhile, activist ranks swell and shrivel.

What Is the American Left?

The American left presents itself as an immense accumulation of movements, advocacy groups, and small organizations that sometimes call themselves "parties" but lack a significant public presence, a political program, and a strategy that matches their ideological orientation; their publications usually have a distinct populist rather than radical bent, and individual "stars" within and without these organizations operate as small entrepreneurs. The stars function as unofficial spokespersons for unidentified constituencies. Having been designated by the media as representatives of the left, sometimes because of best-selling books, or because their celebrity has been earned in past struggles, they speak on college campuses; before peace, progressive, church, and civic groups; and at political rallies; they appear on radio and TV on panels and in interviews; and they sign letters to solicit funds for left and left-liberal organizations. Some, notably Amy Goodman and Jim Hightower, host radio and television news shows that are broadcast on the Pacifica network, on community and college radio stations, and on independent TV cable channels. Others write columns in weekly newspapers or op-ed pieces for the dailies. In most instances their ability to capture political space may be explained not just by the vitality of movements that have propelled them into prominence but as well by the convergence of their message with those of left-turning liberals. Although they are self-identified radicals, their pieces no longer depart sharply from those of left-liberals such as *New York Times* columnists Paul Krugman and Bob Herbert, erstwhile *Los Angeles Times* writer Robert Scheer, and nationally syndicated columnist Molly Ivins whose critiques have adorned otherwise conservative media. Although one should not underestimate the role of prominent leftists who have achieved purchase on a fragment of the commonweal, their contribution is not a substitute for a coherent political formation.

Then there are the discipline-based academic caucuses and groups, especially in sociology, political science, planning, philosophy, geography, and psychology, that, in the main, have secured an official place within their respective associations. At annual conventions of the disciplines, they sponsor panels and often publish a journal. Occasionally, during times of growing political discontent over the generally conservative predispositions of the established associations, one or more of their number run for elective office in the association and win—in which case nothing much changes. The once-vibrant left academy that raised serious questions about the political and intellectual perspectives of the mainstream disciplines, and attempted to organize intellectuals across the disciplines in The New University Conference—a membership organization that was assembled to address large political questions in and outside the academy—has disappeared into the once-criticized mainstream. And, in the past two decades, many have joined unionization efforts in higher education, by no means a small achievement. Some of the three major unions' locals in this sector are led by leftists, but these leaders have not seen fit to form caucuses within their respective national unions or to join together across institutional boundaries, except on specific issues such as the group Educators Against the War.

Finally we note that, in the aftermath of the rise and fall of New Left intellectuals, there emerged a substantial coterie of what at the turn of the twentieth century were once derisively described as "Marxists of the chair." The characteristic that defined this group is their distance from the parties and movements of the left. Their espousal of marxism was, and is, confined to scholarly explication of the works of Marx and the marxist tradition in books, articles (mostly in left academic journals), and in the classroom. To this legacy we may add the recent canonization of "post"-marxists such as Derrida, Foucault, Deleuze, and other luminaries of the French intellectual pantheon whose work has been used as justification for extolling social movements at the expense of class politics.

Now I want to make plain my view that writing can be a public and political act, and that its content need not be contemporary, epistolary, or didactic. Even the genre of intellectual commentary common in philosophy and literary studies can embody the features of public intervention. What is required is that the author understands and demonstrates the salience of her work for broadening our collective comprehension of the way we live and struggle with the tension between the analytic, which Henri Lefebvre and Jean Paul Sartre term the "regressive," and the project of radical futurity, the "progressive." We are all burdened by the past, which tries to impose its categories on the present and future. Political writing as public intervention strives to bring to life the "not yet," that which is nonsynchronous with the homogenous and banal definitions of the everyday that wear us down.

In retreat, the left academy has effectively abandoned the discursive field to the conservatives. Seizing the space vacated by the left, the right is engaged in a serious effort to impose a new common sense on universities and colleges: The liberal arts are depicted as leftist playgrounds, and professors have taken advantage of their authority to proselytize their ideologies and suppress classroom dissent from conservative students. According to this mantra, academic freedom is an excuse for disseminating one-sided worldviews; students should be encouraged to monitor classroom content and expose professorial biases; academic neutrality demands the depoliticization of the professoriate. And the pièce de resistance: Already eroded by the proliferation of contingent short-term contracts of one, three, and five years that remain largely unchallenged, and engulfed by adjuncts who in some public universities teach half or more of the courses, tenure is under siege. According to the right, tenure is merely lifetime protection for a class of political propagandists and burnt-out cases. And even if current tenured faculty members are "grandfathered" mostly for legal reasons, shouldn't tenure be abolished for all new hires except the truly distinguished? For the time being, the extant tenured faculty remain complacent in their putative job security, but the systematic disinvestment by state legislatures in higher education augurs ill for the future. If students are expected to fill the gap left by reduced state expenditures by paying higher tuition, the future of many schools depends on a combination of economic buoyancy and the maintenance of federal and state student aid programs to pay the bills. If the economy falters as these programs are shaved to the bone, enrollments may drop; and even if they remain high, contingent and part-time faculty are likely to assume more responsibility for delivering the curriculum.

The few national organizations, such as those that organized anti–Iraq war mobilizations, deliberately kept their message simple in order to attract the widest possible constituency. While giving lip-service to the wider implications of the war— huge military expenditures that have bulged up the deficit (used as an excuse by conservatives to cut social spending) and severe threats to civil liberties (a concomitant of every war situation)—the leading organizations have chosen to follow the pattern of the anti–Vietnam war movement, short on debate and criticism, long on reductive slogans. The groundswell against the war in Iraq finally reached the halls of Congress in November 2005, when a conservative Democrat from Pennsylvania, John Murtha, a decorated Vietnam veteran and the ranking member of the House Appropriations subcommittee on military affairs, urged the Bush administration to set a short timetable for troop withdrawal from Iraq. It is no exaggeration to claim that, save its ability to mobilize a mass anti–Iraq war movement—which, together with the unrelenting civil war that followed the fall of the Baathist government, has finally aroused a sombulent US Congress to demand accountability from the Bush administration—the left's influence on American politics, even on issues that should be its natural subjects, is weaker today than at any time in the past century. Imprisoned by its own sectarianism, and by subservience not only to the Democratic Party but also to the trade union, liberal, and social movement officialdoms, the left has, in the main, lost contact with the everyday life of a large portion of the population.

At the same time, no vast movement from below has greeted the race to the bottom that marks the economic situation—a circumstance attributable not to the lack of resources of the putative opposition but, rather, to the ideological weakness of the unions, large sections of which are granting concessions to employers even as economists and the media declare economic growth. The inability of organized labor, the liberals, and the left to do more than react to the neoliberal hegemonic strategies of the center as well as the right in both political parties by conceding hard-won past gains to their employers is due, primarily, to the fragmentation and despair of the rank and file and to the absence of an articulate opposition capable of mobilizing against class collaboration within the ranks of labor and the social movements and of offering a strategic alternative to the downward spiral of living standards and good jobs.

I want to examine, in detail, three examples of how some burning questions—the concrete issues that affect the disempowered classes—have been all but ignored by the main detachments of the left. These examples are the deteriorating economy, the ecological crisis, and the crisis in democracy. All three are domains within which a vibrant left can reemerge, domains that, at the material and ideological level, frame our own time. While there are good political and sociological explanations for the left's failure to make these questions central concerns of a hypothetical intervention, the virtual silence of the left, and of the left-liberal press, constitutes nothing less than abdication of the terrain of the cutting-edge dimensions of political/ideological combat to the center and the right.

◇

4

Three Core Domains of Struggle and Alternative

Racing to the Bottom

Readers of the *Wall Street Journal* started their week on Monday November 14, 2005, with a lead story of how the relatively good wages of Detroit's auto workers were about to disappear. Focusing on Chris Brown, an assembly-line worker for the parts firm Delphi, whose $26.09 an hour comfortably supported his three kids, the article predicts that his pay may be cut in half (only a company negotiating position but a distinct possibility, at least in real terms) and his benefits eroded as the company and union "shift down" as part of a program to restore Delphi to profitability. Why should the union go along with this project of restoring profitability? Because its leadership considers itself part of the corporate world. Is what is good for General Motors (GM) good for the workers? As GM and Ford face equally gloomy futures, at least for US manufacturing facilities, the prospects for workers, not only in these giant corporations but also in the vast array of their suppliers, are indeed quite grim. Brown's sister, who works for the auto-seat maker Lear Corporation, has already experienced a $7.76 wage cut from $26.40 to $18.64 per hour as well as a reduction of health benefits. Although GM and the United Auto Workers union had not yet agreed to make similar wage reductions but did agree to the company's proposal to institute a co-pay health care program to replace its once-vaunted, completely free coverage, the handwriting seems to be on the wall.[1]

Union members at Delphi took a strike vote in early 2006, which prompted the company to devise a new plan to offer a buyout ranging from $35,000 to $140,000 depending on workers' seniority. On June 8 the union leadership forged an agreement on the buyout but left open its options regarding wage concessions. But given past patterns, regardless of whether the union members choose to strike over proposed wage cuts, it seems likely that the leadership will opt to "save Delphi" by granting some reductions.

Given the union leadership's concessionary mentality, only a rank-and-file rebellion and some bold thinking about how to save living standards can stem what appears to be an inexorable tide. There were rumblings among some local union officers and rank-and-file members, and a fairly weak but feisty caucus, the successor organization to New Directions, responded to the November announcements of imminent cuts by calling meetings in Michigan and Indiana, two of Delphi's key sites. But it will take considerable effort to reverse the company and union leadership's decision to save the US auto corporations on the workers' backs. In the first place, a militant response would face the argument that "globalization" makes wage and benefit cuts inevitable. And as GM and Ford announce plans to lay off thousands of workers, and move some plants offshore or to Canada, workers must insist that the existing union contract, which obliges the company to pay full wages and benefits whether people are working or not, be retained. However, the traditional concept (embedded in the collective bargaining agreement) that the company has a right to allocate its resources, including the labor force, anywhere it wants sooner or later—and probably sooner—is likely to reassert itself with a vengeance. The union was able to negotiate a measure of job security in a period of general prosperity for the leading corporations. But as the American auto industry continues to sink, the corporations will insist on being relieved of the contractual burdens to guarantee wages, health care, and pension benefits for laid-off workers. The question is whether the labor movement can invoke the radical imagination to seek remedies beyond the conventions of collective bargaining and of corporatism.

The post–World War II command enjoyed by US auto corporations over their home market as well as significant portions of foreign markets no longer exists. In the 1980s and 1990s Japanese and Korean car makers and, to a lesser extent, Europeans, cut deeply into the market share of domestic corporations. In response, the Big Three (GM, Ford, and Chrysler) all but conceded subcompact autos to their global competitors and cut back on their compacts as well, focusing on mid- and full-sized sedans and trucks. In the 1990s, GM and Ford put considerable capital in the very profitable, but gas-guzzling, sports utility vehicles (SUVs); Chrysler absorbed American Motors, which made the best-selling Jeep; and the Big Three were apparently unconcerned as Japanese and Korean rivals grabbed large shares of the US small-car market, which, the American car companies argued, yielded smaller profits, especially since they pay high health and pension costs. The strategy worked for at least a decade, but the combined effects of gas inflation and an eroding reputation for quality have created a crisis for the US industry. As their success in the American consumer market expands, Japanese and European automakers have built plants within the United States, mostly without union representation even as the US giants have shut down numerous assembly plants and removed some of them to Mexico and Canada. Among the closed facilities are GM's in Fremont, California; Tarrytown, New York; Linden, New Jersey; and Baltimore, Maryland. On November 21, 2005, GM supplemented its previously announced plan to render 25,000 production workers redundant by announcing an additional 5,000 layoffs and further plant closings.

The workers at Ford, too, have their share of woes. In the 1980s and 1990s it closed nearly all of its East Coast plants and sharply reduced employment in many of its oldest factories, such as Michigan's huge River Rouge facility. Moreover, in response to a 15 percent reduction in sales during 2005—and having earlier announced a modest 6 percent reduction in hourly employees, when the profit picture began to sag even further—it proposed on January 23, 2006, to cut 25 percent of its work force between 2006 and 2013 by laying off between 25,000 and 30,000 workers and closing fourteen additional North American plants. And even though Daimler-Chrysler's Jeep division has led the corporation to profitability, many of its traditional car lines have suffered sagging sales. This situation, combined with the relative slump in sales of Mercedes cars, threatened to lead to more layoffs. Of course, the decline of the American auto industry was not helped by the severe spike in gas prices during 2005, particularly since the Big Three had staked their fate on gas-guzzling SUVs. Nor was consumer confidence bolstered by the evident superiority of the US industry's rivals—especially in the areas of safety, durability, and design.

But with the media firmly in league with the big auto corporations, and labor and liberal circles otherwise occupied, there was virtually no refutation of capital's claim that the problem was high wages of factory workers; indeed, Japanese and European wage levels were higher than those in the United States—except, of course, for the costs of private health and pension plans. That neither the Auto Workers union (which formally favors universal national health care as a partial solution to the industry's crisis) nor the big auto corporations (which share conservative antipathy to universal health care paid out of taxes) nor, for that matter, anyone else of power and influence saw fit to launch a major campaign for socialized medicine (improperly known as "single-payer") was a sign that ideological concerns trumped cost-saving proposals. The Big Three would not press Congress to relieve their health and pension burdens by instituting a government-paid program, and the major unions were deeply divided on universal public health care proposals because a significant number of them had programs of their own that were politically potent with the membership and provided jobs for favored insiders. Nevertheless, in January 2006, AFL-CIO president John Sweeney delivered a major speech to the National Press Club calling for national health insurance for all. This speech followed a decade of Sweeney's silence on the matter because, among other reasons, his constituent unions were divided. Moreover, only in private rooms did experts notice that, as with the steel industry during the 1970s and 1980s, in the interests of reaping huge profits the auto corporations made a series of disastrous decisions that reduced product quality and abandoned whole sectors of the market to their competitors.

This short-sightedness and managerial incompetence have had much to do with the decline in auto and other major manufacturing sectors. John Hoerr and others have chronicled the long record of stunning but carefully hidden managerial errors by steel employers that contributed to a massive shrinking of the industry. Top executives invested in lapsed technology and found themselves technologically outpaced by German, Italian, and Japanese competitors who used computerized machines to eliminate several steps in the steelmaking process well before these innovations were introduced to the domestic US industry. Although the long years of American dominance in the global steel industry were bound to come to an end because of European and Japanese economic recovery, the depth of the crisis—plant shutdowns, mass layoffs, and the appearance and growth of nonunion mills—was by no means inevitable. Like those in the auto industry, steel union leaders persuaded large sections of the rank and file that concessions were necessary to preserve their past gains. The wager, as in almost all concessionary periods, proved a cruel deception, perhaps a self-deception by the union leaders themselves. In some instances employee ownership schemes were able to forestall plant closure, though typically for only a short time. Major steel, textile, and electrical shutdowns marked the economic landscape from the 1970s to the present, often with the collaboration of the unions that negotiated the conditions of closure.[2]

During the late 1970s and 1980s these concessionary deals were widely publicized in newspapers and the electronic media. This was also a period when organizing slowed to a crawl. Labor leaders and labor experts ascribed the retreat to the conservative political environment that swept the country after Lyndon Johnson's demise. But the slow yet steady erosion of labor's power on the shop floor, at the bargaining table, and in the public sphere resulted as much from the triumph of neoliberal, free market *thinking* as from the decline of the economic power of US-based production and service industries. Despite their generally liberal social and economic sentiments, most of organized labor accepted the inevitability of compromise in the wake of US capitalism's shift to a floating dollar, intensified global investments, and aggressive attack on wages and working conditions. One of the cardinal goals of the modern labor movement, to refuse to put labor in competition with itself, was abandoned at home as well as abroad. Adopted instead, in an effort to save jobs, was a corporatist stance—the philosophy that, despite disagreements over particular issues, the interests of the company and the workers were identical—once-progressive unions such as the UAW in the 1980s had embarked on a Buy American campaign, a sign that the union had become nationalistic and protectionist, and that the old concept of international workers' solidarity was definitively consigned to the garbage pail. But unorganized workers weren't impressed. As they saw the labor movement steadily yield gains, the occasional instances of resistance by organized workers met with the leadership's manipulation and scorn; and with the weight of federal labor policy arrayed against them, they became reluctant to stick their collective necks out because the unions might not protect them against discharge and the blacklist.

Since the 1970s the number of union members has lagged chronically behind the growth of the labor force. The unions blamed their relative decline on globalization and the conservative tide, especially the long reign of Reaganism, even as they refused to draw the lesson of the period: Either organize or die. Many once-viable trade unions died and, in their death rattle, merged with larger organizations. The list is a chronicle of the demise of the CIO, once the harbinger of labor's vigorous bid for industrial democracy and, in some cases, rank-and-file sovereignty: Shortly after the expulsion of eleven CIO unions for Communist domination in 1949, and following a series of raids, one of them, the Farm Equipment Workers (FE), was absorbed by the United Auto Workers; and the Fur and Leather Workers (an expelled CIO union) found a home in the Meat Cutters (originally an AFL affiliate, now called the Food and Commercial Workers)—but not before its Communist leadership complied with the Taft-Hartley requirement by quitting the party. The same action was taken by the CIO Packinghouse Workers, which, years earlier, avoided CIO expulsion by pledging to conform to the Taft-Hartley proscriptions. As the electrical, appliance, radio, and television sections of the industry were cut into pieces by mergers, technological change, plant migration, and large-scale outsourcing to the American South and to Mexico, the International Union of Electrical Workers, born of a Cold War split from its parent, the United Electrical Workers, was among the first to disappear as an independent organization. The much-reduced union merged with the Communications Workers of America, the union of telephone workers; so did the Furniture Workers, a small but plucky former CIO affiliate that simply lacked the resources to follow the bulk of the industry to the South. The Rubber Workers, whose origins are forever linked to the pioneer 1936 Akron Sit-Down Strikes, were absorbed by the United Steelworkers, as were the Mine-Mill and Smelter Workers, the legatee of the legendary Western Federation of Miners, a forerunner of the Industrial Workers of the World (IWW), and an expelled former CIO union that held off Steelworkers raids until it exhausted its treasury—and its energy. The Textile Workers, once 400,000-strong but severely reduced by plant migrations to the South, job-reducing technological changes, and the relative decline of the US industry, were, together with the almost moribund Shoe Workers and Hat, Cap and Millinery Workers (one of the original unions that formed the CIO), folded into the Clothing Workers. And the Oil, Chemical, and Atomic Workers, reduced by automation and cybernation and by the short-sighted corporate decision to shut more than half of all US refineries, became a division of the United Paper Workers, which, in turn, was absorbed by the Steelworkers, today's largest union of manufacturing workers. Of the twenty CIO unions, only Steel, Auto, Communications, Transport, and the independent United Electrical Workers have survived—though, with the exception of the Communications Workers, in severely reduced form.

The wage erosion suffered by workers in nearly every major production industry, combined with the poverty wages that prevail in most of the retail sector, points to a downward spiral in Americans' living standards. In this respect we have a stark example of the consequence of the absence of a genuine left press. Some business newspapers such as the *Wall Street Journal* and business sections of the dailies, particularly the *New York Times*, *Los Angeles Times*, and *Chicago Tribune*, have occasionally run stories about this long wave of union concessions, outright corporate theft of workers' pension plans, plant closures, and ferocious employer abrogation of workers' rights. Only *Labor Notes*, an independent monthly labor newspaper, and some online labor publications have consistently addressed this question. But except for activists these sources have limited outreach and come out too infrequently to have significant impact. On the whole, in the mainstream media the story is buried.

Drowned in debt, many Americans hold two or three jobs in order to pay the most basic bills, are frequently obliged to take out a second mortgage to pay medical and education costs, and live permanently on tenterhooks in fear that their main job will disappear. To ascribe this slide to the prevailing conservative political environment begs the question of why the environment has turned so decisively to the right, such that even the liberal organizations, especially the NAACP and the labor movement, have been reduced in size and influence. Among the questions to be asked are these: Why does neoliberal economic and social policy dominate both major political parties—along with much of the de facto liberal party, which has all but abandoned the workers and the chronically unemployed, and cannot bring itself to advocate even the mildest version of noncommodified social welfare, particularly socialized medicine? Why has the Fundamentalist Christian Right achieved so much influence in the Republican Party that even some old-line conservatives find themselves marginalized or driven out? And why do the center and the left seem unable to mount a sustained opposition to what may be the most right-wing political era since the Gilded Age, or at least since the 1920s?

One overall answer has to do with the restricted scope of most political activity. Entering a dialogue with neoliberal ideology requires a national effort. In order to address falling living standards and the pattern of concessionary bargaining, the left would have to take a serious look at the economy and at the labor movement itself—a measure that requires significant intellectual effort and reorientation away from an uncritical view of organized labor and toward a critical, rank-and-file standpoint. And it requires a critical look at globalization as an ideology, as distinct from corporate investment practice. Such an inquiry might discover that globalization has been employed by capital as a bludgeon against workers and industrial communities. To comprehend the growth of the religious right, we must undertake a critique of the Enlightenment and especially the secular faith in science and technology as substitutes for traditional religion. While individual scientists may be religious, science and technology as ideologies have claimed that the technological fix can solve all social ills, that our spiritual dissatisfactions can be addressed by new scientific discoveries that lead to new consumer products. The antinomy of our culture is that science and fundamentalist religion present themselves as contenders for the soul, and the fundamentalists seem to be winning. We are discovering the limits of a shamefaced secularism—"shamefaced" because the nonreligious left does not defend its own secularity but, instead, feels forced to concede ground to the most potent force on the ideological right. And we must renounce the obdurate refusal of some on the left to take cultural questions seriously. Above all, as some have argued, the spiritual need must be addressed within the framework of a thoroughly secular politics. For the fundamentalists have tapped into a series of unmet needs that grow out of the brutalities of the commodification of everyday existence as well as the "scientism"—faith in the power of rational calculation to solve our deepest emotional needs—that pervades politics and culture. It is not enough to dismiss their appeal by class snobbery—abstract condemnations of consumer society—or to be content with exposing the undeniable fact that the religious revival of the last thirty years has significant commercial and political dimensions.

It is true that a small number of activists affiliated with the World Social Forum and its offshoots have attempted to combat the most egregious features of transnational capitalism. But local interventions predominate: Leftists often play leading roles in fighting real estate development, ensuring the availability of low-cost housing, preserving civil liberties, and organizing municipal or county education coalitions of parents and teachers, and there are numerous left-tinged advocacy groups consisting of physicians, activists, and experts working in behalf of universal health care and children's rights, and against hunger, as well as a few organizing projects among the poor, some of which have trade union sponsorship, some not. The advocates often propose alternatives, but because they lack an independent politics or a forum for sharing experiences with other movement activists, they often function as policy advisors to the Democratic Party and organizations of the liberal establishment such as the unions, the civil rights organizations, and liberal feminist organizations like the National Organization of Women and the National Abortion Rights League, which are themselves caught in the policy vice. In the main, these efforts are not coordinated across issues, either formally or through networks. Also few in number are conferences or forums that could bring together locally based social and labor activists to discuss their common ground as well as their differences. Nor do these activists share a common political orientation, except implicitly. In this respect we note that some of them shudder at the idea that they should have a broad political and intellectual orientation.

The Challenge of the Ecological Crisis

The absence of a politics that links apparently disparate issues is glaringly demonstrated by the failure of the movements for economic justice to address the class dimension of the festering ecological crisis. For there has been no more obvious illustration of the thesis that ecology is a challenge to both the fundamental premise of capitalism itself—economic growth—and the implicate hierarchy immanent in state policy. In the wake of the dire consequences of global warming, among whose symptoms was Hurricane Katrina—part of one of the most turbulent hurricane seasons in memory—progressives were unable to respond with concrete actions to expose the flagrant neglect of black working-class districts by all levels of government, the eerie silence of Democratic Party leaders in the face of this shameless exhibition of racist policy, and the downright incompetence of the Bush administration. In the throes of Katrina, Bush asked for and received billions in aid from Congress but, in the absence of significant protest, was free to squander huge portions of it to reward his friends, especially Halliburton. Moreover, while huge sections of the Gulf Coast languished without assistance (in short order, FEMA—the federal agency charged with the responsibility of providing disaster relief—was out of money), Bush selectively aided cities such as Jackson, Mississippi, where the political payoff would be greater, regardless of the extent of damage. This act of philanthropy benefiting the rich and the politically relevant at the expense of the working class was also executed without significant protest, even as the limited alternative media showed that New Orleans' vulnerable black districts were ignored in the reconstruction efforts. Instead, in the main, the response to Katrina was reactive and typically voluntaristic: Liberal charities and sections of the labor movement raised funds to assist victims by sending food and supplies, but they were unable to mobilize protests or to offer alternative solutions to the obscene responses of the

Bush administration, which has been allowed to get away with reneging on its promise of massive aid.

The ecological crisis is a class issue, among other things, but it also threatens to extinguish many life forms in the next half-century. Virtually no articulate left or militant green component of the ecology movement is persistently sounding the alarm of global warming and the loss of biodiversity resulting from the excessive emissions of carbon dioxide in our environment, except at the local level. On Saturday, December 3, 2005, 40,000 people demonstrated against global warming in Montreal, and similar mass demonstrations have occurred recently in Italy and Spain. But the local level—the space of action—is woefully absent in the face of this catastrophe. Although most leftists understand, to some extent, the dangers of global warming, the East Asian tsunami and Hurricane Katrina failed to stimulate a broad national discussion, much less direct action in the United States about the costs of what Lewis Mumford terms "carboniferous capitalism"—a system of production and consumption that, without an iota of reflection, proliferates hydrocarbons and contaminates the air and water, yet retains its worldwide dominance as a mode of economic life. Nor has rapid Chinese and Indian industrialization—the growth of which has resulted in, among other calamities, the expulsion of tens of millions of rural and urban dwellers and unparalleled pollution in most major cities of Southeast Asia—succeeded in capturing their political gaze. Most salient are the warnings of scientists: that what appear to be "natural" events are, to a substantial extent, the result of human intervention, especially with respect to the choice of energy sources but also to the imperatives of economic growth within a regime of ecologically unviable accumulation. Meanwhile, most of us continue to conduct our business as usual. We are caught in the grip of mass denial. These events should have been the occasion for raising questions about the dire consequences of the way we live.

"Global warming" describes only one aspect of the ecological crisis; equally important is climate instability, a product of the gradual heating of the earth's surface. According to some climatologists we can expect not only gradual warming but unexpected abrupt climate changes that, in turn, might intensify storm and hurricane activity.[3]

Of course, many scientists and ecological intellectuals, as well as a few individuals in Congress and state legislatures, have asked some of the hard questions: Can we afford to employ nonrenewable hydrocarbons as the major energy source of our economic life? Can we trace the cancer epidemic that is afflicting tens of millions of people in all industrialized and industrializing countries to the toxic emissions from cars, oil- and coal-driven power stations, and diesel-driven buses and trucks? Have these pollutants fatally penetrated our water table? For example, should internal-combustion-engine vehicles be replaced with a vast network of buses and long-distance trains that use "clean" sources of power? True, a few states on both coasts are prepared to restrict auto emissions, but this modest proposal has been met by a fierce counterattack on the part of leading auto and oil corporations. That counterattack should have been the occasion for initiating a public discussion on energy alternatives and a militant campaign to thwart the corporate effort—and not just by environmentalists. But neither happened because, among other burdens, activists are overwhelmed with immediate emergencies, most of which involve defensive struggles to hold back the egregious offensives being committed by employers, real estate developers, and state and local governments. At the same time, as I have argued throughout this book, the left is mired in its own disposition—against centralization and unified political interventions—and, perhaps above all, in its unwillingness to draw the threads of apparently disparate struggles into a concrete totality of critique and alternative to transnational corporate capitalism and its captive states.

Liberal environmentalists have urged the Bush administration to sign the Kyoto treaty (which is now facing opposition in developing countries as well), urged executive and legislative action limiting emissions of greenhouse gases, and called for imposing heavier penalties on corporations that violate clean air and water statutes. They have also supported the introduction of auto hybrids; advocated higher fuel efficiency standards for autos and trucks; fought for the introduction of "clean" fuels such as wind, solar, and water-based energy; and, of course, sponsored recycling. Yet, while desirable in the short term, none of these measures can do more than slow the pace of ecological deterioration. What makes them inadequate is that they fail not only to allow radical solutions but also to advance a radical analysis of the crisis. Nor are the liberals prepared to go to the streets to express their opposition and disseminate their alternatives. Moreover, these are measures introduced after the fact rather than being devoted to change the structures that produced the crisis.

For the root of the crisis resides, in part, in the very condition by which the capitalist mode of production reproduces itself: capital accumulation on the basis of nonrenewable energy resources; production of vast quantities of chemically based artificial materials, especially plastics; genetically modified crops, both food and fibers; the engine of postwar economic expansion known as suburban sprawl, an aesthetic as well as ecological blight that entails the spread of single-family homes, each of which requires separate heating systems, appliances, furniture, and building materials extracted from forests and from the earth; and, as already noted, the serious problems posed by diesel-powered truck and gasoline-driven auto transportation. Among the culprits is the capitalist holy grail, "development" itself, which has squandered vast acreage of forest and wetlands by cutting old-growth trees and wiping out wildlife, reduced the number and density of vital rain forests, overrun valuable agricultural lands, and poisoned waters for the purposes of oil drilling and tree cutting. As the waters are despoiled, fish are driven farther from land masses and, together with birds and mammals, are killed. In short, our everyday lives are infused by pollutants, which are creating the conditions for food and water shortages in the future—and, in some parts of the globe, even in the present. These emissions produce old and new illnesses that, given the nature of travel and mass emigration, have become, or threaten, pandemics that transgress cities, regions, and even continents. For example, tuberculosis afflicts 2 million people every year; the AIDS epidemic has worsened, especially in Africa and Latin America; and infantile paralysis is staging a lethal comeback. Meanwhile, we have seen the exponential advance of respiratory diseases such as asthma and emphysema, the proliferation of lung cancer among nonsmokers, and the spread of breast cancer across the class divide.

The ecological crisis is the harvest of 500 years of capitalist development, a system that in its full flower has been able to sustain high living standards for a fraction of its underlying populations—mainly in the most technologically advanced societies and among the ruling, mercantile, and professional classes of the developing countries—even as it has subordinated a huge portion of the earth's human and nonhuman mammals and other life forms under the imperatives of capital accumulation. In the United States, in addition to ecological despoliation (the latest example of which was the erosion of vast sections of the Gulf Coast), the concomitant of economic growth was impoverished public goods—a condition described by John Kenneth Galbraith, no radical, as public squalor amid affluence. These disparities did not go unnoticed but were tolerated as long as their effects were largely restricted to the poor who, by the late 1950s, had become invisible. But Katrina and other manifestations of climatic turbulence augur badly for the upper 20 percent of the populations of advanced societies, whose sense of security was recently shaken in Louisiana and all along the Southern tier as well as in the Midwest where storms have ripped through Wisconsin and Michigan. During these events we should have discovered the mythological character of our sustaining belief in individual fate and in the superiority of the private sector. We learned that the price of temporary affluence for some was to put them at the mercy of our own collective blindness to nature's revolt against human folly. For successive national administrations have consistently short-changed or privatized the infrastructures of major metropolitan and rural areas, and starved or abolished federal and state relief agencies, leaving the task to the Red Cross and various private nonprofits that have failed dismally to adequately address the problems.

Indeed, the federal government's response to Katrina was not only incompetent, a pattern that increasingly takes on the characteristic of policy, but pernicious as well. The ideological and political predispositions of those in power was to redirect scarce resources to private contractors and to direct whatever efforts they could muster to their own—namely, the ruling and middle classes who, nevertheless, did not receive the support they had come to expect. That no major debate occurred in the aftermath of these events is not surprising, given the absence of a genuine ecological left capable of proposing significant steps to address the systemic fault lines, linking global warming and its emanations in climatic instability to issues of economic growth, class and racial subordination, privatization, and administrative and political neglect.

Is the United States a Thriving Democracy?

The third crucial domain of radical intervention is democracy. As we have seen, from Tocqueville to Sheldon Wolin there is a rich trove of political criticism of democracy in America. Contemporary critics have argued that our democratic institutions are undermined by the inordinate power of large corporations whose tentacles have penetrated every branch of government, and that the political directorate has skewed local and congressional districts so that the electorate is deprived of representation. Historians and commentators, too, call attention to the persistence of black exclusion in the economic and political process, despite legislative remedies that are now over forty years old. For example, speaking in early December 2005 on the PBS show *Charlie Rose*, historian John Hope Franklin stated with eloquence that America is still mired in the legacy of slavery. From a political standpoint that "peculiar institution"—a throwback to ancient times but functioning in a capitalist marketplace—rendered the US constitution deeply flawed because, though blacks were counted, they lacked citizenship. He said neither the civil war and reconstruction, nor the Civil Rights movement of the 1950s and 1960s, had fully repaired the flaw.

Linking class and race he argued that democracy and equality were inextricably joined, that despite the formal trappings of opportunity provided by the Voting and Civil Rights Acts signed into law by Lyndon Johnson in 1964 and 1965, the promise had not been realized; in the words of Langston Hughes, it is still a "dream deferred." According to Franklin the achievements of the black freedom movement still do not measure up to the goals of equality and democracy. Blacks have twice the rates of joblessness as whites, they suffer proportionately greater infant and adult mortality, and, despite *Brown v Board of Education*'s mandate of school integration, urban housing segregation and economic inequality force black children to attend poorly funded, segregated schools. That these conditions have grown worse in recent years, Franklin argues, is no accident: The prevailing power structure "is not interested" in addressing poverty, let alone black poverty. To which one might add that the Civil Rights establishment, which embraces Organized Labor and liberal organizations as well as the NAACP

and the Urban League, is not eager—at a moment of conservative hegemony—to upset the apple cart by challenging the
Democrats to live up to their pretensions.

A democratic society cannot be measured alone by its fair
application of the franchise. Voting rights are necessary but not
sufficient to the claims of a representative system of governance
to be democratic. If conditions of life are unequal across the race
and gender divide, democracy is in jeopardy. But the elephant
in the room of American democracy is, perhaps, the autocratic
management of the workplace—a subject of little concern to civil
libertarians, let alone liberal politicians. In America, workers
have few rights beyond the security that may be provided by a
collective bargaining agreement. Even then, if the political and
ideological environment is inimical to the preservation of labor's
gains, the union contract may not defend workers.

We have learned from bitter historical experience that
the National Labor Relations Act (NLRA), which many trade
unionists once considered "Labor's Magna Carta," does not
industrial citizens make. According to its framers, the NLRA
was intended to introduce a system of industrial democracy
into the workplace. They envisioned an eventuality of shop
councils that would work closely with management to make
all sorts of decisions affecting employment conditions. Some,
like Steelworkers' leader Clinton Golden and Harold Rutten-
berg, the union's research director, offered a detailed plan for
decision-sharing that would encompass a much wider range
of questions than conventional collective bargaining. We are
a long way from the hope of industrial democracy that many
associated with the passage of the labor relations law. Together
with a predecessor, the Norris-LaGuardia Act (which banned
"yellow dog" contracts whereby, as a condition of employment, workers were forced to renounce union membership),
the NLRA conferred certain rights on workers, especially to
join unions of their own choosing and to strike to better their
conditions; however, these legislative gains were relatively
short-lived. Almost immediately after the NLRA finally cleared
its last legal hurdle in 1938, the combined effects of three
factors—union complacency manifested as blind faith in the
rule of law, legislative revisions such as the 1947 Taft-Hartley amendments that eviscerated labor's scope of action by
banning secondary boycotts and sympathy strikes, and court

decisions that outlawed factory occupations and granted employers free speech to oppose unionization—reduced workers' statutory rights to the vanishing point.

Federal employees are barred from striking—the price workers paid for the right to engage in collective bargaining—and many states have similar statutes against strikes by public-sector unions. Under a succession of conservative national administrations, the Labor Relations Board has often taken the employers' side in disputes concerning the right to organize. The Board that served during Clinton's term was somewhat more attentive to labor, but it did not take the philosophical perspective, written into the original law, that its function is to protect and defend labor. As a result, even before the advent of the Bush presidency, which further weakened labor's rights, some unions all but gave up using the Board's offices to resolve questions of representation. They tried to use their agreements with multisite employers to coerce or otherwise persuade them to recognize unions through "card checks"—a procedure under which the union is required to show only that a majority of the company's employees have elected to join the union by signing cards authorizing it to represent them. But the law grants employers the right to challenge this form of evidence by demanding an election to determine whether employees actually choose union representation. In the South and Southwest, winning an election becomes a heroic feat; and getting a union contract, a miracle. In 2005 more than 90 percent of private-sector workers were not in unions. Except for sex, race, and disability discrimination (the effectiveness of which depends entirely on enforcement), as well as the provisions of the wage and hour law, which prescribes minimum wages and requires overtime pay beyond forty hours of work, employers may hire and fire at will, set wage and salary levels whose only constraint is market competition, and impose compulsory overtime and other onerous working conditions without fear of legal sanction.

Is democracy possible in a society of stark contrasts of wealth and political and economic power, where, under the doctrine of the absolute right of private property, labor is subordinated at the workplace, and where the state is arrayed against the people? Can we achieve equality in a system where modes of rule exclude them from participating directly in the decision-making processes of the most powerful economic and political institutions, and where citizenship has been reduced to an act of voting that merely confers consent on rulers whose powers are derived from wealth? Perhaps the most striking aspect of US labor law is its consistent sanction of the fundamental sovereignty of private property. Rights are conferred if, and only if, workers have succeeded in gaining union representation. Even then, the right to strike is severely limited. Instead, after signing away this prerogative for the duration of the agreement, they may avail themselves of a rather intricate and prolonged grievance procedure, which, even when it results in a union victory, often comes too late to save a worker's job. In contrast, labor law in France, for example, provides for a mandatory works council that negotiates agreements with employers in enterprises with more than a certain number of employees. The union per se is not the negotiator, but workers may elect union members as well as others to the council. These institutions ensure some representation for nearly all workers, regardless of whether they are union members. And workers may block roads, disrupt traffic in the cities, and occupy government offices until their grievances are addressed. In many countries, factory and other workplace occupations are a tried-and-true method of conducting industrial warfare and are exempt from court injunctions prohibiting them. These practices may be viewed as a sharp rebuke to the claim that America is a democratic society.

As we saw during the 2000 presidential election, committed to the authority of state institutions, liberal protest was muted when Florida's secretary of state disenfranchised thousands of voters, mostly blacks, and stood by as the Supreme Court stopped the recount that probably would have elected Al Gore. We can cite other examples of the erosion of democratic institutions as well: gerrymandered districts; the routine exclusion of black, Latino, and poor voters, no longer through the poll tax and literacy tests but, rather, by administrative fiat; registration rules that restrict the time and place where potential voters may enroll; failure to designate Election Day as a paid holiday or to hold elections on Saturdays or Sundays; and the absence of election law that would give voters for minority parties representation, particularly proportional representation and an instant runoff provision. These injustices cannot be remedied by legislation alone. They require the intervention of organized political formations prepared to take a variety of steps, including direct action to enforce them. In Florida, for example, right-wing gangs entered voting places and frightened voters away from exercising their franchise. But the goal of fair elections is to purge liberal democracy of its inequities, not to challenge the existing system.

Following historical precedent, democracy is conventionally construed as the right and duty of citizens to select representatives to assume the tasks of legislation and of administration. With few exceptions, political philosophers construe the popular will in terms of its minimum intervention: to confer consent on the decisions made by representatives who, nevertheless, are not bound to any particular constituent's position. For in any liberal-democratic political system the polity consists in individuals who cast a secret ballot for a candidate who, at least formally, personifies a political party. The problem is that the postmodern party is no longer unified in its ideology or program, not even with respect to broad principles. These principles have been relegated to largely ignored party platforms, due mainly to the fact that the political parties do not exercise discipline over their legislative organizations, or on elected officials. The congressional or legislative party is accountable to itself and, indirectly, to the electorate, but not to the political party. The two parties retain formal structures such as state and local committees, but they cannot recall representatives who fail to follow party policy. Nor in our primary system do they have ultimate control over nominations. For this reason and others, members of Congress and of many state and local legislatures must, with some exceptions, constitute themselves as a party of one. In the United States they are forced to raise their own funds, build their own political organizations, and construct a platform that corresponds to their own views, the imperatives of business groups that support them, and the perceived positions of their constituents.

These imperatives signify that the party system, even the concept of a legitimate opposition, has broken down, especially in the United States but increasingly in states of the Capitalist West as well. And, as we saw in Chapter 1, the underlying assumption of liberal democracy—that voters have clear choices between competing programs and visions of the not yet—functions as an unrealized ideal. (In this respect, we have witnessed the emergence of a tension, if not a schism, within the Republican Party as conservatives have grown increasingly critical of the takeover of their party by the religious right and by social Neanderthals. Although the Bush administration and its congressional allies claimed the mantle of conservatism, its profligate spending and state interventionist policies, exemplified by the post-9/11 Patriot Act, belie that label.)

One major aspect of the Bush doctrine is that the open avowal of the "national security state," which, since the start of the Reagan era remained implicit, has become public policy. This concept signifies that civil liberties, social welfare, and the democratic process are ultimately subordinate to the permanent war. Whereas Reagan himself announced "it's morning in America," a slogan that signified freshness, hope, and even happiness, Bush has reinvoked the doctrines of the administrations of John Adams: In times of national emergency—which Bush has declared are permanent—individual freedom is subordinate to the interests of security. Remarkably there has been little dispute about this doctrine among a wide spectrum of political opinions. The Congress passed the Patriot Act, which grants the executive branch emergency powers to suspend liberties; only Russell Feingold, a Wisconsin Democrat, voted against it in the Senate, and a tiny opposition was expressed in the House. The fact that the combined forces of Senate Democrats and a few moderate Republicans were able to temporarily postpone the final passage of the reauthorization bill at the end of 2005 may be understood as an exception to the rule that the Democrats cave in at every opportunity.

That Bush, like his predecessor, Reagan, is a military Keynesian there can be little doubt. The role of defense expenditures in propping up an essentially stagnant economy has been sharply reduced in this post-fordist era, when just as the dollar floats on world money markets, almost every form of regulation has been dismantled, and the very concept of a national economy is in question. In these circumstances "growth" and employment statistics would be measurably weaker without the trillion-dollar arms budget. The problem is that many in the left-liberal camp harbor the illusion that they, not the centrists who currently control the Democratic Party, will ultimately prevail and that the old program of the New Deal—minus its reliance on deficit spending—will be restored. Of course, a balanced budget within the context of extensive social welfare is an oxymoron. To preserve their place within the party, the left-liberals have been willing to select a few issues on which to stand; they oppose welfare cuts but, fearing retribution for alleged weakness on security issues, they have objected only half-heartedly to the military buildup and to the Iraq war itself. But there is one question upon which the left-liberals remain strong: They are committed to thwarting the emergence of an independent radical politics that can form a genuine opposition. Read the liberal journals of opinion. There you will find no fundamental challenge to the presuppositions of liberal democracy in an age of the de facto one-party state. What you will find is a steady drumbeat of objections to third parties on the dubious argument that they split the progressive ranks. To which one might reply: What progressive ranks?

While it is true that some liberal organizations, such as the ACLU, having shaken the scales from their eyes, now more or less vigorously defend the institutions of liberal democracy and the first ten amendments of the constitution, the question of democracy cuts much deeper than they, or most progressives, are willing to go. To begin with, much of the fight has been framed by rights discourse. As we have seen, labor and civil rights legislation, and the recent demands of the human rights movement around the globe for the rights to speech, assembly, and organizing, presuppose that the state is a neutral arena within which a multiplicity of competing forces seek to exercise influence. In this reprise, the state is framed in the analogy of the resultant of a parallelogram of competing forces that are obliged to reach a compromise in order to preserve the state's administrative functions. Its mirror image is the notion of the sovereignty of the state whereby, as Pierre Clastres observes, society serves the state rather than the reverse, and civilization itself is measured by whether it has reached the evolutionary stage of sovereign state power. Here we have a version of Hegel's philosophy of the state: Its sovereignty is necessary because of its role of resolving and reconciling the economic and social contradictions of family and civil society, which had devolved into relations of commodity exchange, the site of the war of all against all.

In this conception the state must stand above the conflicts of everyday life, but it reserves to itself the power to confer "rights" and "duties" upon citizens, to which some would add the duty to "promote the general welfare," especially for those unable to take care of themselves. The doctrine of positive law, upon which this conception is based, was first enunciated by Thomas Hobbes, who views "human nature" as essentially aggressive; or, to be more precise, aggression is a property of a significant minority of the population who, without control, will succeed in creating social chaos. Therefore, the sovereign is constituted to suppress the "animal" instincts such as greed and avariciousness by assuming the reigns of power—a standing army, a police force, and a system of laws, courts and prisons to contain the savage beast. Thus there are no unjust laws, if by that term we mean that order is their first obligation. To which Rousseau, and especially Ernst Bloch, counterpose Natural Law, whose essential premise is that humans are born free, have cooperative rather than competitive predispositions, and possess a "natural" orientation toward creating their own future. Both argue for the centrality of nature, which has provided the material basis for sociality and for the achievement of freedom. It is the state, whose task is to hold at bay the oppressed classes and to impose both the value and the institutions of coercive order, which stands as a barrier to the achievement of human freedom. Its ideology of the "rule of law" presents itself as an aspect of natural law, but conceives of nature as "other," as an enemy of humans.[4]

In capitalist societies the bourgeoisie and the state have always privileged law and order over democratic assembly and free speech. But since World War II the permanent "state of emergency" has transformed the United States and the United Kingdom into regimes where, in the interest of preserving "the domestic security" (a contemporary euphemism for the suppression of dissent), national security trumps freedom. This is also an epoch during which, because of its command, through powers of taxation, over substantial quantities of capital, government has become a treasure house for private appropriation. Privatization consists not only in the huge contracts awarded to corporations to produce and deliver public services such as roads, education, and prisons, but also in the active intervention of corporate agents in writing the laws that sanction their loot. In short, we have entered an era of legalized piracy. Corruption is no longer the exception but has become the rule, and the stakes are enormous. Given this state of affairs, the prattle about spreading democracy as a justification for an overblown arms budget and for global military interventions, uttered with numbing regularity by the US government and its allies, has a hollow ring. But patriotic slogans rule the political system. That both sides of the aisle in Congress dutifully appropriate these funds is one more indication of the absence of a genuine opposition.

That said, it would be foolish to abandon the field of conventional political struggle altogether. However much the constitution is flawed and ignored in the service of national security, a task of the left must be to defend and extend representative democracy, to provide some backbone to liberals to join in the fight against voter disenfranchisements and the violation of civil liberties. But this is only one side of the equation. In this period of fierce ideological combat the left must contest the one-party duopoly by forming parties that can participate in elections, mainly at the local level. These electoral vehicles would propose a new radical municipalism to reverse the long-term giveaways such as tax cuts for business and the rich. They would oppose real estate commercial development that reduces the supply of moderately priced rental housing and monopolizes urban space, fight gentrification, and oppose the introduction into neighborhoods of giant, low-paying retail chains such as Wal-Mart. And they would fight authoritarian schooling and invent new forms of universal health care at the local level. At the same time, as discussed earlier, radicals would engage in the struggle to produce new urban space by proposing and implementing alternative forms of horizontal power such as community gardens, encouraging squatters to occupy and renovate abandoned buildings, converting some buildings to community centers available for recreation and educational activities, and promoting and sponsoring community economic development to provide jobs and income to blacks and other oppressed groups who suffer chronic unemployment.

But the left goes further: It must defend society against the state. A New Left would transform our collective understanding of democracy by expanding the scope of popular decision-making to the workplace, the neighborhood, and every corner of social space. It would combat the pervasive notion that the state is the sole, or even the primary, arena of combat, and would oppose the idea of its neutrality—that is, of political pluralism.

It would recognize that the state is not only a series of institutions including, as Louis Althusser has argued, a phalanx of "ideological" apparatuses, but also consists of repressive state apparatuses whose leading function is to control the underlying population. The concept of ideological apparatus is the materialization of what in other discourses are termed "legitimating" institutions of the state—those organizations that present the state in the image of public safety and a series of social services. These include religious institutions, trade unions, schools, the media, and certain types of civil and cultural organizations. Such apparatuses contain and configure aspirations and expectations within the system of domination. For example, the state guarantees the right of every child to free schooling until the twelfth grade but has the power to determine what constitutes an adequate education. And if the state's provision of a child's education is deemed adequate, if she fails to find a secure job in the marketplace she has obviously not worked hard enough in her studies. In this context, "rights" implicitly concede to power because power has conferred benefits. The machinery of concession is not only coercion but the subject's internalization of the state as a natural institution. In the era of welfare capitalism (1935–1980), the "legitimate" state, which provides services and especially education and income security, was internalized by individuals as a social fact. Even as the welfare state began to recede, people still looked to the state for security; welfare capitalism was so deeply embedded in the social unconscious that it had become part of everyday life's habitus long after the state ceased to provide services.

The left's chief intervention in the struggle for democracy is to shift from the discourse of rights to the practices of horizontal power, to contest the content as well as the form of knowledge, especially education, as well as to propose new modes of social rule. A civil society that acted on its own to create new forms of economic and social power would not concede to state sovereignty without a fight and might proceed to create these forms without the limitation of state veto. These initiatives may occur with the approbation of the state or may take the form of occupations of vacated or underused lands, factories, and public buildings, depending on the relationship of political forces.

Recall that in the 1960s through the first half of the 1990s, squatters occupied vacant apartment buildings in several major

New York neighborhoods, residents started community gardens on vacant lands, and the homeless constructed modern-day "Hoovervilles"—shantytowns in public parks consisting of houses made of cardboard and discarded wood. In most cases these individuals acted on their own, without seeking or winning substantial public support, even among the organizations of the homeless, which, by the early 1980s, had been co-opted by "liberal" city governments and disdained civil disobedience. Ultimately, most of the occupants were expelled from their apartments and from the parks, ending the squatters' movement, at least for the time-being.

In the late 1960s the New York City administration of John V. Lindsay advanced proposals to decentralize the far-flung but fragmented city government and confer new powers to neighborhoods, even as the Black Panthers and other political formations were making demands for community control of the schools, police, and other services. Needless to say, the political and corporate establishment launched a huge media campaign to disqualify these initiatives and succeeded, except for the community school boards. Throughout the last thirty years they were systematically infiltrated by the Catholic Church and the teachers' union and shorn of most of their powers by state and local officials. By the 1990s most school boards were regarded by many parents and other school activists with some suspicion. The boards survived into the first year of the twenty-first century, but quietly disappeared when a new mayor, taking the school system under his authority, abolished them with little dissent.

The project of encouraging popular civil empowerment from below, such as occupations in vacated but technologically viable factories to create workers' co-ops, is a massive educational undertaking as well as a program of practical interventions. For since the advent of the welfare state, people have looked to government to address a wide variety of issues from income maintenance to health care and education. And in a number of instances, such as those involving the doctrine of the separation of church and state, they have looked to the courts to inhibit the initiatives of religious fundamentalists to turn the public schools into propagators of the faith. That the state's functions have shifted sharply to its coercive functions—witness the military buildup, the expansion of police, the legal framework addressing criminal justice that has decisively adopted the stance of retribution, and the introduction of electronic surveillance as official policy—seems to have eluded the understanding. But the withering of rights and of democracy in America requires a approach entirely different from the largely defensive and frequently futile effort to reinsert the past—which, from the standpoint of blacks and other ethnic minorities and union organizing drives, was an example not worthy of emulation.

The traditional revolutionary left sought to "capture state power" and, in Lenin's classic formulation, to replace the capitalist state with a transitional "dictatorship" of the proletariat—transitional because, in the marxist as well as anarchist conception, the two central goals were to abolish the proletariat itself and the state. And since the state is inherently an instrument of class oppression, when bourgeois property has been abolished it "withers away." But the function of administration will be retained. The Marxist formula was to replace the administration of people by the administration of things. Marx's idea of the new society was framed as a "free association of producers." The people will still need services such as education, health, and sanitation. These will be cooperatively run.

The core distinction between marxists and anarchists is the notion of the transition. Anarchists have always argued that any state is bound to adopt the characteristics of hierarchy and domination, that the state itself is the problem and cannot be part of the solution. Marx and Lenin were well aware of this danger but insisted that private property and the state were so deeply imbedded in society, its institutions, and its members that a period of time was required to dismantle them. Among other problems the marxists envisioned the necessity of a struggle to consolidate the gains of the revolution against determined counterrevolution by the bourgeoisie and its retainers. This consolidation would require the use of force. Among the contradictions of the transitional state is the question of who is to be the vehicle—the existing armed forces or the people's militia? In this respect, accommodation to the traditional military carries great dangers; only when the entire working population has been armed can these dangers be (partially) addressed.

Which raises the crucial question: Does the left advocate within the labor and social movements a goal of "capturing" state power and retaining it after toppling the former political regime? Or have we learned from the experience of the revolutions of the twentieth century that the state itself, especially in its coercive form, is implicated with having taken bureaucratic control, with suppression not only of private property but of the oppressed classes? On the other hand, how to consolidate the gains of the "revolution" without preparing to defend them against the inevitable counterattack by the ancient forces? We may recall that, in the interest of waging a war against both the old hegemonic forces within the Russian empire and the foreign armies that invaded the Soviet Union in 1921, the Bolsheviks felt obliged to suspend (indefinitely, as it turned out) the Soviets, or workers' councils. By 1923 Trotsky would write that the process of bureaucratization had reached dangerous proportions and was threatening the revolution.[5]

The anti–Bolshevik council communists proposed to reconstitute political society on the basis of workers' councils. Aware of the problem posed by a hierarchical division between decisions and administration, they proposed that these functions in all sectors of public life be combined—that higher bodies (say, the administration of an entire industry as opposed to a single workplace) be elected, with regular accountability of the higher to the lower bodies, and with the right to recall representatives at any time. In this proposal the concept of state power is jettisoned, but the need for administration retained. Needless to say, such an arrangement requires a massive reevaluation of work and working time. As Ernest Mandel argued, real workers' control entails reducing working hours by half in order to enable the people to actually make necessary decisions at the workplace, in schools, and in other institutions of everyday life. But Mandel was a leninist insofar as he agreed with the notion of the transitional state. In effect, council communism became as suspicious of the state as were the anarchists.

I pose these questions because they cut to the heart of the problem of what radical futurity would look like. I cannot avoid the suggestion that some kind of transition is necessary before the state can be completely overcome. At the same time, the danger of the formation of a new technocratic, bureaucratic layer of society is very serious. This is a real contradiction in complex societies that have experienced thousands of years of the coercive state, but the underlying population has internalized its beneficent role. Between here and there, we need a lot of debate. However, it would be foolhardy to follow the example of social-democracy and its left adversary, communism, to defer the question to some far distant future.

Instead we could entertain the notion that horizontal forms of institutional life can be initiated within the framework of capitalism and the capitalist state as *dual powers* where grassroots organizations at the local level and at the workplace undertake initiatives to challenge and sometimes to replace established authorities. This is a way of addressing the question of how to overcome perpetuating the division between present and future. Indeed, we must build a political formation and initiate forms of work relations and social life that, despite their necessary limitations, given the political and ideological context, reach toward the prefiguration of a society we would like to create.

In this regard, one might consult the recent factory occupations in Argentina. There, a decade-long disinvestment program by local and foreign capital had left scores of industrial facilities shut down for years. Rather than accepting the inevitability of capital's dominance, at the turn of the twentieth century an organized movement formed to reopen the factories and operate them as workers' cooperatives. To be sure, the reopened plants produce within the market system, which obliged them to reduce wages. But if the purists remained skeptical, the employers and the Argentine government fully understood what the stakes were in these initiatives. Although, in the main, the patronat had no intention of resuming production, they understood this "reform" as a dangerous abrogation of *their* property rights, and some of the courts agreed. Besides, the workers learned that profit was not the natural motor of production, that their mutual cooperation could make the enterprise run on a more egalitarian basis than privately run competitors, with respect to both decision-making and wages. Soon workers from all over the country and parts of Latin America were visiting some of the larger enterprises to learn how to start and maintain production and distribution on a cooperative basis. And a network of occupied factory councils emerged to coordinate, among other tasks, their legal defense, their production needs, and even their finances. That there were setbacks goes without saying. But many of these experiments have survived because resistance to the concept that capital defines the natural order of things took the form of alternative.

The Argentine factory co-ops are businesses but also a social movement whose relation to the existing party structure is, at best, kept at arm's length. The movement, which embraced more than 10,000 workers and dozens of fairly small factories in the production sectors, created its own federation, fought for and won legal status, and has become a beacon for, among others, Venezuela's new Bolivaran labor movement and a model for similar government-sponsored initiatives. In stark contrast to most other countries' working classes, a section of Argentine workers refused to accept the fate of either permanent unemployment or employment that paid a fraction of their factory jobs. Imagine if some of the 9 million-plus displaced industrial workers in the United States had taken similar steps. While in the 1980s some plants were reopened, or sold by owners because they were lemon enterprises under Employee Stock Option Plans (ESOP), in nearly all cases these were run by highly paid managers who remained sovereign—in all decisions regarding financing, choice of product, and the conditions of production—from the workers who technically owned the enterprise. There are almost no instances of workers' councils actually running the plant. Boards of directors, consisting of investors and union officials, hire management on the same terms that a privately held corporation would, signing contracts that guarantee market salaries for management but have no voice in the day-to-day running of the plant. At United Airlines, for example, employees were the "owners," but the airline remained firmly in the hands of managers until the company was returned to private hands.

I can hear the objections. When workers run their own enterprises within a market system, aren't they exploiting themselves? Won't wages and benefits be cut in order to address foreign and domestic low-wage competition? Insofar as the workers must deal with labor costs in order to keep the workplace viable, aren't they thereby transformed into capitalists? What is the role of the union in a worker-run enterprise? If a member is unfairly treated on the job or discharged, who will protect her or him?

Cooperatively run enterprises can scarcely avoid the contradictions inherent in the capitalist mode of production. The decision by a workers' co-op to equalize pay and benefits will not circumvent grievances. Even a much-reduced occupational hierarchy lends itself to differences between supervision and line workers, between the more skilled and the less skilled, between engineers and the skilled and unskilled. These differences can be mitigated by a comprehensive program of scientific and technical education and upgrading, as well as education about the principle of cooperation in the self-management of enterprises; by rotation of tasks to alleviate long-term boredom and burnout, including assignment to line workers some of the tasks assigned to line supervisors and professionals; and by rigorous enforcement of codes that guarantee workers' rights, including the right to choose more than one union within the workplace. The union remains the institution of workers' protection against the likely appearance of bureaucracy and hierarchy within the works council. And the concept of workers' self-management must replace the traditional sovereignty of management. This means that when decisions are made as to the choice of product, introduction of new technologies, and other changes in the labor process, wage and benefit levels reside in the councils rather than in the technical and professional staff, although they, too, should have representation on the council and be free to present their arguments.

Needless to say, under a market system where the cooperative is surrounded by traditional capitalist corporations and practices, and where wages are under siege from domestic and foreign low-wage labor, the path forward will not be strewn with roses. To combat the thorns, workers will require considerable education in the terms and conditions of business and have available to them the experience of similar efforts elsewhere. Under some circumstances it may be necessary for the co-op not only to operate on a nonprofit basis—reserving a portion of accumulation for maintenance and technical improvements—but also to create its own market. In this regard we have a possible model in the health and organic food industries, which actually did create a market niche that permits them to sell at a premium price to a growing but still restricted group of relatively well-heeled clients. Such an arrangement may not be feasible for co-ops that engage in mass production goods such as metals, moderately priced clothing, and appliances. But in some cases they would be better advised to seek a unique market niche compatible with their technological mix and labor process, and to identify a consumer pool prepared to support them with purchases. Here the example of retail food coops, which rely on the closed market and voluntary labor of their members, might be worth consulting. Voluntary labor may not be an option for producer co-ops, but what might be feasible is a system whereby membership entitles the consumer to purchase, at reduced prices, higher-quality products than are available at commercial supermarkets and wholesale and retail outlets. This relationship might result in the organization of worker-consumer councils to decide a number of issues related to production such as what should be produced and at what prices.

Beyond Fragmentation

Given the long fallow period of left disappearance and disarray, it is likely to be years before an organized left can expect to have more than marginal influence on the course of political events and to earn public legitimacy to address the serious decline of education, the health care crisis, the assault on abortion and other womens' rights, and, as organized labor continues to decline, deepening class and racial inequality. But absent a national political formation capable of addressing politics in a timely way by instituting the means of theoretical and practical work, and of forms of communication that enter the public sphere in order to call attention to the nature of events and public issues, their interconnections, and their consequences for the everyday lives of most Americans, the path to deteriorating living standards—economic, social, and ecological—becomes almost inevitable. Under these circumstances we can foresee the consolidation of the already insurgent authoritarianism of the federal government, the displacement of its welfare functions by its police function, and more openly violent attacks on labor and social movements.

Inevitability is the outcome of the vacuum created by various forms of inaction at the level of system and structure: postmodern politics, which has fetishized the primacy of local struggles at the expense of national and transnational questions; the libertarian left's legitimate suspicion of authoritarianism, but which has been confused with rejection of all forms of centralization; the abdication of the search for alternatives to current state policies and the consequent elevation of protest and resistance to a political principle, and also to the substance of political practice; the dogmatic refusal by some of the forms of electoralism and its reverse, the reduction of all politics to electoral politics and to legislative policy. As a strategy, "protest and resistance" concedes the power to innovate to the prevailing hegemonies. It is suspicious of all forms of institutionalization that entail interventions within the capitalist state, even if framed as alternatives that it identifies, incorrectly, with moderation because alternatives invariably become reforms within the system. The anarchists criticize those who choose to "participate" or, in the words of Gramsci and the German New Left tribune Rudi Dutschke, who take the "long march through the institutions." Yet without the long march, without taking control of these institutions, even within a broad framework of capitalist social relations, how can large sections of the population gain the experience and the political confidence to run society? And we are left with the further question: How to disarm, neutralize, and eventually win over the military so that opponents of social change will not have at their command the force of violence to overturn the future?

Notes

1. Jeffrey McCracken, "Shifting Down: A Middle Class Made by Detroit Is Now Threatened by Its Slump," *Wall Street Journal*, November 14, 2005.

2. John Hoerr, *And the Wolf Finally Came* (Pittsburgh: University of Pittsburgh Press, 1988).

3. Kim Stanley Robinson—one of our best science-fiction writers, whose Mars trilogy won almost every available award in this genre—has produced two volumes of a projected trilogy on global warming: *Forty Signs of Rain* (New York: Bantam Books, 2004) and *Fifty Degrees Below* (New York: Bantam Books, 2005). As these are based rigorously on cutting-edge scientific knowledge, the reader might learn as much from them as from any nonfiction text—if not more. For those wanting a definitive scientific assessment by a distinguished climatologist, see Stephen M. Schneider, *Global Warming: Are We Entering the Greenhouse Century?* (New York: Vintage Books, 1990).

4. Thomas Hobbes, *Leviathan,* edited by C. B. Macpherson (Hammondsworth: Penguin Books, 1968); Ernst Bloch, *Natural Law and Human Dignity* (Cambridge, MA: MIT Press, 1986).

5. Leon Trotsky, *The New Course* (New York: Pioneer Publishers, 1947).

◇

5

The Shape of Practice

What would a new political formation do that is not now being done by the left-liberals and by the single-issue movements? For an answer we might start by considering a national news-weekly with local supplements. For example, take the New York City transit strike at the end of 2005. In December of that year, militants in New York's Transport Workers Union Local 100, the union of subway and bus workers, tested their power in a dispute with the system's operator, the Metropolitan Transportation Authority (MTA). Attempting to reverse years of concessionary bargaining among municipal employees, and in their own contracts, the workers rejected the MTA demand for a two-tier pension system and were fighting to reform management's punitive discipline policies. In the face of steep penalties under New York State's Taylor Law, which bans strikes by public employees (a judge ordered fines of $1 million a day for the union and two days' pay for each day of the walkout for members and a day later threatened jail for the union leaders), workers mounted picket lines during the early morning hours of December 20. Three days later they returned to work without a contract but had exacted a major conces-sion from the MTA that it would withdraw its two-tier pension demand. On December 28, however, on the union president's recommendation the executive board overwhelmingly approved a settlement that required workers to pay 1.5 percent health insurance premiums without securing a public commitment from the MTA and the mayor that it would seek to rescind the fines. And the proposed agreement pushed back the expiration date from December 15—the height of the holiday season—to January 15, when New York stores are usually begging for customers. It appeared that the mayor had drawn his pound of flesh from the union's leaders, but the press almost uniformly greeted the deal as a union victory.

As the strike loomed, all metropolitan area dailies mounted a huge anti-union barrage. With the exception of the pro-worker Pacifica radio station WBAI, and the NPR affiliate in New York City, WNYC (which tried to remain nonpartisan), the radio and television coverage was firmly in the MTA's camp. Nor did liberal politicians, many of whom relied on labor's money for their campaigns, step up publicly to support the workers, except when given the opportunity for photo ops. The day after transit workers returned to work, the *New York Times,* whose reporting was occasionally illuminating regarding strike issues, especially its coverage of the under-the-radar-screen question of work discipline that has resulted in thousands of penalties for workers, ran an editorial calling the strike "useless" as if the union's main demand—forcing MTA to drop the two-tier pension system—was a minor matter, and that the issue of dignity and of race (a majority of the workers are black, Latino, and Asian) was trivial. On another occasion a *Times* editorial repeated the old charge that the union was "holding the city hostage."[1] Apart from appearances by the union president Roger Toussaint, and occasional commentary by sympathetic labor intellectuals on the media, Mayor Michael Bloomberg's vicious attacks—in numerous public appearances he called the union "thuggish" and "selfish"—dominated the airwaves and the print media. Despite all of this, an ABC poll showed that 52 percent of the public approved the union's cause and other polls ranged up to 70 percent in favor of the workers.

What was missing was a newspaper consistently analyzing the strike's issues, making labor's case against concessions and two-tier contracts, assessing its impact, and providing detailed information on the transit system's finances and leadership. And although a well-known right-wing think tank, The Manhattan Institute, presented the employer's and government's arguments on all media, since there was no left institute the union's side was woefully outgunned in the battle of perception and of ideas. During the strike Toussaint repeated the refrain that the union was seeking not to make dramatic gains but merely, in his words, to "hold the line." But the union was unable to disseminate information to the public or to the small number of labor-oriented intellectuals who appeared as "experts" on talk shows and in newspaper interviews. (And, of course, one of the key roles of a new political formation is to get the word out when the mainstream press refuses to perform its role as disseminator.) As a result the workers may have missed the chance to mobilize a much larger labor and public protest against the governor and the MTA's concessionary program. On December 28 the local's leadership voted to end the strike but accepted a management demand that workers contribute 1.5 percent of their wages to the health plan, which reduced their wage gains below the inflation level. But in a secret-ballot membership referendum, the rank and file defeated the contract settlement by 7 votes out of the 22,000 cast. Still, the press persisted in its prediction that not much would be changed by the narrow rejection. The dissidents had no strong public voice to counter the MTA and the union leadership's version of the situation. Imagine if, on the day after the vote to approve the contract was announced, there appeared at subway stations and bus stops a four-page bulletin discussing the reasons for the rank and file's rejection of the deal. Tens of thousands of MTA riders would have gotten a viewpoint different from that of the MTA, the union leadership, and the commercial media.

There are other signs that workers have grown weary of twenty-five years of retreat and are preparing to fight. For example, in the fall of 2005 the United Auto Workers' leadership responded to GM parts maker Delphi's proposal to cut wages by more than half by taking its case to a bankruptcy judge rather than initiating direct action on the shop floor and in the streets. The fact that these forces cling to the illusion that the slowly grinding wheels of legal procedures, especially the courts, are adequate to address the catastrophies that have already occurred, and that lie ahead, controverts the palpable truth that legal and parliamentary contests are at best a second line of defense and may even prove detrimental if the courts render anti-worker decisions that can become precedent in other fights. Yet, by the new year, rank-and-file activists within the union were putting heavy pressure on a reluctant leadership to strike against the company's plans to impose draconian wage and benefit reductions. Delphi felt the heat; fearing a crippling walkout as the year ended, it announced that it was withdrawing some of these proposals. But the demand for concessions remains on the table. In January 2006 the company asked a bankruptcy judge to vacate the provisions of the union contract. And the union seems unable to get its message out in any public way.

The stark alternative that I previously suggested—that without resolute resistance on a broad front, we are rapidly sinking into an authoritarian morass—implies that we have largely left behind the chance for incremental reforms to address the rapid deterioration of liberal democratic institutions, the flagrant attack against workers' living standards and working conditions, America's aggressive war policies, and the ecological crisis. Congress and state legislatures are busy granting generous tax breaks for the rich by ruthlessly cutting aid to the poor; reducing education budgets, especially for public higher education; forcing public workers to accept reductions in their living standards by requiring increases in their co-payments for health and pension benefits; and leaving parks, coastal rock formations, rivers, and other recreation areas in disrepair.

The erosion of these aspects of the natural environment has already had catastrophic effects in New Orleans, on the Gulf Coast, and throughout Northern California. Some cities have responded to state and federal aid reductions by closing hospitals, restricting library hours (especially neighborhood branches), and reducing garbage pickups and the size of sanitation crews. In most cases, unions as well as education and neighborhood groups are fighting, like the New York Transport Workers, to hold the line rather than proposing advances. But as the New York Giants' coach Steve Owens once quipped, "The best defense is a good offense." Unfortunately, this message has failed to penetrate most social movements and civil society organizations, which remain on the defensive. Before us is the urgent necessity of launching the anti-capitalist project in the United States and, with great specificity, making plain what we may mean by an alternative to the authoritarian present. We are faced with the urgent need to reignite the radical imagination. We simply have no vehicle to undertake this work—a party that can express the standpoint of exploited and oppressed that, in the current historical conjuncture, must extend far beyond the poor and the workers, since capital and the state have launched a major assault on the middle classes. In short, we need a political formation capable of articulating the content of the "not-yet"—that which is immanent in the present but remains unrealized.

Creating a new political formation requires careful preparation and a lot of work because, among other things, most active leftists—anti-war, labor, and social movement activists—have little or no experience in radical political organizations. Indeed, the context for participating in such a project is absent from most of our lives. Nor, for the most part, do we possess the collective memory, historical knowledge, or historical experience of engaging in the struggle for a radically different future. Later in this chapter I want to address what "socialism" might mean in the post-Soviet, postsocial democratic era. Certainly we cannot rest content to repeat the past; but, as I have already argued, we must take seriously the distortions, misconceptions, and outright betrayals of both Marx's and the anarchist conception that the new society will be a "free association" of producers, free of the bureaucratic domination that has thwarted the base of society from inventing new forms of life. The invocation of the conception of the new society as a free association challenges the prevailing modern socialist and communist privileging of the state as the key arena of both struggle and of radical futurity. It suggests that we need forms of politics different from those we have inherited.

We also need to discuss the problems involved in getting started. As I have already indicated, it would be naïve and certainly premature to call for a new radical organization instantly. Given the long duration of postmodern and relativist politics in the United States, the first task is to persuade many activists who have settled for working in single-issue movements that renounce "grand narratives" such as are expressed by the concepts of the totality, class and class struggle, capitalism itself as an object of political contestation, and other large ideas. And many intellectuals teach and write as individuals because they see no chance of working collectively except on scholarly research projects that require funding, the sources of which are usually government agencies, corporate foundations, or private corporations. The tasks associated with persuasion are likely to be protracted. Paradoxically, it will take an organization, or at least an organizing committee, to undertake these tasks. We cannot wait until people are "ready" to make a start. Arguably, they may never be ready without the provocation provided by a proposal to act differently. This is the chief meaning of the term "leadership." It does not override self-activity, but neither does it take the position that we are fated to remain in a state of suspended animation until a rhizomic rebellion occurs.

The main ideological obstacle to the project is the habitual adherence of many activists, intellectuals, and other leftists to the "grand" strategy of transforming the Democratic Party, or at least pushing it to the left. Here is an example: In late December 2005, former Texas Agriculture Commissioner, radio commentator, and author Jim Hightower sent an e-mail message saying:

> My wish is for a Democratic Party that chooses to reconnect with its populist roots, recognizes that its only real reason for existence is to be the unabashed, unequivocal unrelenting representative of its core populist constituency, including America's working stiffs, the middle class (this means the 60% of the country who have incomes of less than $55,000 a year). The poor (a fast growing constituency, unfortunately), old folks, and children, grunts and veterans, and proponents of clean air and water.[2]

This combination of lament and invocation comes in an era when, as Hightower and his fellow left-populists well know, the Democratic Party is firmly planted on the center-right, unabashedly pro–big business as well as pro–free trade, unequivocally centrist, and relentlessly dedicated to budget balancing; and in the service of neoliberalism, most Democratic leaders have shown themselves on numerous occasions to be more than willing to bash the poor, the working stiffs, and the so-called "middle class" who, I would argue, are mostly working stiffs themselves. Apart from independent farmers and small-business people, they work for wages and salaries, are insecure in their jobs, and are facing mounting indebtedness because their incomes do not match necessary expenditures. These are not people who take extended vacations to Caribbean retreats. If they manage to go away on vacation for two or three weeks every year, they count themselves lucky.

Although the Democrats have shifted steadily to the right since the short-lived progressive takeover of the national party in 1972, the legacy of retreat is much longer. In his homily Hightower repeats one of the myths that, along with the obsessional fear of the extreme right, helps sustain the Democrats' hold over a sizeable constituency. The myth is that the Democratic Party (DP) was once a populist and unrelenting representative of workers. Hightower differentiates between workers and the poor, but, historically and increasingly in our own time, this distinction describes different and fluid strata of the same class; neither the workers nor the professional/managerial class are secure in their situations. The stratification system within wage and salary earning groups is extremely porous. Notice that for Hightower women, blacks, and Latinos do not rate a separate classification whereas "grunts and veterans" do, even though it could be easily shown that they also fall into several of the other categories. This is a stunning illustration of Thomas Frankism—the populist doctrine that urges the left to focus on economic issues and to soft-pedal its cultural and social positions for purposes of either social conservatism or, as in Frank's case, strategic convenience.[3]

But the claim that the Democrats have populist roots is misleading and relies on two historical periods: the era of Southern agrarian insurgency at the turn of the twentieth century that gave rise to figures such as Southern Senators Tom Watson and Pitchfork Ben Tillman and, most famously, William Jennings Bryan; and the progressive era that once competed with the populists for the support of agrarians and workers, and that culminated in the Woodrow Wilson tradition of top-down reform, whose main legatee was the "second" New Deal of the mid-1930s. What distinguished populism and progressivism? While both were class movements, they expressed different political orientations and different classes. The populists were the expression of disenfranchised farmers at a time when half the population lived in rural areas and whose living standards were attacked by large rail and processing corporations in the last third of the nineteenth century. In his masterful revisionist history Lawrence Goodwyn argues that populism was a de facto working-class movement since many of populisms' agrarian adherents were drowned in debt (mostly to the banks), owned their land in name only, and were pitted against a very powerful fraction of capital—finance capital. Frustrated at their inability to win national political power, they developed horizontal forms of organization such as producers' cooperatives of various sorts and focused on state legislatures rather than on Congress to adjudicate their grievances.[4]

Populists entered into electoral politics in 1880 as an independent party, opposed to what they considered to be the two parties of big business. But desperate to regain some national footing the Democrats abandoned their me-too stance of the Gilded Age, nominated a Midwesterner for president, and convinced many populists to surrender their political independence. With William Jennings Bryan's Democratic presidential campaign of 1896, populism disappeared as a national movement when the candidate adopted a populist plank, replacing gold with silver as the measure of money, although it survived in several states of the upper Midwest: North Dakota, Minnesota, and in hybrid forms (where populists coalesced with the Republicans) in Nebraska, Wisconsin, and elsewhere. Until Franklin Roosevelt's presidency, Progressives split their loyalties between the two major parties—after all, Theodore Roosevelt, the Progressive Party presidential candidate, was a scion of Old New York money and a powerful representative of its class interests ran on that label in 1912—and it can be argued that, given the segregationists' dominance of the Democrats and the fact that its urban political machines were geared to tempering working-class discontent, they felt more comfortable in Republican ranks.

The progressives, whose formation is coincident with the decline of the "populist moment," co-opted some of the populist rhetoric, especially during the three losing presidential races of their standard bearer, Bryan. But as many historians have argued, progressivism was not a movement of and by the underlying population of workers and farmers but, rather, an alliance of a fraction of small and large business enterprises and the growing "new middle class" of managers and professionals that, fearing working-class insurgency but also the dire effects of monopoly power, attempted to thwart it through a program of incremental reform. While the "progressive" Sherman Anti-Trust Act preceded the Wilson presidency, with the Clayton Act (1913) this administration, and Franklin Roosevelt's as well, assumed the populist mantle of "trust busters" (they succeeded very rarely, but their reputations exceeded modest expectations). Roosevelt and his secretary of agriculture, Henry A. Wallace, cobbled a farm policy ostensibly to help poor farmers retain their land during the Depression. But the various programs it carried out actually accelerated the corporate industrialization of American agriculture. To this day, federal farm subsidies and land conservation benefit the largest farms; small farmers have never gained substantial income from these programs.

The best the New Deal was able to do for poor farmers was to regulate freight rates, provide rural electrification, and, in some instances, support the organization of grain and dairy cooperatives, even though this movement had emerged earlier in the century as an anti-statist populist initiative. But many small producers lost their farms during the Roosevelt era because Wallace's Agriculture Department devoted the lion's share of its efforts to saving the larger producers. In retrospect, Roosevelt's main accomplishment was to enshrine the state as a virtuous institution rather than as the enemy of the people. This was a crucial ideological move because many perceived during the Gilded Age that, as James Truslow Adams observed, "the business of government is business." From the 1930s on, a large fraction of small and medium farmers, and an even larger fraction of workers who had come to distrust the government and understood it to be an adversary to their interests, became fervent supporters of government intervention to improve their lives. This new faith was founded on Roosevelt's relief programs, which fed millions during the Depression; on the proliferation of public works, which created a modest number of jobs for hundreds of thousands of unemployed but was mythologized as the New Deal's solution to the job crisis; and on the powerful image that Roosevelt projected of a government that was on the side of the "forgotten man," a deeply emotional appeal that referred directly to the Hoover years. In this connection we should not underestimate the weight of the president's command of populist rhetoric. Railing against "economic royalists" on the heels of one of the administration's most humiliating defeats—Roosevelt's attempt to pack the Supreme Court to get his agenda approved—he also was famous for adroit phrases such as his response to the Depression ("All we have to fear is fear itself") and his frequent expressions of sympathy for the labor movement, even as he opposed its most militant actions.

Yet, throughout his administration, but especially during the first two years, the so-called first New Deal, Roosevelt never wavered from the view that his primary objective was to help business revive. His populist reputation was enhanced by the obdurate opposition of a significant section of capital to his expansion of welfare reform beyond relief to Social Security and unemployment insurance, which were mainly responses to the industrial working-class rebellions of 1933–1937. But Roosevelt's chief emphasis was to expand Herbert Hoover's proposals to provide capital resources to business through agencies such as the Reconstruction Finance Corporation. Roosevelt went further by sponsoring the National Industrial Recovery Act, which set up boards to regulate prices, profits, and wages, which, with the exceptions of mining and apparel boards on which strong unions sat, were adjusted to the needs of business. And throughout the 1930s there was continuity between the imperial foreign policies of Republican administrations from McKinley to Hoover and the New Deal. It is easy to forget that both Hoover and Roosevelt pursued the Open Door to China (i.e., engaged in "gunboat" diplomacy) and fiercely promulgated the Monroe Doctrine in Latin America, which led to several invasions of Central and South American countries. (For example, Nicaragua was invaded in 1934 in an attempt to suppress the Sandinistas, who had challenged the country's status as a "banana republic.") This period also witnessed the organization of international cartels of German and US capital in the steel and electrical industries; indeed, it was during the 1930s that a stunning rise of monopoly capital occurred, becoming the object of a famous congressional inquiry led by the progressive Robert Lafollette of Wisconsin.[5]

I have already argued that the National Labor Relations Act proved to be a mixed blessing for American labor. But Roosevelt constructed the pension system (Social Security) on the basis of employer and worker contributions, not on that of taxes, because he knew that every welfare program that relies on general revenue might eventually suffer draconian cuts. This is exactly what has occurred since the Reagan revolution; and, as noted, it was the Democrat Bill Clinton who signed the welfare reform act that drove nails in the coffin of one of the New Deal's most important features: income support for the long-term unemployed. At the same time that successive, right-wing Republican-dominated congressional majorities have continued their assault on a wide array of social programs, the Democrats have backed away from their own historical policies and refused to make these human insults an electoral issue.

As Paul Krugman has pointed out, they were even reluctant to defend Social Security from the Bush administration's and Wall Street's attempt to construct a slippery slope by privatizing some of the funds. Their backs were finally stiffened by the grassroots outcry of protest from (among others) retirees who, contrary to the common-sense view of human nature, refused to be moved by the administration's promise to "grandfather" them into the previous deal. Rather, fearing they would be smeared with the label of big spenders and socialist sympathizers, the Democrats wax proud of their own miserly fiscal conservatism. From the socialists, many of whom, in 1936, defected from their own party, and the Communists, who after 1934 supported the New Deal and its Democratic party successors, to the current crop of apologists, anti-radical liberal organizations, and intellectuals, like Hightower, who issue regular pleas for a mythical revived Democratic populism, we can discern the tragic consequences of their choices. The wages of their collaboration with the centrist establishment have left the people largely defenseless, except on the few occasions that they have raised their voices without relying on politicians' support.

We must convince those leftists who opt, one more time, for a politics of the two-party system that they have backed the wrong donkey for the better part of this century. Hightower, a good person, is a representative figure in perpetuating that calamity. The principal reason for an organization that links specific domains and struggles to a center of analysis and alternative is that, without an explicit radical political formation, single-issue movements necessarily function within the limits of the dwindling opportunities for incremental reform. Even if reform politics remain viable in certain domains such as health care—largely because the privatized systems are disintegrating before our eyes—we must acknowledge that the general prospect is dim, that liberal hopes for a new New Deal are bound to be frustrated, certainly without a left that provides the spine that is ordinarily lacking among the liberal leadership and its institutions. Recall the celebrated Jules Feiffer cartoon whose caption reads: "Why do the liberals have no ideas?" They always get their ideas from the left. But the left has no ideas that go beyond the statist solutions. For if it is true that the contemporary capitalist state has been transformed so that its coercive, police functions overwhelm the "legitimating" functions such as social welfare—in the event that, for example, it has been so fiscally starved and its functions so privatized that it can no longer address social needs—we must face the possibility that only a new perspective will point the way forward.

The first requirement for a new perspective is that there be a political formation that stands outside the system. It must be radically intransigent while holding out its arms to other forces such as left-liberals working in the Democratic Party and its base organizations who want to fight capital and for significant social change. What might the "new perspective" look like? From the socialist tradition it would retain the view that private ownership of the basic means of material production and mass communications are, in these times, incapable of addressing the underlying economic and social needs of the vast majority. During the last half-century capital not only has become socially irresponsible but, in order to solve its profound economic stagnation, has actively entered the public arena to sponsor anti-popular economic and political regimes directed at reducing workers' living standards. Capital has broken the social contract and supported rightist efforts to restrict social and political freedom. Capital has invoked the mantra of "cost cutting"—its euphemism for solving its accumulation problems on the backs of the working class—to justify plant closings, massive job cuts in major sectors of the economy, and support for a national administration that has radically curtailed labor's rights. Even as the auto industry disintegrates before our eyes the Democrats remain silent, as if to criticize the large corporate establishment would subject them to charges of being socialists.

These interventions demonstrate the degree to which big capital has forfeited the limited legitimacy it acquired during the late New Deal period when its main corporations entered into a historic compromise with labor. In the new society the basic means of production—already partially decimated by capital—would become public goods. Shuttered steel mills and auto, electrical, textile, and other production plants might be reopened to produce for domestic markets and cooperatively work with developing countries to meet their needs. The producers, though now managing their own labor, would recognize that since these industries were built by the collective labor of society they have become labor's collective responsibility to operate in the public trust. These enterprises would collective private property, but not state owned. Of course the broad distribution of management functions to the entire workforce would make necessary the significant reduction of working hours and a new division of labor.

What of small commodity producers, such as farmers and small industrial enterprises, small retail establishments and independent professionals (e.g., physicians, artists, publishers, lawyers, architects), and self-employed mechanics such as plumbers, auto repair shops, and the like? These activities are best conducted in the regulated local markets that they serve, except for artists, publishers, and small manufacturers who require larger markets. By "regulation" I do not mean a government-controlled price system but a system of inspection to ensure quality, public support for cooperative markets, and refusal of space to large retail chains. These enterprises would be subject to a maximum- as well as a minimum-income rule and, if they employed workers, wages would correspond to the historical level of material culture. That is, employees of small as well as larger enterprises should be able to live comfortably, have the unconditional right to withhold their labor, and participate in the management of the enterprise.

These local markets might, in lieu of money, have their own instruments of exchange. For example, in Ithaca, New York, some commercial products and health services are exchanged with local currency. At the same time, national chains would be broken up and transferred to former employees, who might operate them on a local basis as cooperatives. These suggestions imply a limited role for the market at the local and regional levels. But large corporations such as Wal-Mart, Microsoft, and United States Steel, which currently exercise oligopolistic control over their respective markets, would be expropriated and their owners offered jobs and compensated at the level of a living wage.

Needless to say, the issues associated with the state and with power must occupy a central place in the new perspective. As I indicated in Chapter 2, while the "transition" to a new society remains an open question, we can no longer derive our inspiration from either the bolshevik or the social-democratic past. In plain words, we have learned that bureaucratic socialism creates as many problems as it purports to solve, and the prospects for reform within a system dedicated to a relentless reduction of labor's power and its living standards are no guide for the future. We must discover the forms embodied in radical and revolutionary literature and, equally, in the social practice of the movements both of the past and the present, especially those that invented social arrangements that show the alternatives of collective and cooperative self-management of the workplace, the neighborhood, the city, and, by extension, society. The main question is: How can a new series of social arrangements transform the state from an institution of hierarchical repression and control into a series of agencies of coordination of a series of self-managed cooperative enterprises that organize the production and distribution of material goods and the dissemination of knowledge and information—in which case the state is no longer the state but something else?

Contrary to the stasis that afflicts most labor and social movements, which still look nostalgically to a benign interventionist state, the new political formation would advance new ideas. These would not entirely renounce the prospect of social reform through state intervention but would soberly assess its chances and take new initiatives that might be forced to bypass traditional routes. For instance, we might consider horizontal ways of meeting social needs. Can we envision a central funding source but decentralized self-managed services? This recalls the critique of the welfare system made by community organizers and activists in movements of the poor and New Left intellectuals during the 1960s. None rejected the notion that funds for schools, welfare, and health care facilities should be funded collectively through central administrations. But they challenged the ability and the wisdom of designating city, state, or federal governments to set policies, let alone to operate these domains. In fact, privatization has flourished on this critique, which, unfortunately, has prompted some who were once effective critics of the liberal bureaucracy, out of fear that past gains will disappear, to become apologists for that system. Until the 1980s movements counterproposed "community control" as an alternative to the control of large bureaucracies. But in the anti-poverty era, "community action"—an arm of the Federal Office of Economic Opportunity, the main anti-poverty agency—gradually came to mean transferring control to local bureaucracies that, with some exceptions, dispensed these services in a manner that resembled the discredited government agencies because they operated within federal guidelines. Local control might take the form of cooperatives acting as service providers, in which the users as well as the producers of the services would have decision-making powers. They would not manage people but would administer services.

If these concepts were to be broadly instituted, one of the most problematic aspects of the New Deal—professional management and executive domination of social services—would become an artifact of history. It would transform our collective understanding of the state and begin to implement the transition from its characteristic administration of people to the administration of things. And, as is well known, we live in an economic and political environment marked, in many ways, by national and global integration. While it may be banal to remark that we are more closely interconnected across national and regional borders than ever before, this development must have implications for the scope and character of political movements. Without a radical formation that adopts the standpoint that—even as it defends and extends local autonomy, recognizes the imperative of addressing the specificity of the United States and its history, and allows the scope of its struggle to go beyond our own borders—this project is likely to remain indefinitely deferred.

Linking concrete struggles to an anti-capitalist project and, beyond resistance and refusal, proposing new modes of life necessitate creating organizations that have varying degrees of *centralization*. Centralization does not require directives from above. It is not a question of having central organizations of power that dictate to the intermediate and lower levels of organizations what their strategy must be. But it does require the accumulation of human, financial, and physical resources of organization without which, in complex societies, effective interventions are next to impossible to implement. The need for centralization has at least three imperatives:

First and perhaps foremost is the need to create organs of communication and analysis that become the embodiment of the relation of theory to practice, and of issue struggles to the concrete totality. For instance, the political formation would launch a news and opinion weekly and eventually a national daily newspaper in hard copy and online, with local supplements—which at first will be the primary means, at the level of news and ideas, of providing linkages among activists and sympathizers, and reaching beyond the already convinced. And the left media would at the beginning be modest, but increasingly powerful, counterweights and alternatives to the virtual conservative and right-wing media monopoly. While not abandoning efforts to intervene in the corporate media, I argue that creating our own has priority. The formidable tasks associated with starting, raising funds for, and building the circulation of newspapers, magazines, Internet blogs, television and radio programs, and other forms of media dissemination will require aggressive and closely coordinated organization. Regarding the funds for such an effort, we cannot expect large contributions from any except a few wealthy individuals or, given its explicitly political nature, nonprofit foundations—two of the main sources of material support for a myriad of organizations and movements. Much healthier but equally daunting is the task of raising smaller amounts from thousands of activists and sympathizers of the political formation that sponsors the fund drive. For example, if 25,000 people contributed an average of $100 each, the effort would raise $2.5 million, enough to launch the newsweekly and other publications some people might pledge more, and as the party grew they would tithe themselves on an annual basis.

Second is the work associated with *interventions* in the course of current events and efforts to link labor and social movements and coordinating efforts to forge these links. I want to underscore the concept of *coordination* because the movements should retain their autonomy to decide questions of strategy and tactics. The role of the center is to organize solidarity efforts during strikes; to help spread knowledge about the issues in these and other struggles; to disseminate new ideas; to conduct or encourage major campaigns such as anti-capitalist globalization protests and other events; to help organize new caucus movements within the unions in which members work and render support to those already in existence; to assist issue organizing in sectors such as ecology, feminist, and freedom struggles; and to make available knowledge from around the world that might assist the movements. In this connection the political formation would recognize and support efforts outside the trade unions to create workers centers whose activities are directed to workers' interests, especially immigrants, and go beyond collective bargaining. These centers, together with some unions, especially the Service Employees, provided the basic support for the organization of the massive demonstrations in behalf of immigrant rights in Spring 2006.

Third is the intellectual work needed to analyze, on an ongoing basis, the relationships between political power and social movements, the configurations of capital on global and local levels, and social developments; to discover efforts in the United States and elsewhere to forge alternatives to neoliberal policies; and to combat militarism and other forms of authoritarianism. These efforts require the organization of centers of inquiry into a host of issues:

- One issue involves the revival and elaboration of economic, social, and cultural theory, including initiation of a wide-ranging discussion of questions of economic and political relations in a new society; and the establishment and development of a comprehensive educational program such as left schools, conferences, and pamphlets on theoretical issues, current events, and popular struggles. In this respect the new political formation would—beyond fundamental principles of equality, democracy, and the struggle for new social relations based on the free associations of producers—regard no past idea as a settled question. For it is abundantly clear that while there are reasons to take good theory from the past, there is an urgent need to reexamine some of it and develop new ideas, even new theoretical paradigms.
- Another issue has to do with encouraging the development of cultural forms and organizations of visual artists, writers, film makers, and practitioners of other art forms. Such organizations would advance the interests of those working in cultural fields, but they would also undertake projects such as concerts, documentary and feature film production, exhibitions, and publication programs.
- A third issue concerns support of the educational, child care, and cultural institutions that exist and creation of those that do not. These would include radical schools for adults and teenagers, radical Sunday schools for kids, theater groups, book and movie clubs, and reading groups.

While the anarchists have insisted that left- as well as right-wing statism—which they often confuse with centralism—is an obstacle to the emancipation of humanity from oppression and exploitation, it would be a grave error to ignore the historical evidence that many anarchist movements have formed vertical (i.e., centralized) as well as horizontal, decentralized organizations. That these organizations do not call themselves "parties" refers to the ordinary signification of the term: a political organization that seeks power within or over the state, through either elections or other means. Although anarchists usually favor the federated principle of political organization, which affords locals considerable autonomy, their federations—like those of the nineteenth- and early-twentieth-century labor and socialist movements—maintained a center; published newspapers, books, and pamphlets; sent organizers to assist strikes and other struggles; organized armed forces during the Spanish Civil War (although these armed forces refused to submit to hierarchical decision-making models); and tried to enforce democratic discussion. Were there anarchist leaders who set the ideological and political direction of the movement? To deny that this was the case is to have one's head in the sand. These activities required money and central coordination, and the historical anarchist movement—no less than the marxists—knew that serious political organization required an apparatus capable of linking local, sectoral, and national struggles to a global framework.

Yet the anarchists' case was reinforced by the tendency of socialist and communist parties to drift toward bureaucratic instead of democratic centralism, and to consider themselves parties of government within the capitalist state, leaving behind the radical and revolutionary traditions from which they sprung. It is no wonder, given the history of these parties, that centralism itself was intimately fused with oligarchic and authoritarian practices. But the tie is by no means intrinsic to the concept of centralism. Centralism can connote either the administrative and coordinating apparatuses or bureaucratic centralism and institutions of command.

As we have seen, the social-democratic movements of the twentieth century often took the reins of government and came to accept the idea that the state not only was an arena of struggle but was neutral and, especially in the era of welfare capitalism, could be useful for the steady improvement of the working-class standard of life. In time, the state was viewed by the socialist and communist left as an unconditional good; the traditional idea of its transitional role was buried in the euphoria of welfare capitalism. As a result, socialists became habitual parliamentarians. When the political environment veered to the right, most of the social-democratic governments—which, after all, were managing the capitalist state—drifted to the center. For decades after World War II their working- and middle-class constituents held the parties' noses to the grindstone of supporting the welfare state. But since they had become parties of government when, in the 1970s, neoliberal ideologies and policies began to dominate statecraft because transnational corporations engaged in outright blackmail, most of them—even the vaunted Scandinavian Social-Democratic parties, slowly bent to versions of neoliberal economic and social governance. Today, in government, most social-democratic parties have presided over the steady erosion of the welfare state, differing from the conservatives in the pace, but not the substance, of their mutual agreement that the rich postwar compromise is now simply too expensive to assuage capital's peripatetic tendencies.

While the Communists retained Marx's concept of the state as the executive of the capitalist class whose principal mission was to serve its general interests, especially against labor and other insurgent classes, many of its national parties, including the Communist Party of the United States of America (CPUSA), entered coalitions with liberals because of the imperatives of the anti-fascist struggles of the 1930s or, in the postwar era, joined with the center to prevent the right in France and Italy from regaining power. Since the 1930s they have soft-pedaled their anti-capitalism and even tempered their critique of the liberal-democratic state. By the late 1960s most CPs in Western Europe and North America were part of the center-left and relegated their revolutionary ideology to the back-burner. For example, in the 2003 French elections, the center-left, which now included the CP, gave open support to sections of the right that were prepared to resist the most authoritarian parties and movements. A year later, the French CP participated in organizing the "no" vote, the successful campaign against the European constitution. In 2005 and 2006, it became, in fact if not in theory, a party of government. In preference to joining a coalition of the "left of the left," which included two parties of trotskyist leanings, it agreed to form an electoral coalition with the centrist Socialists. Perhaps because of their history as the main target of an insurgent right, the American Communists, parallel to the left-liberals, have compulsively given priority to the preservation of the liberal state through the defense of civil liberties at the expense of any kind of genuine advance in the direction of an emancipatory politics. The CP is today largely irrelevant to radical politics, due not only to its history of uncritical support of the Soviet Union but also to its abandonment of independent radical politics. Internally, with the exception of the former German party, most of the Communist parties in the West are bereft of serious discussion concerning their stalinist past or the steps needed to forge a qualitatively better future. And their public presentation lacks verve and insurgency; they remain in most nation-states tired and defensive and they lack the most elementary characteristics of a movement that intends to change the world.

On the other hand, contemporary anarchism in the United States and some parts of Europe have at times exhibited inventiveness, a spirit of resistance to established authority, and a healthy suspicion of doctrinal and organizational rigidity. Mostly composed of students and youth, they have been in the forefront of struggles against globalization. Among the tactical innovations, anarchists have formed decentralized "affinity groups" to conduct civil disobedience during global justice demonstrations, notably during the now-legendary 1999 Seattle anti-WTO protest. Refusing to engage in protracted negotiations with the police to ensure legality and collaboration to control crowds, the affinity groups mastered the element of surprise, which caused official disorientation (since the police were looking for a center with which to negotiate), even as highly disciplined union contingents circumvented the civil disobedience and adhered to the law by marching peacefully through the city. And even though Organized Labor has stayed away, the tiny remnant of the anarcho-syndicalist IWW has distinguished itself in organizing campaigns at Starbucks and Borders, two of the leading retail chains.

But American anarchists are woefully, even deliberately, ignorant of their own history; they have often carried their rejection of organizational rigidity to a refusal of theoretical and strategic thinking and their elevation of resistance and protest to a political principle. Having adopted the postmodern stance that ignores or refuses to make links between specific struggles to problems of future society, most anarchists have also forfeited the search for concrete alternatives to the prevailing economic and social order. As a consequence of having paid little or no attention to problems of organization after an initial upsurge of interest and loose affiliation by some activists, American anarchism has again become largely publicly invisible, except in a few cities. Its press is small or nonexistent, and while anarchists have sustained a number of bookstores that sponsor talks, book-signings, and poetry readings, and some groups and individuals have joined local Social Forums, their activities are mostly reactive.

The Immediate Tasks

A new radical political formation would draw inspiration from several intellectual traditions: marxism, especially its deep respect for theoretical and strategic thinking; utopian thought—both its socialist and communist variants—which holds that the present is the time to consider the "not-yet" of an egalitarian democratic society, and that the movement in its internal life must be prefigurative of the new society; and the anarchist/councilist traditions, which combat bureaucracy within the movement and in society by insisting on "self-activity of the masses"—radical democracy at the workplace and in forms of left organization—rather than on elite vanguards.

And, in contrast to earlier left parties and other political formations that have tacked ecology to their rather traditional programs aimed at more equality, the new political formation would take ecological thought absolutely seriously. In this respect, at a time when scientific consensus has determined that global warming and abrupt climate change threaten to envelop the planet, the political formation would, of necessity, be required to offer a more profound critique of industrial society, not only of its capitalist variant. It would undertake a serious reevaluation of the alleged neutrality of the "forces of production," questioning the conventional view of their unassailable creative and progressive character. This reevaluation entails revisiting the accepted view that science and technology are, unalterably, instances of progressive reason and have, in effect, the force of "nature." Recognizing that science and its entailment, technology, are produced under conditions whereby all knowledge is ineluctably linked to power, both over nature and over humans themselves, and has become an instrument of the reproduction of that power, would be a first step in freeing knowledge from the thrall of capital.

This inquiry is far from being solely academic for, alongside the struggle for equality, it would raise significant questions about the very conditions that have produced our collective version of material comfort. We would recognize the limits of human intervention in nature, especially the rarely assailed notion of capital accumulation as the main form of economic expansion; for example, we would ask whether the vast suburbanization of material space in the United States on the basis of one- and two-family homes and our prevailing car and truck culture are ecologically sustainable, and whether we need to rapidly move away from reliance on nonrenewable sources of energy, and from processed and especially genetically modified organisms in foods. Reducing the carbon dioxide content of the air and maintaining a healthy water table would, perforce, place severe restrictions on real estate development, especially near reservoirs, as well as on the production and distribution of automobiles, trucks, and buses that are equipped with internal combustion engines—even hybrids of electricity and gasoline.

Taken individually, none of these proposals is particularly novel except, perhaps, the one about curtailing suburban development. Yet together they would threaten many interests: a sizeable proportion of large industrial corporations, their investors, and their workers; the bulk of the real estate and construction industries and the powerful unions and their members who rely for their living on new buildings regardless of kind or consequence; and the huge constituency of working- and middle-class people who have been habituated to a carboniferous mode of life—two or three cars, one-family houses that burn oil and use coal-driven electricity, and easy-access shopping at malls whose concentration of autos and trucks generate pollution.

In short, to contemplate waging a large-scale struggle to make the United States ecologically rational goes far beyond the effort to convince Congress and the national political directorate to sign the Kyoto treaty or to agree to standards that reduce CO_2

in the air over time. It requires a major campaign to persuade Americans that, without a radical shift in the ways of life to which we have become accustomed, we are on a slippery slope toward self-annihilation. This is by now the conclusion of 95 percent of climatologists, meteorologists, biologists, and environmental scientists. That the urgency of their appeals has been consistently ignored or, worse, rejected—not only by the Bush administration but also by large segments of the public—reveals the limits of expert influence over the political and economic process. Amazingly, leading oil corporations such as Exxon Mobil and some influential congressional acolytes have brazenly labeled global warming a myth and have succeeded in defeating even the tiny steps represented by the McCain-Lieberman bill toward raising greenhouse emission standards. The key task is to persuade the public—trade unions, civic organizations, and public opinion—of the urgency of major changes in our collective ways of life. To literally save the planet requires more than dire warnings, because sheer inertia and short-term self-interest generally outweigh apocalyptic, long-range thinking. Persuasion would require developing alternatives to the way we currently live and advancing new ways that can be adopted without considerable reduction in living standards. Or, to be more exact, the party's theoretical and practical work would consist in redefining what we mean by a good standard of living, which would raise questions about profligate consumption of goods that emit vast quantities of carbon dioxide or are produced in an ecologically dangerous technological regime. Of course these are not small matters and would involve taking stock of the vast ecological literature, mostly ignored by the entire spectrum of political opinion, including the left.

In this connection the new political formation might revisit some older proposals: partially replacing global and national economies with relatively compact regions capable of producing their own energy, food, manufactured products, and distribution networks; replacing the massive national highway program with mass transit; and implementing the concept of import substitution developed in the 1950s and 1960s by Latin American economist Raoul Prebitsch, among others. In those years Prebitsch advised incipient democratic regimes in Brazil, Chile, and Venezuela to adopt a development strategy alternative to the prevailing policies of encouraging large-scale foreign investment, which is often used to purchase goods from abroad. He urged them to build their economies by sharply curtailing imports, especially of food and fiber, and instead to undertake a government-sponsored agricultural and manufacturing program aimed at internal markets. The notion of smaller-scale economies has been described and advocated by US writers such as Kirkpatrick Sale, E. L. Schumacher, Frances Lappé, Murray Bookchin, and many others. Recent suggestions by the leftward-turning governments in that region indicate that, after more than three decades of being ignored by US-backed authoritarian regimes, Prebitsch's ideas are, indeed, receiving a sympathetic ear. We need to repudiate the air of inevitability that surrounds the term "globalization" and refuse to bow to the criticism that import substitution is a version of "turning inward." Is it time to discuss such ideas as regional economies based, in part, on organic and cooperative farming and locally based production and retail co-ops in the United States? Must we accept the inevitability of the Wal-Martization program of poverty wages that pay for discounts and the growing monopoly of retail chains over available land in metropolitan regions? And what about our own import glut?[6]

Since the left political formation takes the standpoint of the totality, it must be deeply involved in global as well as domestic questions. In this regard, there is a plethora of empirical description of the new configuration of unilateral US global power, but little theorizing concerning imperialism and what some argue is a postimperialist world order. The exception is Hardt and Negri's recent argument that the old Western imperialism has been transformed by postcolonialism; the breakup of the Western alliance; the emergence of Japan, China, and India as world economic powers; and the collapse of the Soviet Union and the Eastern European Communist states.[7] The term "Empire," in their view, signals a new search for "order" by the leading powers, especially the rule of international law. But this formulation preceded the Bush presidency, 9/11, and the Iraq war. While there is a pronounced tendency to claim that a new "imperialism" has appeared on the world stage—particularly in the work of David Harvey, Samir Amin, and Alex Callinicos—these conceptions require more study and debate.[8]

Nor are we engaged in discussion of the status of nation-states in the wake of the increasing integration of transnational corporations and what some have described as a "global" or "meta-state" that appears to ignore or bypass the established authorities. State theory has fallen on hard times perhaps because most analysts, like Hardt and Negri, assume the state is all but eclipsed by globalization, which transcends the limits of the laws of the nation-state. They argue that capital knows no borders but, nonetheless, needs a new world order to regulate its economic, political, and social relations. Others, like Peter Bratsis and Bob Jessop, insist that although the old role of the national state has been weakened by the transnationals—for example, under pressure from the neoliberal doctrine of free trade and free markets, the subtext is that the state must be relieved of its interventionist role in providing a rich safety net for the underlying population—capital still relies on the state for many functions. The state is still called on to bail out corporations considered vital to the economy and to provide the material infrastructure of roads and rail systems. And, under the sign of anti-terrorism, its coercive functions have taken on increased importance: to police domestic and foreign populations, control demonstrations, and incarcerate or bring under control troublesome sections of the population from the subordinated classes—particularly blacks, Latinos, and white working-class people who are convicted of crimes under the law, regardless of whether they are violent or not. In any case the theoretical work of assessing historical and structural economic and political power must not be allowed to degenerate into scholasticism; it needs to be put in the context of the political practices of anti-globalization, labor, and other movements.[9]

Moreover, the Hardt/Negri thesis, deriving largely from the influence of Spinoza and Deleuze, that the designation "multitude" replaces the traditional proletariat and peasantry as new agents of revolt, has received scant attention on the American left for reasons having to do with the relative stalemate that afflicts Western European and US left political and social theory. Elsewhere I have criticized this concept for lacking specificity and direction toward practice and, for this reason, it remains an assertion without much substance. Yet at least Hardt and Negri are thinking, unlike many erstwhile marxists and radical intellectuals who have lapsed into various forms of liberal democratic theory in which class and class politics plays a minor role, or none at all. In reaction, others have insisted upon a slightly updated version of the old marxist faith. It may be broken, but Hardt and Negri argue that it is a sin to try to fix it.[10]

Elsewhere I have advanced the idea that the class divide must be arranged along the axis of power, about which questions of ownership of the means of production are constitutive but mediated. If this conception were to be followed, class and class struggle would designate an emerging alliance among different fractions of the powerless of all social strata, rather than the agency of a single fraction of the disempowered formations. From this perspective, "class" as a concept is reconfigured historically, thus precluding reversion to conceptualizations that refer to eighteenth- and nineteenth-century capitalisms. Class theory would be required to take account of the integration of the state and the economy, which, despite transnationalism, has changed in form but not in its degree of integration. Against a static economic metaphysics, class formation would be regarded as an outcome of struggles rather than a preexisting state of being. These struggles are forged in both defensive and offensive contexts, and whether classes form cannot be predicted in advance. The criterion for class formation, I contend, is that demands succeed in dividing society so that it must address them. The outcome of this process is, short of revolutionary upheaval, nevertheless to change the shape of social relations. Such were the results of the black freedom struggles of the 1950s and early 1960s, the feminist movement of the late 1960s and 1970s, and the ecological movement of the same period. In each instance society was, and in the case of ecology remains, cleaved. Moreover, I argue that the distinction between labor and "new" social movements is historical and does not refer to essential differences in terms of either their respective relation to power or their interests. That in the past labor's compromises with capital (a class that surely knows itself as a class) have tempered class as an emergent formation goes without saying. Given changed circumstances, the past is only one influence on the future. More significant is the ability of political and social actors to invent new alliances and alternatives that point to a different future.[11]

The question of nationalism and its continuing appeal requires considerable theoretical and political discussion. Recall that Lenin, Trotsky, and the Austrian Left Socialist Otto Bauer questioned the traditional marxist antipathy to nationalism in the context of Eastern and Central European countries, where, at the turn of the twentieth century, the revolutionary movement confronted the reality of ethnically based movements for national independence against the Russian and Austro-Hungarian empires. While not ignoring the class contradictions that persist in colonial and semi-colonial societies, they declared that in the subordinated nations of these empires struggles for national self-determination were both progressive and necessary concomitants to the struggle for socialism, and that in the new society the revolutionaries would support the "right of nations to self-determination" even as they argued against separation, and for a federation of nations with the broad framework of a socialist society. "The Union of Soviet Socialist Republics" was a strategic expression of the Bolshevik adherence to the notion of national self-determination; it flagrantly reversed Marx's dictum that the working class has no country. On the other side, Rosa Luxemburg vehemently rejected any capitulation to nationalism, pointing to its corrosive, bourgeois character. She argued that in a world in which imperialism, aided by nationalism, had often divided the working class, Lenin's formulation would only exacerbate the splintering of the world proletariat. Her analysis and prognostication were, unfortunately, richly vindicated at the outbreak of World War I, when, with few exceptions, Socialist parliamentarians from opposing countries took a patriotic stance and voted for war credits. Since the vast majority of soldiers in any war are from working-class backgrounds, her and Lenin's worst fears were realized. Instead of an international working-class opposition to the war, worker was pitted against worker.

In the United States and several Western European countries such as France and the UK, where nationalism's appeal is intimately intertwined with racial subordination and specific forms of class oppression of African, Afro-Caribbean, and (in the United States) African American, Puerto Rican, and Latin American immigrant groups, especially Latinos and East Asians, the left has been deeply divided. While communists, not only members of the Communist Party but trotskyists as well, have largely won the argument on the left that racial oppression cannot be subsumed, as Socialists once did, under class categories without serious mediations—that race is a relatively independent social and political force and must be addressed specifically by radical movements at both the ideological and political levels—the history of the nineteenth and especially the twentieth centuries are marked by a significant rift within black and Latino communities between forces of racial integration and separation. After World War II, armed with an integrationist ideology, the civil rights movement dominated the black freedom movement. Despite its earlier insistence that blacks constituted a special social and political formation within the class structure, the communist left aided its program to secure rights for blacks but also the integration of schools and other public facilities. Its claim was that the legal abolition of segregation and the creation of the legal framework for broad access to education was both a necessary and a sufficient condition of black freedom.

In the 1960s, although the black left fought for liberal democratic advances such as ending forced segregation, winning voting rights, and gaining access to public accommodations, organizations like the Student Nonviolent Coordinating Committee (SNCC) disputed the liberal reliance on legal means to achieve these goals, but not the sufficiency of the goals themselves. In the 1960s, save a small minority of black revolutionaries who questioned integrationist thought (but not the fight for rights), the debate was joined over the alternative tactics of direct action and bringing the fight mainly to courts and to Congress. Thus the decision by the NAACP to pursue a Supreme Court decision in *Brown v Board of Education* to declare that racial integration was the only legitimate way to guarantee blacks equal protection under the constitution, thereby overturning its 1896 decision in *Plessy v Ferguson* that a policy of separate but equal facilities was constitutional. But there were influential, if somewhat marginalized, voices of dissent.

From the writings of Alexander Crummell and Martin Delany in the nineteenth century to the Garveyites and Muslims, which were twentieth-century social movements, the appeal of cultural nationalism to all classes of blacks has waxed and waned but remains an underlying theme of African-American and African-Caribbean politics and culture. Even W.E.B. Dubois, whose writings may be considered the most influential in the camp of racial integration, arrived at the conclusion in his middle and twilight years that integrationalist ideology may have surrendered too much black autonomy. To be sure, the ambivalent outcome of *Brown* is still felt. Although blacks have gained access to formerly all-white institutions of higher education, and found places within managerial ranks in the private and public sectors, the past half-century has witnessed the enfeeblement of traditional black institutions in both grade school and higher education. Today once-proud black colleges struggle to survive. Cultural nationalism has a claim in black neighborhoods and professional communities precisely because of the failure of integration, the severe blows that have been absorbed in the past quarter-century by affirmative action programs, and, especially, the success of capital to create an expanded black middle class while leaving the black working class behind to suffer the effects of deindustrialization, mass unemployment, particularly among black men, and, for a rising fraction, hunger. As national retail food chains penetrate black communities, local merchants, white as well as black, are crowded out. And the absence of a vigorous small-business class often leads to the hollowing out of neighborhood culture, which traditionally has been a source of solidarity. Recall the barber shop, the shoe repair shop, the neighborhood bar, and the grocery store as places where people congregate, pass the time of day, and often discuss politics. These are really the working-class and middle-class public spheres of black and Latino neighborhoods. Will they become objects of art, or museum pieces? Or is there still a chance for their revival and survival?

In the wake of these developments, lacking a sophisticated effort to articulate the common links of the exploited and oppressed with the precarious position of a black middle class which, like the new middle class generally, is beginning to slide downward, we can expect nationalism to revive and even flourish. What would a new left political formation say to these developments? What are the consequences of the refusal of the civil rights establishment to fight for black economic development in rural and urban communities as a partial solution to unemployment and underemployment, and to the growing incursion of monopolistic retailers? While collaborating with large corporations and local and state governments on the argument that they are making room for more black managers, administrators, and scientific and technical professionals, the NAACP, many church leaders, and the Urban League have all but abandoned the black working class. When and where can we expect efforts to organize the black unemployed to demand jobs or income? What role should the labor movement play in the organization of the jobless in general and the African American unemployed in particular? The proposal for an effort to create jobs on the basis of locally based co-ops and neighborhood-sponsored small business, as well as to make demands on the local and national government for work projects (community services as well as construction), needs to be discussed and debated.

In the 1930s Communists and other left organizations paid particular attention to organizing for jobs and income, and against evictions, in black communities throughout the country. In the 1960s and 1970s organizations such as Harlem Fight Back and similar groups in Chicago and Los Angeles fought to gain entrance by blacks into well-paid union construction jobs. Harlem Fight Back still exists, but there is virtually no organized force to take up cudgels to combat poverty, unemployment, and underemployment in a new and creative way—and one cannot expect the traditional liberal civil rights organizations to take the lead. If not them, who will?

What Will the Party Look Like?

We have had two major articulations in the history of the left: parties that have settled for strategies of incremental reform and for becoming institutions of government within the existing capitalist system and parties that announce their revolutionary character. That is, they declare that their ultimate goal is to lead wide sections of the exploited and oppressed to capture state power in order to abolish private property in the means of material production, and to dismantle the repressive machinery of the capitalist state. Until World War I, whatever their current struggles for reform, while arguing that a "peaceful transition" to socialism was desirable and even possible, socialist revolutionaries expected that the use of force would likely be necessary to achieve these goals because, in most cases, capital would not simply surrender power through the electoral process and other peaceful means without a fight. The experiences that people underwent during the Russian revolutions of 1905 when the tsar brutally assaulted peaceful demonstrators pleading for bread—and in 1917 when the so-called White armies (elements of the Tsarist regime and twenty-one foreign armies, including that of the United States) conducted armed combat against the new Soviet society—seemed to vindicate this perspective. Beginning in the 1920s Communists and socialists assumed the mantle of the opposition to authoritarian and liberal bourgeois regimes but, with few exceptions, retained the rhetoric of revolution without engaging in a concrete practice that fulfilled this aspiration. Apart from their differences regarding the Soviet Union and questions of how to fight fascism and imperialism, the two main socialist tendencies defined their "socialism" in terms of a program of limited nationalization of the main means of production, universal decommodified health care, and a state pension system—the latter two of which, unlike in the United States, are based on citizenship rather than on employment. For example, British Labor's nationalization of the mines and the steel industry after taking governmental power in 1945 as well as its introduction of a national health scheme, and of a comprehensive social welfare system, have remained to this day its main accomplishments. These measures were termed "democratic" socialism to distinguish the reformist parties from the Soviet model of the now-abandoned revolutionary dictatorship by the party and a state bureaucracy.

Except for colonial and postcolonial societies, which conducted a series of post–World War II nationalist revolutionary uprisings, in the West we are living in the aftermath of this sea change in left politics of more than eighty years. European countries where the postwar compromise with capital was in full effect (the left pledged to respect the processes of liberal democratic capitalism and to not engage in revolution, if the bourgeoisie conceded an extensive welfare state) have experienced deterioration in the welfare state and a gradual shift to authoritarian state rule especially, but not exclusively, against immigrants. In this respect, recall the content of the Patriot Act and the Bush administration's interpretation that it possesses constitutional power to spy on American citizens without a court-issued warrant. Americans struggle to achieve some of these reforms in the wake of the collapse of private pension systems and privatized health insurance. (In the last decade the proportion of corporations sponsoring health and pension programs has declined from 80 percent to 60 percent; millions lack pension plans supplementary to Social Security; and the number of health-uninsured has skyrocketed to nearly 50 million, including millions of children.) Of course, in the wake of neoliberalism's ideological triumph, no European Social-Democratic government has undertaken new nationalization

programs in decades. On the contrary, some formerly national-
ized industries have been privatized, notably in France.

With the end of "really existing" Eastern European socialism
under Communist auspices, one of the untold stories of the
past two decades has been the virtual extinction of Western
social democracy, even in its whittled-down mode. Ironically, as
despised as was the authoritarian Soviet regime by democratic
forces and by its own people, one cannot avoid ascribing the
utter triumph of neoliberal ideology in part to the collapse of
the Soviet Union. For despite its odious features, it represented
a putative alternative to the most callous features of capitalism and stood as a barrier to a frontal assault on the welfare
state. For hundreds of millions of people in the developing
world, even as the Soviet regime began to disintegrate in the
1970s and 1980s it was the closest approximation of a practical utopia, at least with respect to issues of equality, universal
health care, public education, and economic security. After its
expiration in 1991, social democracy and its US variant, modern liberalism, all but capitulated to the neoliberals. The claim
by neoconservatives that America was the world's democratic
guardian was largely uncontested in the public sphere. In this
regard the signal consequence of the Bush administration's
brutal military intervention in Iraq, and its refusal to honor
a host of humanistic global treaties, was to shatter America's
reputation as a beacon of hope. The widespread hatred of
American transnational capitalism has opened the gates to a
new conception of a utopian future free of its Soviet variant,
but also of the market utopianism advanced by writers like
Francis Fukuyama and Milton Friedman.[12]

A new left party confronts the question: How to distinguish
itself from the legacies of these collapsed traditions? Throughout
this book I have used the term "radical" to connote a party that
defines itself in terms of ideas that point in the direction of social
transformation. As I have argued, the term "revolutionary" has
come to signify not only intention but possibility. It expresses
the imminence of fundamental social change and a change of
strategy from the struggle for reforms within the existing setup
to the struggle about power. But it must be accompanied by
conceptions of what the nature of the new society will be. In its
traditional form it implies that the proletariat "seizes" and retains
state power until the defeat of the counterrevolutionary forces

of the right and of capital. Thus the revolutionary dictatorship continues for an indeterminate period, and in the actual history of those parties influenced by Lenin's program, individual dissent and oppositional forces outside of as well as within the revolutionary movement are more or less ruthlessly suppressed. These betrayals of the emancipatory project may not have been an inevitable outcome of the difficulties of consolidating state power under conditions of relative backwardness and of military and political isolation, but the practices of the Russians and the Chinese revolutions, in particular, have had the effect of discrediting the revolutionary tradition, save its underlying impulse. But there is a more salient reason to avoid the term "revolution" at this historical moment. If we agree that we live in nonrevolutionary times, to proclaim the movement's revolutionary character condemns the party to sectarian pretense.

The term "radical" suspends and would not renounce the revolutionary goal, but only in practical terms. The concept and its consequences for issues of power, the state, and the problem of force would remain topics of active discussion and political education in the radical party. In the nations of Latin America where parties and movements are seeking, in various degrees, to bring about social change, marxists, ecologists, and other leftists have generally avoided characterizing the movement as revolutionary. Venezuela's president Hugo Chavez uses the term to describe what would otherwise be understood as radical reform. His government has proposed to take over abandoned factories and other workplaces and return them to the workers who would operate them as cooperatives within a market system. And his government has undertaken a limited economic redistribution program to assist the poorest sections of the population in raising its living standards. By the standards of the Russian, Chinese, and Cuban revolutions, these are modest measures; nonetheless, they are radical insofar as they challenge the sanctity of private property and the prerogatives of capitalist wealth for the first time in decades and open up new possibilities for popular democratic power. Similarly, in the United States, legal and political challenges to the process of Wal-Martization of the suburban and urban landscape, squatters in the cities who occupy vacant houses, and the experiments in communal living, community gardens, and cooperative farming that have appeared periodically tacitly reject the idea that in the end corporate capitalism and its huge resources unreservedly rule.

"Radical" means that the party refuses to accept the clientization of workers and the poor, in unions as well as in the delivery of social services. And train and bus riders are not "customers" of public transportation, as Amtrak and municipal transportation authorities call them. They are the owners of these services, and the bureaucracy and managers who operate them are public servants and should be accountable not just as participants in ritual public hearings but as members of elected citizen boards. "Radical" is a demand for the selfmanagement of the institutions of everyday life. In this regard, while contesting seats in legislative institutions, radicals expose their undemocratic nature and propose alternative modes of governance that empower the people to directly make crucial workplace and neighborhood decisions. Here "radical" means proposing for the United States a comprehensive system of proportional representation and instant runoff voting when none of the candidates for public office receives a majority of the vote. "Radical" means opposing a labor bureaucracy that does not "give a rat's ass" about union democracy. "Radical" signifies that a revived health care and pension system would be based on citizenship rather than on employment and would conduct a struggle to enable the undocumented to become citizens for the purposes of social benefits, but also to participate in elections, at least at the local level before citizenship certification. And the party would oppose all attempts to restrict immigration by quotas, even as it recognizes that, except for political refugees, the movement of large numbers of people to developed societies and to the cities of developing societies is a symptom of what Pierre Bourdieu has called "the tyranny of the market." In the developing world this is a consequence of, among other causes, the tyranny of international financial institutions that force heavy debt and mass unemployment on these societies. The ultimate "solution" to immigration is the transformation of the centuries of dependency and oppression these societies have suffered under the yoke of colonial and neocolonial rule. So we will find ways to express solidarity with efforts by left democratic movements everywhere to overcome the widening gap between rich and poor, to create new forms of radical democracy, and to resolutely oppose efforts by the US

government and its right-wing allies to subvert leftist governments and movements for equality and democracy.[13]

"Radical" is a movement for social and economic equality in
employment, education, housing, and other everyday needs.
But it also opposes meeting this goal on the basis of bureaucratic domination. So, just as the party fights for a democratic,
self-managed workplace, it fights for the radical democratiza-
tion of public services. Among them, education plays a crucial
role. We have witnessed a long history of efforts by parents,
teachers, and neighborhood residents to make public schools
responsive to children's needs for learning. These have often
been thwarted by politicians, conservative ideologues, and,
in some large cities, such as New York, by a defensive teachers' union leadership that, in the past, frequently preferred to
deal with an entrenched school bureaucracy rather than the
neighborhood's residents. Recently the union has softened its
stand, but it has never declared itself a proponent of democratic
and inclusive school governance. In this respect the example of
more than 100 small schools that have been established during the past fifteen years points to some change. Some of these
were organized by a coalition of parents and teachers. Most,
however, are the product of a top-down program sponsored by
the school chancellor and have many of the earmarks of the
failed larger schools. They must meet the draconian requirement of standardized tests in all of the lower grades and in
the high schools. Thus there is little room for curriculum or
pedagogic innovation. Since teachers are held responsible for
results, they tend to "teach to the test"—and very little learning, in the true sense of the term, takes place.

In nearly every American city and suburb, this regime has
become the rule; exceptions are confined to schools with
largely middle-class student populations. In many instances,
working-class kids, many of whom are black, Latino, Arab,
and Asian, are subject to strict discipline, including expul-
sions for various infractions of the rules. Following the lead
of liberal as well as conservative social science, the authorities argue that these kids need such a regime because their
homes and neighborhoods are chaotic. Needless to say, the
presupposition of social disorganization among poor children
of color as a foundation for educational policy—especially as
it relates to the differential treatment of kids with respect to

curriculum, pedagogy, and discipline—is subject to dispute. While some intellectuals in education schools and the liberal arts institutions have criticized "No Child Left Behind," the Bush administration's legislative codification of this approach, and parents and politicians in affluent districts have openly defied the unfunded mandates to implement testing without end, there is very little discourse about alternative conceptions or pedagogic innovation in the working-class districts. Among the reasons for the lack of protest, or even debate, is that an important fraction of socially conservative liberal, black, and Latino educators has supported the notion that poor kids need "structure" and discipline that is lacking in the rest of their lives. I would argue that this question needs urgent attention by a radical democratic left that will not concede the schools to the social authoritarians.

Finally, "radical" means a determined effort to go beyond capitalism to seek alternatives to the authoritarianism of the political and economic system, and to create a democratic, self-managed workplace and everyday life. Proposals offered by Michael Albert, Gar Alperovitz, and Seymour Melman are instances of practical alternatives to capitalism that deserve serious scrutiny for the project of encouraging a new radical imagination. Each argues that the unprecedented wealth of US society makes possible the realization of what may be called a practical utopia. Each opposes the view that what is, is eternal. Each asks us to follow this country's hallowed practice of reinvention, not only of the self but of the main institutions of society.[14]

Problems of Party Organization

I have argued throughout this book that without a political organization that unifies theory and practice, we cannot thwart, let alone reverse, what is fast becoming an authoritarian political regime and a seriously fragmented and defeated opposition. But the organization cannot be left to a wish list of ideological and programmatic ideas. What follows is a series of concrete suggestions, each of which needs to be adapted to the outcome of discussion and debate.

Like any other political party, the radical party or political association would be based on local units. Some of these locals would be organized geographically—in towns, counties, cities, and regions. They might address issues such as land use (especially development), housing, recreation, industrial and commercial facilities, schools, health, and other questions of vital concern to their neighborhoods or areas. In the first place, outside the electoral field they would participate in campaigns to fulfill popular needs and to oppose commercial efforts to appropriate local land and other resources that are better used to meet public needs by producing public goods. As workers and parents, they would participate in struggles to make workplaces and schools the centers of democratic life. And the local would be a site for conducting struggles against transnational corporations, against the war machine, and for solidarity with various workers and other popular struggles in other parts of the United States as well as in other countries and on other continents.

The local might participate in elections, including running candidates under their own banner. The question of the relation of the party to other parties depends on conditions of time and place. However, I would argue against permanent alliances with local organizations of the two major parties. This would not preclude backing individual candidates on the basis of their positions on specific issues during a particular election campaign. Given the reluctance of the Democrats to oppose commercial development at the expense of better land uses, and their support for business interests, the radical party may take the lead in helping to form a local independent electoral vehicle to address local issues together with other movements. And the local might undertake to start or support efforts to organize new cooperatives, energy initiatives, radical schools for adults and children (a left Sunday school, as was common at the turn of the twentieth century comes to mind), summer camps, and cultural activities such as choruses, film and book clubs, and drama groups.

The struggle for a democratic workplace, including rank-and-file control of unions, requires that some locals would be located in industries and occupations, for which the underlying units are the factory or industry, the hospital or regional health sector, the school system, the university, the town, county and city government employees, and the large retail or administrative establishment. In the case of occupations—social workers, physicians, and nurses, scientists and engineers, writers, musicians and film makers, visual artists and media workers, many of whom would be in scientific and technical occupations who have been cast in the role of "consultants" because they cannot find real jobs and, of course the long-term unemployed, one of the most neglected fractions of the disempowered class—the political formation would be required to invent novel forms of organization that correspond to the specificity of the conditions of these occupational groups. These groups would be encouraged to become active in their unions and professional associations, to help form caucuses where the leadership is undemocratic and unresponsive to rank-and-file needs. But wherever possible these activities would be a collective rather than an individual responsibility. Whether on a geographic, sectoral, or occupational basis, locals would select delegates to coordinating bodies (e.g., various caucuses and individual activists working in a local or regional labor movement, a local of party members working as teachers or administrative workers in a town or city board of education, or a local of creative artists in a large or medium sized city). But eventually there would also be a need for city, county, or state organizations to organize and coordinate campaigns that go beyond the purview of locals. These bodies would consist of delegated representatives of the local bodies. Whether they would employ full-time organizers cannot be decided in advance.

If the party is not chiefly an electoral vehicle but seeks to mediate specific struggles and sectors with "history," its intellectual tasks—including education, maintaining its own media and other means to influence mainstream and alternative media, and creating "think tanks" to provide systematic knowledge to the public and its affiliates—take on an importance that is equal to its participation in everyday struggles. The political formation would, of necessity, publish journals and a discussion bulletin that provides the opportunity for the membership as a whole to debate fundamental theoretical questions such as the state and its role, new classes, race and gender configurations, science, technology and power, as well as to join a forum for discussion of immediate strategic questions. These groups might organize their own locals or branches of a city or county organization, or affiliate with a national body devoted to addressing sectoral issues, depending on the circumstances. But the objective is to encourage all members to join and participate in the work of collectivities, which, in turn, have a structured voice in the decisions taken by the party. Thus the concept of the neutered "staff" is rejected.

In the beginning, the political formation would not be a "mass" organization. Such an organization presupposes a long period of development, both of the political formation and of its constituents. Mass parties come into existence when tens or hundreds of thousands share a body of rich experience of struggle and of cultural formation. Absent this historical experience the mass organization tends to reproduce some of the conditions of liberal groups. By the term "mass" I mean an organization with members who are not activists and who affiliate only because they agree, in a general sense, with its theoretical and political orientation. They attend meetings and might contribute money but are not part of the process of fleshing out the theoretical and practical perspectives of the movement. However, given the history of the left over the last half-century, it would be foolish to expect that, because a person has been a union or community organizer, or an activist in the anti-war or social movements, they can join a radical political formation without participating in discussions and study circles that are dedicated to fleshing out what this might mean for their own political practice. Thus the recruitment of cadres entails undertaking a significant internal education program.

Clearly, the center takes on the tasks that cannot be undertaken by locals: a clear and effective response to national and international events and its dissemination to members and to the media; national and regional schools for activists; and publications, national communications, international contacts, and organizing new locals in industries as well as geographic areas. The national committee must be elected from among the lower bodies so that its decisions reflect the grassroots of the movement and its practices as much as the ideological and political perspectives of the center. The question of whether these committees are elected by national and regional conventions or by referendum of the entire membership cannot be decided in advance. The general election is usually held to be more democratic—and, indeed, in the history of liberal democratic regimes and union politics, insurgents have pressed for this form on the ground that conventions are more easily controlled from a self-perpetuating center. However, it is arguable that political formations are better off with conventions than with general elections. Parties are not identical to mass politics. If the political formation has a highly conscious and active membership, delegates are likely to reflect the views of the active locals. If the convention is preceded by a rich discussion of the issues and permits different positions to be freely articulated, on the basis of broad participation from the membership both in the discussion bulletin(s) and in the locals, prior to the selection of delegates, these safeguards might prove as democratic as, if not more democratic than, individuals voting and sending their ballots in. To guard against bureaucratization, members of the central or national committee must be subject to recall at any time by petition of a relatively significant fraction of the membership or the body from which they have been delegated.

How to address issues that include but transcend the limits of local action? These include education, health, the labor movement, transportation, energy, the status of women and immigrants, and the fundamental economic, political, and social freedoms of blacks and other oppressed sections of the population. And beyond its own media, the political formation would form a commission that would offer regular analysis, and make proposals to democratize mainstream and alternative media institutions.

There are a fair number of national independent committees, coalitions, and professionalized advocacy groups that address specific domains. The party would not attempt to supercede or compete with these in any way. In fact, if successful, many of the leading actors within them would be party members and members of the commissions. But there are issues that left-liberal groups do not usually address. These concern not the proposals to improve services on the basis of current power arrangements but, rather, the burning questions associated with a radical democratic transformation of these power arrangements. Since a radical political formation would always make the connections between otherwise fragmented sectoral struggles and the totality, our "grand narratives" would function not to stifle innovation and autonomy but to help encourage the formation of the alliances that need to be built in order to win on any front.

On the premise that a movement grows not only in number but also in quality, largely as a function of the vitality of its links with youth, the radical party would encourage the formation of youth and student organizations with close relationships to it. But history has some lessons to teach. It may be better to encourage these organizations to remain autonomous. Arguably, SDS was the closest intellectual and organizational expression of a generation. By "generation" I mean Karl Mannheim's definition of the term: a cohort of people born and raised in the same era who come to share a set of values and a worldview that expresses itself in political and chiefly in cultural terms in ways that influence and change the prevailing modes of life. Thus a generation is not simply a cohort that shares common links of birth and maturity. We cannot predict that such a generation will emerge in the context of the development of a new New Left; but in order to encourage it, the radical party would be well advised to respect its autonomy and to rely on persuasion rather than command or intimidation to come to political agreement.

If there develops in the early years of this new century a clamor to organize a radical political formation, and if, on a related front, the more radical contingents of the Greens, the Labor Party, and other left organizations try to form a new electoral vehicle to oppose the two-party monopoly, we can expect to hear echoes of earlier objections. As occurred during the 2000 presidential campaign of Ralph Nader, the left, once again, will be accused of splitting the "progressive forces." The left-liberal establishment, which has shown a disturbing predisposition to vehemently attack its left even as it remains supine as the center regularly betrays it, will most likely once again close ranks to vilify and otherwise discredit any radical democratic movement that threatens its futile efforts to nudge the Democrats leftward. If any have learned the lessons of 2000 let alone the 1960s, we simply cannot afford to acquiesce to the backtracking of these forces. The stakes are too high. Given their sorry record, the tried-and-true methods of disrupting a radical turn among the young and veteran political activists and intellectuals, this might be the moment when their interventions will prove futile. For what is at stake in the formation of a new radical party that reaches across national borders is the future of humankind, even of the planet.

Notes

1. "A Useless Strike," *New York Times* Editorial, December 27, 2005.

2. Jim Hightower, "Christmas Message," *Alternet,* December 23, 2005.

3. Thomas Frank, *What's the Matter with Kansas?* (New York: Metropolitan Books, 2004).

4. Lawrence Goodwyn, *Democratic Promise: The Populist Moment* (New York: Oxford University Press, 1976).

5. Temporary National Economic Committee, *Report on Economic Concentration* (Washington, DC: United States Government Printing Office, 1937); Lloyd Gardner, *Economic Aspects of New Deal Diplomacy* (Madison: University of Wisconsin Press, 1970).

6. Raul Prebitsch, "Dependence, Development and Interdependence," in Arthur Lewis et al., eds., *Papers of a Conference on the Current State of Economics* (Oxford: Blackwell, 1986).

7. Michael Hardt and Tony Negri, *Empire* (Cambridge, MA: Harvard University Press, 2000).

8. David Harvey, *The New Imperialism* (Oxford/New York: Oxford University Press, 2003); Samir Amin, *Accumulation on a World Scale* (New York: Monthly Review Press, 1975); Alex Callinicos, *The New Imperialism* (London: Pluto Press, 1996).

9. Peter Bratsis, "Unthinking the State: Reification, Ideology and the State," and Bob Jessop, "Globalization and the National State," in Stanley Aronowitz and Peter Bratsis, eds., *Paradigm Lost: State Theory Reconsidered* (Minneapolis: University of Minnesota Press, 2002).

10. Michael Hardt and Tony Negri, *Multitude* (New York: Penguin Books, 2004).

11. Stanley Aronowitz, *How Class Works* (New Haven: Yale University Press, 2003).

12. Francis Fukuyama, *The End of History and the Last Man* (New York: Free Press,1989); Milton Friedman, *Capitalism and Freedom* (Chicago: University Chicago Press, 1961).

13. Pierre Bourdieu, *Against the Tyranny of the Market: Fighting Back* (New York: New Press, 1999).

14. Michael Albert, *Paracon: Life After Capitalism* (London: Verso, 2003); Gar Alperovitz, *America Beyond Capitalism: Reclaiming Our Wealth, Our Liberty and Our Democracy* (New York: John Wiley and Sons, 2005); Seymour Melman, *After Capitalism: From Managerialism to Workplace Democracy* (New York: Alfred A. Knopf, 2001).

◆

6

Alternatives to Market Capitalism

The Revival of Liberal Political Philosophy

Since the collapse of the Soviet Union and its Eastern European client states in 1991, the formation and maintenance of liberal democratic state institutions has become normative in virtually every corner of the world. Of the major powers only China remains openly authoritarian, and those African and Asian states that continue to resist the transition to a version of Western liberal democracy (i.e., parliamentary governance and "free" elections) risk courting pariah status. Of course free specch is quite another matter: In most countries the press remains free for those who own one; in the United States and elsewhere citizens are routinely subject to surveillance and sometimes arrested by intelligence agencies; opposition parties and dissident organizations are harassed, their offices occasionally raided or pilfered of vital documents. In sum, it is enough for a political regime to be elected by a version of popular mandate to be considered legitimate by the United States and other leading powers.

The almost universal demand for "democracy" combined with the end, in practical terms at least, of the socialist project has resulted in the revival of the dominant version of liberal political philosophy. The main idea in this tradition, which stretches back to the dawn of the bourgeois era in the seventeenth century, is the autonomy of the political and the urgency

199

of state sovereignty—that is, its freedom from influence, let alone reliance, on the practices of civil society (the economy) and of the family. Even though many writers still claim lineage to Aristotle's *Politics,* they conveniently forget that the presupposition of his conception of citizenship is that politics can be a vocation only for those freed from the burdens of labor. Yet, the Greek state and its decision-making citizenry stand on the shoulders of women, artisans, and slaves who run the household, which, in Aristotle's notion, includes the entire sphere of the production and satisfaction of fundamental material needs. Therefore, the social is the precondition but can in no way be a component of political decision-making.

From Hobbes to Hegel the spheres of family and "civil society" (commerce) are viewed as too tumultuous, too subject to perennial conflict, to secure social peace. For traditional political philosophy these spheres must surrender a significant portion of their autonomy to the state, lest society itself descend to the war of all against all. Communitarians like Alisdair McIntyre urge us to bestow sovereignty on "communities" in which the state plays a steadily diminished role. Hannah Arendt did not subscribe to Hobbes's doctrine but regarded the realm of the social, especially production and consumption—indeed, all material relations—as the fulfillment of functions that humans share with other animals. In contrast, politics is potentially a creative practice that, together with art, meets the standard of the truly human. Consequently, the human condition is admirably fulfilled when politics—that is, public life—rigorously separates itself from the private or social spheres.[1]

At the same time, in contradistinction to this precept, in the interest of preserving the prerogatives of the individual over his possessions nearly all of contemporary political philosophy agrees with its bourgeois antecedents that there must be a strict separation of the private and the public. Of course, among the motivations for this position is the pervasive fear of the state shared by activists, commentators, and theorists; in order to preserve individual liberties, the scope of state action in the political sphere must be severely restricted to issues of public safety and national security. Each term can be interpreted to mean the executive's right to intervene when these are threatened. Political philosophers are aware that some liberties may be suspended in the face of security threats, but they are loathe to surrender individual freedom except under dire circumstances. In this vein many liberals as well as conservatives argue that the property owner must be free to dispose of her or his possessions, to enter into contracts with other property owners—including owners of labor power—without interference from the state. Recall that Locke argued that property ownership should be restricted to the outcomes of a person's own labor. But this idea was renounced by Locke himself in the wake of the transition from predominantly artisanal labor to manufacturing. Hiring wage labor became legitimate in his discourse as property ownership was endowed with the powers to command another's labor, under the doctrine that free labor could also dispose of its property for a limited period of time during which the worker forfeited her or his rights except to agree to certain terms and conditions of employment, including hours of labor and quantity of wages. And as we have learned from recent experience, in the public interest, under the rules of eminent domain the state reserves the right to violate private property rights, with reasonable compensation, even when it takes property from one owner and transfers it to another rather than reserving the property as a public good.[2]

The struggle of labor to seek, in turn, factory health and safety conditions, restriction or abolition of child labor, and legislation limiting hours of labor was universally viewed by owners of capital as an outright abrogation of their fundamental rights. That these demands languished in legislatures for centuries signified the power of capital over the political process. More to the point, historical experience challenged the prevailing view of the autonomy of politics and the institutions of the state in capitalist states. In time, many theorists recognized that in the industrializing era politics and economics had become intertwined. Deploring the incursion of institutions of civil society over politics, some, such as Arendt, called for the return of political activity to the Aristotelian model whereby politics is freed from its dependence or influence on the social realm. As we saw in Chapter 1, others, such as John Rawls, recognizing the salience of the social, sought "redistributive justice" through moderate state intervention while refusing to challenge the system of private ownership of the means of material production to achieve more equality.[3]

It may be argued that social theory began in the eighteenth century with Vico and Rousseau, but it certainly attained a new stature in Hegel's *Phenomenology of the Spirit,* where the category of labor is elevated to primacy in the unfolding of the dialectic. Refusing what he understood as Hegel's retreat from his own explication of the logic of domination, in which labor achieves self-consciousness of her or his own subjugation but cannot advance to the realm of freedom, Marx argued for the primacy of the social, and for the transformation of social relations in the quest for liberation from the thrall of alienated labor, the heart of class exploitation. In opposition to Hegel's contention that the state is constituted to overcome the contradictions of the family and civil society, he insisted that the state is an executive of the ruling (capitalist) class, and that neither the state and its institutions nor political parties could achieve independence from social or class relations (not "economics," as the vulgar interpretation would have it). The spheres of production and consumption are intertwined with political power (as Karl Polanyi puts it, the market has never been free of the interventions of the state since capital cannot survive on its own). Thus the state was no mere "nightwatchman" to protect property but was routinely mobilized, albeit indirectly, by capital and its minions, to intervene in the economy in forms such as provision of the means of communications such as roads, railways, and, in modern times, access to airwaves and to virtual space. However, the idea of the state's relative autonomy remains one of capital's valuable ideological assets. The discourse of its neutrality with respect to the capital-labor relation led to the widespread belief that when labor faced an impasse on the shop or office floor, as it inevitably did, and when conflicts occurred within the family and among neighbors sharing geographic space, the mechanisms of lawsuits and arbitration (both of which were mediated by the state) might secure individuals a measure of justice. This doctrine of the equanimity of law and the apparatuses of justice remains a cultural as well as political influence over the underlying population. It has also served to inhibit and delegitimize collective action in the realms of social life. Or, to be more exact, in the absence of a culture of collective action, individual recourse to courts and the law becomes a substitute. In recent years this avenue for justice has gradually been narrowed as leading sectors of business have petitioned Congress and the courts to reduce citizens' ability to bring certain lawsuits and juries' ability to grant large awards to complainants.[4]

The rise of social theory was accompanied by and, in a certain sense, an expression of the growing recognition by workers as well as philosophers during the eighteenth and nineteenth centuries that state institutions, including those of representative democracy, barely scratch the surface of freedom. Regardless of the success of reform movements during the late nineteenth and first half of the twentieth centuries in prompting legislatures to pass bills to ameliorate the terms and conditions of employment and extending free speech and the right to self-organization to workers, liberal democratic governments will, only under the duress of wars, depressions, and mass working-class mobilization, take possession of the privately owned means of production. But if nationalization is a necessary condition of change, it has proven countless times not to be the sufficient condition. Public ownership that does not, in itself, change forms of authority in the workplace, nor alter the rule of market relations over production and consumption, can result in the extension, rather than the rescinding, of tyranny. As long as the arbitrary authority of management remains unchallenged from labor's standpoint, state ownership has generally meant exchanging one group of masters for another. As we have seen, workers' movements have recently turned to worker-owned cooperatives to address problems of unemployment resulting from plant migration and to enlist the state, where possible, to ratify rather than supervise their initiatives.

Yet, recognizing that liberal democracy stops at the factory and office doors, since the end of World War II labor and socialist movements in Western Europe have fought and, in some countries, won a measure of industrial or workplace democracy. Whether the enterprise is state-owned or in private hands, the law of labor relations in Germany and France, for example, limits the rights of capital to hire and fire at will, manages the workplace unilaterally, and establishes works councils that bargain with employers. Nor can the employer and its managerial staff unilaterally direct the workforce with respect to issues of job assignment, layoffs, and plant closings. Indeed, during the spring of 2006, when the conservative government of Jacques Chirac of France attempted to abrogate the law protecting employment by rescinding these protections for workers and allowing an employer to fire a worker under the age of 26 at will, the government was met with mass protests that threatened the survival of the prime minister and potentially the government itself. These hard-won constraints on employers' prerogatives have in recent years invoked the wrath of neoliberal economists and policy-makers who argue that such "arcane" restrictions, introduced as part of a post–World War II compromise between capital and labor, thwart economic growth and maintain high unemployment rates. They point to the United States as a shining example of relatively unrestricted free market economics—"relatively" unrestricted because, until about 1980, the manufacturing workplace, especially in basic industries, was largely subject to worker protections afforded by collective bargaining agreements. In contrast to Western Europe, in the United States the state intervenes, putatively, to protect the rights to organize and to enter into collective agreements, but these rights are enjoyed only by those workers whose union has been certified as a bargaining agent. Similarly, in contrast to most of Europe where the provisions of social welfare are citizen based, in the United States all benefits, except for the pitiful income-maintenance programs for the chronically jobless, are workplace based. In nonunion enterprises, which now constitute 90 percent of the private-sector workforce, only racial discrimination, some types of disability discrimination, and sex discrimination are subject to the rule of federal law. Beyond that, employers are free to hire and fire or otherwise discipline any employee without the employee's recourse to the courts or to government protections.

In the American democratic tradition the political system has disdained legislative mandates that would provide workplace democracy. During the unionization era, workers exercised considerable powers at the workplace without the aid of legislation or administrative agencies. In some industries the right of employers to fire a worker was severely limited by collective agreements that codified shop-floor workers' activity, including job actions and short-term protests. Although taylorism and fordism were introduced as management's tool to reduce workers' power, these methods were not entirely effective. It was not always the result of formal agreements with employers that workers were able to determine the pace of work, modify the technologies to their requirements, alter work methods to make the job easier, and successfully restrict management's right to unilaterally direct the work forces and completely dominate the labor process. During working hours, labor tends to invent methods of job performance that suit it, both cooperatively and individually. While the assembly-line is harder to alter, machine labor, although subject to taylorist segmentation, often lends itself to shop-floor innovation because there is no automatic belt governing the production process. And, historically, workers have ably resisted management's efforts at speed-up by establishing informal quotas, which may or may not find their way into negotiated work rules. Yet forms of resistance become a key impetus for the introduction of labor-destroying technologies whose logic is to disrupt traditional intraworker arrangements, as well as to reduce or eliminate labor entirely. But workers' control on the shop floor was an effect of labor's solidarity and willingness to take direct action.

The shredding of the social welfare state in the United States was preceded by the erosion of historic legislation that purportedly guaranteed workers' rights. As early as 1939 the Supreme Court ruled that factory occupations to seek union recognition were illegal. And the courts recognized employers' "free speech" to oppose union organization, even though the stated purpose of the law was to facilitate workers' ability to form unions "of their own choosing" free of employer interference. These and other court decisions were codified in the Taft-Hartley amendments to the labor relations law in 1947 following the most widespread strike activity in American history. But the amendments further restricted labor's rights by banning sympathy strikes, secondary boycotts, and Communists from holding union office.

The Reagan revolution and its aftermath have witnessed a dramatic transfer of powers; labor is rapidly losing even the limited power in the workplace that it painfully sought and won in more than a century of struggle. For the past quarter-century the United States has become the model for emulation by other capitalist states. After President Ronald Reagan fired 11,000 air traffic controllers for daring to disobey a federal law prohibiting strikes by public employees, and the AFL-CIO leadership failed to respond with large-scale strikes and demonstrations, emboldened employers began an unrelenting campaign, still in progress, to cut unions down to size and restore their virtually unchallenged reign over the workplace. At the beginning of this drive in 1981, unions still represented 25 percent of the workforce—down from 35 percent in 1953 but still potent in all but a handful of basic industries.

Today unions represent less than 10 percent of the private-sector workforce. And as we have seen, the citadel of industrial unionism, the United Auto Workers, is facing erosion if not complete destruction of its power to protect workers' job security and living standards. Foreign auto corporations have built and operated assembly plants, mainly in the South, and have successfully resisted union organization, even those that are joint ventures between unionized European and Japanese corporations and similarly unionized American corporations. Many car parts for domestic corporations are made in nonunion plants at home or abroad. And, as we have seen, General Motors as well as its de facto subsidiary parts maker, Delphi, are preparing drastic cuts in wages and benefits for their respective work forces. At this writing, United Auto Workers has threatened strike action to prevent such a catastrophe; but given the prevailing labor and political climate, even if a strike ensues, we can expect a "compromise" settlement that will reduce wages and benefits.

The United States arguably has the most authoritarian workplaces of any advanced industrial society. Union contracts, no less than labor laws mediated by court decisions, fiercely protect property rights. The typical union contract, for example, grants to management the prerogative to determine by what means the product is produced; management, acting for the principal owners of the enterprise, assign the workforce to specific tasks, decide on methods of production, and determine the pace of work. Union contracts somewhat constrain the rights of management and, in a few instances (as discussed below) give workers some autonomy in work assignment and performance. And as Seymour Melman and his colleague Lawrence Cohen show, even when there is no formal agreement many industrial enterprises are operated, not by supervision, but by workers on the shop floor.[5]

In 90 percent of American private-sector workplaces that are nonunion, the management's rule is "Do it my way or there's the highway," which, in a time of relative shortages of good jobs, means that many workers have been inhibited from exercising their own power at the workplace. In this era of globalization, many unions that earlier negotiated agreements giving workers some rights over the pace and intensity of their labor have, in fact if not in contract, surrendered these rights in order to keep a beleaguered company afloat or, in many cases, especially during the 1980s and early 1990s, suffered lost strikes over these issues.[6] Concessionary bargaining during that period was not only about wages and benefits but, as well, about hard-won work rules. In some instances unions surrendered control over outsourcing; in others they granted management more "flexibility" in directing the workforce by agreeing to compulsory overtime that saved the company the expense of making new hires to accommodate expansion, agreed to enforce higher production norms, and accepted tiering wages in violation of one of labor's most sacred principles: equal pay for equal work.

The triumph of neoliberalism as the dominant economic program of global capital—which coincided with the ascendancy of British Prime Minister Margaret Thatcher and of Reagan in the United States—was signified by its intention to break the social compact in countries where the historical compromise had been in effect since World War II and in the United States since the mid-1930s. In many European countries the terms of this compact entailed capital's concession to insurgent labor and socialist movements of considerable powers at the workplace and a fairly broad scope of economic and social security, including universal health schemes, state pensions, at least a month of paid vacations, at least a week of holidays, and paid sick and maternity leave. The main field of politics since the late 1970s has been labor and other popular forces' struggle to retain elements of this compact. Given the intensity of capital's offensive, labor has been forced on the defensive, which means that there is almost no question, anywhere in the most industrially advanced societies, of labor proposing and winning new social space. On the contrary, labor in the widest sense is merely trying to preserve past gains. Starting from a much more modest base, Americans are engaged in similar battles. However, despite the diminution of labor's power, the last decade has witnessed a resurgence of utopian thinking, especially in the form of ideas that have historically been associated with socialism.

Three Utopian Proposals

The devastation of living standards in developed and developing countries wrought by global capital's pursuit of neoliberal policies has evoked four principal responses: (1) movements of protest and resistance; (2) efforts, especially in Latin America, to bring protest into the electoral arena by electing opponents of the prevailing neoliberalism; (3) the World Social Forum and its regional offshoots, which have brought together anti-globalization forces with nongovernmental organizations (NGOs) in a grand dialogue about values and strategies for popular forces attempting to repeal, or to mitigate, globalization; and (4) ecologists and anti-capitalist utopian thinkers who are trying to propose alternatives to the current setup.

First, on the left we have seen the emergence of anti-globalization movements. Many anti-globalists are also anti-capitalist; others seek to democratize global institutions to make space for the social base in the decisions that affect their lives. They conduct mass demonstrations that are supported by some unions in the United States and Western Europe against the transnational corporations and agencies of their control such as the World Trade Organization, the World Bank, and the International Monetary Fund. This is the substance of the strategy of resistance and protest, whose goal is to disrupt the neoliberal program though it does not necessarily have a program of its own.

Second, in Latin America opposition to globalization and neoliberal economic policies has taken the form of mostly successful socialist and nationalist electoral and extraparliamentary insurgencies, which are struggling to articulate alternatives that would, at the minimum, free their countries from the ravages of dependency. As we have seen, the Brazilian Workers Party government has chosen to observe austerity policies in order to raise funds to pay its debts to the big banks. Most of the new governments call themselves socialists but have not yet figured out how to address what Pierre Bourdieu has termed the "tyranny of the market." This has also been the case in Argentina and, more recently, Venezuela, where workers have made dramatic efforts to seize and operate abandoned plants.

Third, in the last five years the World Social Forum and its regional offshoots have initiated a series of very large assemblages directed toward finding alternatives to neoliberalism. Within this space are those arguing that the interests of transnational capital and its institutions are irreconcilable with those of popular forces, especially the poor who have borne the main burden of debt and austerity. Others, associated with the professional staffs and leadership of many NGOs (many of whom are funded by corporate foundations such as the Ford Foundation), are open to dialogue with global institutions such as the World Bank and with states whose governments are sympathetic to finding solutions to the problem of mandatory debt payments. These debts have resulted in near bankruptcy for many and have forced others to impose severe austerity on the populace, a policy that results in reduced wages and the loss of already-meager welfare state services. Between intransigents and compromisers stand those who, like the bulk of organized labor and constituents for social benefits, strive to hold the line.

Fourth, into the tangled wood of denial a small but growing coterie of intellectuals has entered the fray with the bold announcement that our relation to nature matters and that humans are a part of natural history. Natural scientists and ecologists have weighed in with proposals for reducing the carbon dioxide content of the air and have discovered that the so-called greenhouse effect is due to human intervention in such forms as carbon-belching power plants and pollution-spewing autos and trucks. Anticipating (by several decades) the world-shaking, raging debate over global warming, theorists such as James O'Connor, Joel Kovel, John Bellamy Foster, and Murray Bookchin have declared that capitalism itself is the chief obstacle to any possible long-term resolution of the crisis.[7] Each in his own way argues for a new relationship between humans and nature that problematizes the rationality of the capitalist mode of production. As the source of the crisis they point to our current industrial system, which is predicated on the domination of nature. To which some, including me, have added the suburbanization of social space, and the persistence of fossil-fuels as the basis of our electrification and heating plants. I have already addressed this question in some detail, but I invoke it again briefly to exemplify the inadequacy of the postmodern turn in social and political philosophy and the blithe, uncritical acceptance of the fruits of modernity in Habermas and his followers' refusal to follow Frankfurt School mentors to interrogate the darker side of the Enlightenment. Of course the same may be said of preponderant liberal and modern social-democratic political theory, which remained ensconced in problems of inequality without considering its relation to the ecological crisis of our time nor, for that matter, the reproduction of inequality in the production sphere where wage labor—even of the most qualified, "professional" kind—is exploited.[8]

In the context of the rise of global movements that challenge transnational capital, a small but growing group of social theorists and economists have opened a discussion of alternatives to capitalist hegemony. Of these I want to discuss Seymour Melman, whose work on conversion from the permanent war economy to peaceful uses of our national resources remains a classic in its field; Michael Albert, the editor of *Z* magazine and a prolific writer on economic issues; and Gar Alperovitz, an economist who formerly served on congressional committees and as an aide to Wisconsin Senator Gaylord Nelson and was a founder of the Institute for Policy Studies, a left-liberal "think tank" that is over forty years old.[9]

First Utopian Proposal

Of this recent crop of studies that purport to consider the nature of work, consumption, and their impact on the prospects for democracy, the most far ranging is Alperovitz's. Invoking the concept of the "pluralist commonwealth" as a countervision to the growing concentration of wealth and power, Alperovitz argues that in order to secure our democracy and our liberty, we need to find ways to share the wealth and thereby achieve more equality. His main proposal is to provide a direct "worker stake in economic life" by supporting institutions such as Employee Stock Ownership Plans (ESOPs) and other programs. He argues as well that democracy is possible only if the community engages in wealth-producing activities that build community solidarity and provide them with a measure of economic autonomy. These arguments are neither novel nor particularly controversial, but the link made to liberty and the chances for democracy is powerful and well-made. Thus he advocates decentralizing public functions to smaller government jurisdictions such as cities and transforming them into entrepreneurs of locally based businesses such as sports and municipally owned energy companies, and, perhaps most controversially, organizing development corporations that can attract private capital, especially in areas of advanced technology. This proposal regurgitates a fairly long history of local development efforts that, in many cases, have proven to be little more than a boon for investors but have had at best mixed results for the communities, which have often provided start-up funds through municipal and state bonds.

Unfortunately, while Alperovitz rehearses the concept of local development corporations and its proliferation over the last four decades, he does little to allay fears about the drawbacks of this strategy. For example, the reader does not learn that, in many cases, companies have taken a variety of public subsidies including gifts, loans, and tax and land breaks, but have closed shop and disappeared when the field looks greener elsewhere. In fact, the experience of publicly supported development projects such as industrial and business zones that are protected from the usual costs such as taxes, construction of plants, and provision of necessary infrastructure has been deeply ambiguous; for every success, where employers remained over a long duration, there are two or three outright failures, in the form either of plants that were built with public money that have left town and remain vacant or converted into "factory outlets" retail stores, or of companies that insisted on remaining union-free and have paid substandard wages and offered poor or no benefits. Doubtless Alperovitz does not have WalMart in mind, but this retail giant has frequently been a beneficiary of the public trough. By invoking the example of high-tech firms, he also does not let the reader in on the dirty little secret about computer-mediated enterprises—namely, that they employ far fewer employees than low- or intermediate-technology manufacturing companies or retail stores. Besides, while the production and maintenance of software are extremely lucrative for large corporations, the record for smaller companies after 2000 has been at best mediocre and often dismal. Indeed, for the bulk of this industry, the era of prosperity is over. Only the giants have prospered in recent years, but in the wake of the relative saturation of their markets they are following many conventional industries in seeking lower-wage labor abroad—in this case, in India and Thailand. But even some of these industries, notably

Microsoft and Sun Systems, face rough sledding ahead. For highly qualified scientific and technical people, their jobs are still some of the best in our occupational structure, but we have not yet measured the effects of the emergence of some countries in the developing world that are capable of supplying qualified technical and scientific labor. Regarding those employees who are not in technical and professional occupations, if the job has not disappeared in the 2000–2003 bust it is routine and not particularly well-paid.

Alperovitz does not rely on argument alone; his book is laden with many examples of ESOPs that have saved businesses and jobs from extinction; collaborative efforts that have been undertaken between universities, and locally based development corporations and high-tech start-ups (specifically in Massachusetts, California, and Maryland). Moreover, he argues for redistributing the costs of health care and Social Security and for addressing housing through a more progressive tax and banking system. And he suggests that in the United States, "the wealthiest nation in the history of the world," we can strengthen family life, promote more citizen involvement in community affairs, and provide more personal comfort by reducing the workweek to as few as twenty-five hours. This is perhaps the most significant proposal in the entire book because it raises the question of how democracy might prosper when two or more members of a household work forty or more hours a week.

There are three major unanswered questions in this generally upbeat picture of a wealth-sharing future. The first is the virtual absence of a discussion of the problem of the authoritarian workplace that prevails both in the private capitalist sector and in the more than 11,000 workplaces where worker ownership exists. As we have already seen, worker ownership does not necessary entail worker control of the labor process. In fact, most ESOP workplaces have simply transferred ownership, but not management, to the workers. And in most cases, their having assumed ownership means only that they now share the burdens and, in some cases, the profits after taxes; the costs of paying management's salaries, which are often similar to those at companies with more traditional ownership schemes and investment costs; and, more generally, all of the risks of enterprise. But daily life at the workplace is no more democratic than when the enterprise was privately owned or was a public corporation.

The second question is closely linked to the problem of workers' self-management of the workplace. Elsewhere in this book I have acknowledged the difficulty of achieving democracy in the workplace without dealing with the market framework, which almost all proposals for transforming the "life world" take for granted. Markets are not identical with the process of exchange that preceded them. The division of labor in society has reached a point where it can be altered to share more desirable work among a wider section of the labor force, but cannot be reversed. The division of labor tends to be hierarchical and can be overcome only by a prolonged process of education of the least qualified in any workplace. But to subject labor and its products to markets tends to defeat the best efforts in any single workplace. Any future society concerned with overcoming the concentration of wealth would have to address the overriding fact that markets are sources of inequality. Competition may result in lower prices and greater variety of products, but competition among labor in this global economy results in lower wages and gives capital the upper hand. When a worker-owned and -controlled enterprise offers its commodities to the market, it will immediately be confronted with this problem of competition. The norms imposed by the market may be incompatible with workers' self-management. Even if managerial salaries are kept below the norm for the private sector, the costs of raw materials, distribution, and marketing, as well as the competition from much larger and better-financed corporate competitors, may have an impact on the workplace and on pricing. The answer is not an easy one to come by, but it is difficult to understand why this question is ignored in Alperovitz's book.

The third unaddressed question is common to all three attempts to address the problem of life after capitalism: What are the political conditions for arriving at that place? I will reserve my discussion of this issue until I have reviewed all three.

Second Utopian Proposal

Michael Albert has written profusely on alternative economics, focusing on the question of workers' control of enterprises. But

Parecon, his latest entry, is perhaps the most thorough and uncompromising utopian proposal of all the recent efforts to come to grips with globalization and massive inequality. It is uncompromising in that it does not presuppose the market but challenges its efficacy—and efficiency—in being able to allocate resources on the basis of strict equality. He not only advocates the abolition of private ownership of the means of material production but suggests that planning at the local and national levels should replace the market for allocation of all sorts of resources and distribution. Put simply, *Parecon*'s central idea is consistent with the tradition of councilism and its American variant, the concept of the "cooperative commonwealth." According to Albert, society should be organized around workers' and consumers' councils—participatory institutions that would share decision-making within the economy, allocation of resources, and determination of what should be produced, how and in what manner it should be distributed, and by what criteria consumed. Consumers, as the most basic societal units—the individual, the family, and the neighborhood—would play a large role in deciding and communicating their "needs and wants," even as workers themselves determine how long and by what methods they would work.

Within this broad scheme Albert discusses a variety of problems: how to ensure participatory production, consumption, and planning; how to solve the problem of "too many meetings," an oblique reference to the tendency of activists to dominate even the most intentionally egalitarian institutions because they do not mind meetings; the issue of "permanent" revolution, an exhausting prospect for all but those engaged full-time in politics; and, finally, the question of human nature. Refuting the argument that humans are by genetic makeup or otherwise inherently greedy and therefore could not work cooperatively to achieve an egalitarian society, he nevertheless does not explicitly endorse the Rousseauian view that humans are inherently cooperative and good and are deformed only by the hierarchical structures of class systems. What he does say is eminently sensible: We don't know enough to come up with a rigorously scientific explanation of human nature, but there is considerable reason to believe that people can work together when the conditions are right. But he argues—persuasively, I believe—that in comparison to proposals to leave decisions to the market (proposals that are rife in the contemporary social environment), and relative to the bureaucratic solution (that planning and control be invested in a technical elite), trying workers' and consumers' self-management and broad participatory planning is more consistent with democratic and egalitarian values.

Parecon was written in the grand tradition of Etienne Cabet, Charles Fourier, Henri Saint-Simon, Ernst Bloch, Anton Pannekoek, and others who declare, frankly, that without utopian thought there can be no transformation of the authoritarian and hierarchical present to a qualitatively different and better future. Like Bloch and Pannekoek, who arrive at their models from an examination of the history of workers' movements as well as of social relations, Albert grounds his utopian model in the categories of how our present society works. It is not about the impossible but, rather, about the "not-yet." The distinction is important. The not-yet signifies that another world is possible but is suppressed by current social and political relations. For given the level of development of our scientific and technological mastery—whereby knowledge of nature, of the labor process, of social relations, and of the tools of social organization has been widely, if inadequately, disseminated—we are surely in a position to imagine another world. What Albert has done admirably is to offer one step in that radical imagination. If *Parecon* often lacks discursive sophistication—that is, if it does not sharply imagine its interlocutors and reproduce the best of their arguments—it nevertheless detracts little from the effort. That Albert does not offer a serious analysis of either the history or the current movements toward self-management, and depicts self-management as an ideal state of being, presents problems of credibility for his argument. For it may be that situating the proposal for workplace democracy in the long struggles by workers themselves is the necessary condition for rescuing the discourse of self-management from the appearance of abstraction and ahistorical conceptualization.

Third Utopian Proposal

In this regard Seymour Melman fills the bill. Melman, a professional industrial engineer and professor at Columbia University, became well known during the 1960s and 1970s for his exposure of the close links between the federal government (especially the Pentagon) and major industrial corporations, and for his work to offer alternatives to the war economy that could meet basic human needs. Of course those holding the reigns of political and economic power all but ignored his suggestions, but his ideas became influential in the public sphere and among wide sections of the peace and nuclear disarmament movements. In the last forty years of his life Melman distinguished himself as a constant fount of ideas and a prod to citizens to take action to free the economy from its dependence on war and destruction.

Consistent with past efforts Melman's last major work, *After Capitalism* (2001), combines an analysis of the ways in which contemporary capitalism remains dependent on war and has produced a widening worldwide gap between rich and poor. Much of this analysis will be familiar to students of the adventures of monopoly capitalism and its imperialist permutations. It offers few new insights and introduces the dubious concept of "state capitalism" as a description of current power. But halfway into the study the emphasis changes from what Melman once called "Pentagon Capitalism" to what he now more broadly terms "*state* capitalism," which signifies that his critique has extended to the alliance of the state and corporations to manage a wide range of economic, political, and social relations. And in this context Melman turns his attention to the fate of democracy under capitalism and concludes that liberal democracy is limited by its failure to address the workplace.

After Capitalism is one of the best, maybe even *the* best, treatments of the history of the struggle for workers' control. Certainly it ranks as one of the most comprehensive. Like Albert, Melman is a stalwart proponent of workers' self-management and employs this as a criterion for evaluating competing paradigms. Melman sternly rejects the view that ESOPs constitute a major breakthrough because, in his words, it is an example of workers' "ownership without control"—a program instigated by industrial management to secure the perpetuity of its power. He advances a persuasive critique of the Soviet Union, whose name owes its origin to the 1905 Russian Revolution, which in turn invented the Soviets—that is, workers' councils. Under the strain of foreign invasion, civil war, and bureaucratic domination from above, the Communists cast the workers' councils aside while perpetuating the myth that a society was ruled not by bureaucratic state, managerial, and technical elites but by the workers themselves. Melman is unsparing in his criticism and proceeds to show what self-management is and can be.

In particular, Melman articulates the concept of a nonmarket system of workers' self-management and, drawing on the practical and intellectual work of his Columbia University colleague Lawrence B. Cohen—who demonstrates that the textile factory's shop floor is in fact, if not in law, largely under the control of the workers—as well as on his own long experience, he shows that, at least incipiently, this concept already exists in the system of capitalist production. Melman and Cohen call workers' self-management "disalienation" in contrast to the hierarchically based capitalist industrial system, where workers are alienated from the product of their labor, from other workers, and, ultimately, from themselves. Drawing on the experience of Mondragon—the mammoth Spanish cooperative banking and industrial organization that, although ensconced in the market system, has made significant advances in the direction of workplace democracy—Melman concludes his study with a critique of various pessimistic prognostications of the chances for a participatory, democratic workplace.

It may be that the political problems associated with the task of transition to a new regime of workplace and system-wide democracy are beyond the scope of these studies, but it is difficult to imagine that many will be convinced of their arguments without a discussion of how the present is linked to the future. Alperovitz assumes that it is possible to initiate change through reform processes that presuppose the liberal democratic political system. Many of his examples refer to existing national, state, and local power structures and legislative reforms (especially those designed to legally sanction ESOPs), and he takes pains to demonstrate that Republicans as well as Democrats are favorably disposed toward enabling legislation. To be frank, he probably needs no political road map because he believes the existing framework is adequate to the ends of creeping post-capitalism if, by that term, we mean a mixed economy in which "beyond capitalism" signifies structures parallel to the dominant forms and to a legislative program of "progressive" measures that somewhat even the economic playing field. I believe Alperovitz can be convicted of a version of "crackpot realism," C.Wright Mills's apt phrase to describe liberal thinkers who disdain bold, radical thinking.

Melman and Albert recognize the need for a new politics, but it is never clear, at least in Albert's argument, whether this refers to the anarchist position, in which the state plays no role because it has already been dismantled. While Melman does not embrace the unions as they are presently constituted, he places some reliance on their ability to put into practice some of his proposals for worker decision-making. Yet, despite the evident point that capitalism cannot, in the long run, accommodate a system of workers' self-management that also rejects the market as a regulative instrument in the last instance, none of the three are willing or able to suggest a politics that can lead beyond capitalism.

A new political formation that sets about the tasks associated with a new map of global and national politics would surely embrace the spirit and some of the details of these proposals and engage intellectuals who are making them. Criticisms aside, the eco-socialists and the democratic radicals who have rejected the concept that democracy stops at the workplace door have made enormous contributions to the project of the radical imagination. The stark reality of globalization—whose central objective remains, even given the prospect of possible compromises with insurgents, to subordinate labor to the imperatives of transnational capital—has failed to provoke a response from established political philosophy. Is this silence due to Jurgen Habermas's influence? Recall that in the years of preparation for his theory of communicative action Habermas had to settle accounts with his own marxist legacy. His key move was to renounce the founding premise of social theory, the centrality of labor in the constitution of society. Habermas begins by separating the sphere of production and, concomitantly, the labor process from the sphere of the "life world." His main argument is that the realm of production and the relation of humans to nature were subsumed under the concept of rational purposive action rather than in a sphere of conflict and transformation and, for this reason, no longer constituted an engine of history. Production had been reduced to a series of technical problems while the key issue of the "life world," communications, remained conflictual because of distortions inherent in speech acts. These distortions constitute the scene of a new social project. Rawlsian political liberalism, the most influential political philosophy of the last decades of the twentieth century, also carefully avoids addressing the sphere of production. In concert with theories of "consumer society," Rawls seeks only to ameliorate inequalities without addressing its source.

Or is the silence of political philosophy and its sister discipline, political theory, a symptom of the postmodern turn in which totalizations are denied—namely, the contention that master narratives of the nineteenth-century capitalism are overtaken by the multiplicity of largely incommensurable contemporary discourses? Since they have reduced society to a series of autonomous intentional communities, are the communitarians, against their wishes, simply a variety of postmodernism? Have they ignored the labor process and social life in general because they are part of the tendency, most forcefully articulated by Arendt, that views the sphere of necessity as classically unworthy of philosophical reflection?

The reason I have written this book is to address the failure of political theory to come to grips with the realities of twenty-first-century global capitalism and the tendency of social theory to reconcile itself to the givens of the economic and social world. I have insisted on a historical perspective because the condition of opening a dialogue is to comprehend where we have been in order to know where we are going.

Notes

1. Hannah Arendt, *The Human Condition* (Chicago: University of Chicago Press, 1961); Jurgen Habermas, "Technology and Science as 'Ideology,'" in Jurgen Habermas, ed., *Toward a Rational Society* (Boston: Beacon Press, 1970).

2. John Locke, *Two Treatises on Government* (New York: Hackett Publishers, 1965).

3. John Rawls, *A Theory of Justice* (Cambridge, MA: Harvard University Press, 1971).

4. Karl Polanyi, *The Great Transformation* (New York: Reynal and Hitchcock, 1944).

5. Seymour Melman, *After Capitalism: From Managerialism to Workplace Democracy* (New York: Alfred A. Knopf, 2001); Lawrence Cohen, unpublished manuscript.

6. Hardy Green, *On Strike at Hormel* (Philadelphia: Temple University Press, 1990); Peter Rachleff, *Hard-Pressed in the Heartland: The Hormel Strike and the Future of the Labor Movement* (Boston: South End Press, 1993)

7. James O'Connor, *Natural Causes* (New York: Gilford Press, 1998); Joel Kovel, *The Enemy of Nature* (Nova Scotia: Fernwood Books and London/New York: Zed Press, 2002); John Bellamy Foster, *Marx's Ecology* (New York: Monthly Review Press, 2000); Murray Bookchin, *The Ecology of Freedom* (Seattle: Bay Press, 1993).

8. Max Horkheimer and Theodor W. Adorno, *The Dialectic of the Enlightenment* (Stanford University Press, 2002).

9. Melman, *After Capitalism;* Michael Albert, *Parecon: Life After Capitalism* (London/New York: Verso Books, 2003); Gar Alperovitz, *America Beyond Capitalism* (Hoboken, NJ: John Wiley and Sons, 2005).

Index

◆

About the Author

Stanley Aronowitz is distinguished professor of sociology at the Graduate Center, City University of New York. A former steelworker and labor union organizer, he previously taught at Staten Island Community College, the University of California–Irvine, the University of Paris, and Columbia University. He is author or editor of twenty-four books, including *The Knowledge Factory* (2000) and *How Class Works* (2003). He was the Green Party's candidate for governor of New York State in 2002 and is a member of the Executive Council of the Professional Staff Congress, which is the union of faculty and staff at CUNY.